THE GENERATIONS OF MEN

'*The Generations of Men run on in the tide of Time,*
But leave their destin'd lineaments permanent for ever and ever.'

BLAKE: *Milton*

JUDITH WRIGHT

The
Generations
of
Men

Illustrated by

ALISON FORBES

MELBOURNE
OXFORD UNIVERSITY PRESS
LONDON   WELLINGTON   NEW YORK

Oxford University Press

OXFORD LONDON GLASGOW
NEW YORK TORONTO MELBOURNE WELLINGTON
NAIROBI DAR ES SALAAM CAPE TOWN
KUALA LUMPUR SINGAPORE HONG KONG TOKYO
DELHI BOMBAY CALCUTTA MADRAS KARACHI

*First published 1959
Reprinted 1960, 1964
First paperback edition 1965
Reprinted 1966, 1967, 1970, 1975, 1979*

NATIONAL LIBRARY OF AUSTRALIA CATALOGUING IN
PUBLICATION DATA

Wright, Judith Arundell, 1915–
   *The generations of men/by Judith Wright;
   illustrated by Alison Forbes. – Melbourne,
   Oxford University Press, 1959.*
   ISBN 0 19 550295 7.

   *1. Wright family. I. Forbes, Alison, illus.
   II. Title.*

929.20994

PRINTED IN HONG KONG BY BRIGHTER PRINTING PRESS LTD
PUBLISHED BY OXFORD UNIVERSITY PRESS, 7 BOWEN CRESCENT, MELBOURNE

CONTENTS

INTRODUCTION

MY GRANDFATHER, Albert Andrew Wright, and my grandmother, then Charlotte May Mackenzie, were born in the Hunter Valley of New South Wales, in the comparatively early years of settlement there—the first in 1840, the second in 1855. My grandmother's family had already lived for a generation in the valley, her own grandparents having arrived there from England in 1828 and built their home, Dalwood, with assigned convict labour brought from the then small port of Newcastle. (Dalwood and the Wright stations are shown on the map on the opposite page.)

During their lifetimes, which were spent partly in the Hunter Valley, partly in the Dawson Valley district in Queensland about a hundred miles inland from Rockhampton, which lies on the Tropic of Capricorn, and partly in the New England tableland district of New South Wales, the pastoral settlement of inland and northern Australia took shape, until at my grandmother's death in 1929, a century after her grandparents' leaving England, the pattern of Australian pastoral land use was fairly complete. I have tried to sketch in, as accurately as I can, this background of their personal story—for instance, the great and almost unchronicled pastoral migrations in which men and cattle spread gradually from the coastal settlements, northward and westward over the inland grazing country, followed by the bullock- and horse-teams of the waggons that brought supplies.

For my knowledge of the lives and personalities of my grandparents themselves, I am indebted not only to their own writings (the diaries of my grandfather for the years from 1866-1890, and of my grandmother in later years, and her unfinished reminiscences), but to my memories of her and my knowledge of the influence of their lives on their surroundings and on their descendants.

Though to this extent, at least, my grandparents may be said to have written this book themselves, any errors of fact or interpretation are, of course, to be imputed to their grand-daughter only.

Judith Wright

To the children

of

MAY and ALBERT

1   AT RICHMOND VALE 1854-1865

OF HER CHILDHOOD, May Mackenzie remembered two houses.

The first was the small cottage where she had been born, and where, for some years after her birth, her parents continued to live. It lay somewhere near a swamp; for, as she recollected, the frogs croaked very loudly at nights, so loudly that she could not sleep, and the nursemaid who generally came when she called (for Mama was busy in the evenings with the family sewing) told her to be quiet, or the bunyips would come for her, the bunyips that lived in the mud, deep under the leaves of the big blue water-lilies.

The cottage faded later in her memory like a dream; but of it she remembered that Papa was often there and often laughing, that when he came into the little sitting-room a warm smell of horses came with him from the big yards on the flat beyond the house. For Arthur Mackenzie dealt in horses for the Indian market, or for the French Army officers in New Caledonia, or indeed for anyone who would buy, and sometimes buyers were few. He was daring, but not often lucky, shipping mobs from Valparaiso, buying wild horses, brumbies running in the back country, and breaking them in by the Rarey method for quick sale. She remembered, too, Mama's face in its golden ringlets, smiling and strangely young; for in her later memories Mama often looked weary, fretful or forlorn.

As the small cottage receded in her mind, the second house of her memories began more and more to dominate her life. At first infrequent, her visits there grew more prolonged and came more often, as her mother, unable to bear the loneliness of the cottage at Richmond Vale, packed up her household and fled back to the comforting shelter of her old home.

Weeta Mackenzie, who had been Weeta Wyndham, perhaps rather enjoyed these homecomings to the Wyndham stronghold—the welcome, the fuss made over her five pretty children, even the discreet sympathy. For Arthur Mackenzie, the Wyndhams knew, deploring the fact in silence for the most part, was 'not as steady as he might be'. His expeditions up the country, his horse-dealings, his ventures into cattle-buying or station-buying, had about them a rather flamboyant air which disturbed the Dalwood atmosphere of solid prosperity, the almost English serenity of establishment.

Dalwood, in May's early memories, was a great house of cool stone corridors and high-ceilinged rooms, of wide iron-barred doors opening on a stone-flagged courtyard where servants pumped water splashing into pails; down the passages and through the windows wandered scents from Grandmama's garden—summer roses, lemon-hedge, lavender and sage and queer herbs for *tisanes* (for Grandmama was partly French). In the long red-curtained day-room was a continual soft murmur of voices as the women of the household sat stitching. Grandmama would be there, talking to Mama; perhaps Aunt Tishy paused there awhile (but she was impatient and went off soon, down to the stables, being not so many years older than May herself); perhaps one or more of the uncles' accumulating number of wives and fiancées.

But mostly, as May remembered it, the voices belonged to Grandmama and Mama, left discreetly to talk it out.

'My dear girl,' Grandmama would say, heeling a sock while her daughter sorted the pieces of the twins' dresses cut out for sewing (they had just come out of long-clothes), 'is there no way of keeping Arthur settled? And where is he gone now?'

And Mama, conscious perhaps of cutting a rather interesting

figure, would begin low-voiced to pour out that stream of confidences in which May, though sitting fascinated at first, soon lost interest. Then she would slip out behind the heavy door-curtain, find a brother or some cousin perhaps, and run through the courtyard to the long stables where noble-headed mares and colts whickered over the stall-doors. Lauristina was there, and Lunelle, the lovely racing-mare whose value May's young uncles were never tired of boasting about, and others no less beautiful. Or they would go to watch the work at the winery with its deep stone cellars, where perhaps the vintage was being racked; or perhaps harvest was in progress and the vineyard was full of grape-pickers, most of them convicts whose terms had expired. Dalwood's wines were old George Wyndham's proudest achievement, and twenty men were employed all year round in wine-making and tending the vines. Everywhere was order, business, the pleasantness of cool whitewashed stone.

If May could find Grandpapa, her day was made. He made a pet of this grand-daughter, pretty and brown-eyed and ready with her tongue; he would swing her up into the gig and off they would go, round the property perhaps to see to some work that was under way, fencing or timber-splitting, ploughing, or work with the handsome red and white Hereford cattle that the Wyndhams bred, and that were young Regi Wyndham's particular care, though his father had as keen an eye to their welfare.

Or perhaps Grandpapa would order his guns. 'It isn't every day I have my grand-daughter here. Let's play truant for the afternoon, May.' And they would spend the day on a shooting expedition, when to May's delight she was taught to load the guns.

George Wyndham, hale and neat and very much the English squire in his leggings and his uncompromisingly well-cut clothes, seemed to May the kindest, though the most august, of men. How different was the life of Dalwood from the life of the cottage, and how meagre and dull seemed her days at Richmond Vale, Papa away!

Indeed Dalwood, the big stone house, set among vineyards and fields of crops, had in the thirty years of its life attained a personality. Those thirty years, which stretched back almost to the beginning of the life of the settlements in the fertile Hunter Valley, were like the first years in human growth in their rapid and spectacular development. Already the pattern of the valley's life was set. It was growing now more and more narrow, repetitious, avid of prosperity; year by year it left farther behind it the raw and painful struggle of its first beginnings.

The house, built in 1830 of stone convict-quarried from the nearer hills, and of the lovely timbers of the forest that was now vanished from the valley, had seen great and definitive changes in the landscape and in the way of living that its settlers had imposed. It had survived much in those years; much had been accomplished in and around it, and this, rather than the mere passage of time, had aged and matured it. The house now smiled triumphantly over its vineyards and cattle, secure of its serenity at last.

When George and Margaret Wyndham had arrived in the small outpost settlement of the lower Hunter Valley early in 1828, they had seen the reign of almost untouched forest over all their land. It had been strange indeed to Margaret, used to the cared-for fields and woods of France and England, to look out into that green alarming depth, from the door of the earth-floored one-roomed hut to which she came. The orchids and parasite plants that flowered on the tall trees were all strangers; the blacks, the animals, and particularly the insects frightened her—the big green mantises, their heads turning eerily to watch her movements, the many-legged creatures that lived in the bark roof, the moths that blundered into the weak flames of the tallow-dip candles at night and left her in the dark.

Yet even then the axes of the assigned men—twenty convicts George had brought from the settlement down-river at Newcastle port—were forcing their way into the ranks of trees. Nothing was to remain of that forest; the swamps where Margaret had gathered the flowers of the gigantic lilies, which, pressed and sent home to England, caused the aunts such wonderment, were all to be drained, ploughed, and planted with wheat.

It was difficult, thirty years having passed, to believe that the tame and fertile valley, obediently bearing its annual crops, had ever seemed such a place of danger, or had ever been the limit of settlement. Men's minds had now swung hundreds of miles beyond it: the valley, dominated and forced into prosperity, was no longer a place of hardship and adventure. This made her grand-parents' tales as fantastic as fairy-stories to May, to whom it seemed that Dalwood must always have existed. So remote from reality were those stories that they invested Dalwood, and her grandfather and grandmother, with the quality of legend brought into daily life.

And Margaret and George, both of them authoritative and dignified figures, filled out quite satisfactorily the characters with which her mind invested them. It was not necessary to look further for a tradition, or for an aim that she should set herself. Accordingly George and Margaret, their lives and their achievements, took on for her an authority that made them, for their grand-daughter, a point of reference which she retained all her life.

Indeed, there was about their story something of the atmosphere of the Book of Genesis, and some aura, too, of supernatural descent clung to them—since it was an axiom that in Australia existed no beauty and no tradition, no art and no aristocracy, and since all things good came from a country unknown to their children and grand-children. Of all that large and growing clan, none except the founders had ever seen England; yet the life of Dalwood still had constant reference to things English, and George and Margaret wrote and received by every English mail long family letters.

Now, however, as George and Margaret aged, the alien influence of their adopted country began at last to flood more and more strongly into their lives. It began to loosen old bonds, to threaten the house that George had dreamed of as outlasting the generations—a monument to a foreign tradition, a house such as Dinton had been, that great stone mansion in its grove of oaks, with the Adam staircase, the Wyndham portraits. . . . He had built Dalwood with that model in his mind.

Yes, it was strange how he, the rebel third son, whose Godwinian ideas, whose Shelleyan dreams had sent him from Dinton's county conservatism to the new countries to realize them, had altered with the years. All his own Englishness, his innate conservatism had re-asserted themselves, as he sensed the spirit of this country hostile to them. The equality of man, a theory so attractive at Oxford, had lost its charm for him here, where it came so dangerously near to realization. . . . And the lives he and Margaret had planned, the care-free gipsy wanderings, when they resolved themselves into fact were somewhat different from the dream.

He had built Dalwood, old George saw now, as a bulwark, a protection against the very ideas he had come to Australia to realize. And his twelve sons, his two daughters—were not their numbers another bulwark? It was reassuring, in this wild undisciplined colony, to be surrounded by sons brought up in English traditions of family duty, in English views of the rights of property and the responsibilities of children to their parents. For it made him uneasy to watch the growth, in these levelling days when servants deserted their masters at the call of the gold-mines, and when ex-convicts could not be told from free men, of the colony's dangerous devil-may-care spirit that whistled tradition down the wind, that cared nothing for discipline nor for England, seeing only that England which exported convicts, soldiers, triangles and whips, and not the England George remembered.

Now he wore his meticulous clothes of an English squire, walked the hot furrows of his vineyard as though they had been English fields, wrote his regular letters to his sisters and brothers still, dreamed of return. But Australia, he feared obscurely, had conquered. His sons, grown now, were not all he had hoped of them; their marriages were not such marriages as they might have made in England—suitable girls were scarce. . . . The third generation? He wondered. He talked often to his grandchildren of England; but though they listened, he knew that England was unimaginable to them. Now, in his old age, he began to feel himself a foreigner among people who belonged here, in his own house, as he himself did not.

Even May, his favourite grandchild, when she asked him for stories asked always for the stories of his Australian wanderings; not for those of his English childhood, which he liked best to tell. Well, it was natural, he thought with a sigh. The child's life would be lived in this country; he himself had, in a sense, brought her here. It was useless to regret England. Yet, without Margaret, how lonely he would be now! One's children—what contact had one with their lives, in the end?

For May, the English stories were to be listened to politely. The

Australian stories she understood. But it seemed that England was so different that one could not see it clearly.

'One day your great-uncle William and I were playing in the oak woods.'

'Yes, Grandpapa?'

'Do you know what oaks look like, May?'

But they were not like river-oaks at all—those dark long-needled pines that hushed in the wind along the creek-edge. And Grandpapa would shake his head.

'Tell me about building Dalwood, then. Or the time when you went in the waggons, like Abraham.'

Accordingly George sighed. Something was awry with his plans, though it was hard indeed to put one's finger on it. He had planned to establish a great house. Well, in face of all the difficulties, he had done it: Dalwood stood there where the forest had been, stone-built to last, loopholed and turreted against bushranging bands, but endowed with such grace as, here at the ends of the earth, he had been able to give it. He had planned to establish a family which should carry on that house and make of it an influence in his chosen country. Had his sons any such talents? He began to doubt it; yet they were strong and self-reliant enough, well-taught considering everything. His friends told him that he was lucky in his family.

But the country, he could not trust it. It had something up its sleeve, he felt obscurely. 'We should have left the place to the blacks!' his old friends would sometimes burst out, half-seriously, at news of droughts, bushrangers, speared cattle, rust in the wheat. . . .

Yet he should have felt a sense of triumph few men achieve. In thirty years he had won his victories, over the forest, over debt and misfortune, over fevers and disasters. Driven from Dalwood, in the bad times after transportation had been abolished, when the valley was almost deserted and there was talk of abandoning the whole colony, he had set out with all his household, his cattle and his horses and a few trusted ex-convict servants, to travel northwards through virtually unknown country, and among hostile tribes. With their herds, their rifles and ammunition, their horses and waggons they lived off the country. The upkeep of the big house, its stables and the cattle and horses that now were worth nothing, would have been

B

impossibly expensive; but travelling nomad-wise they needed little beyond their food, and taking up land as they went, where it seemed worth while to do so, they could stock it with the increase of their herds and leave it in the charge of a trusted man or of an elder son while they travelled on. They left Dalwood closed and deserted, with a servant as caretaker, intending to return there if the markets should mend and wheat, wine and cattle be salable again.

Margaret and the children had travelled in one covered waggon, the stores had been packed in another, and a third held a cook and his kitchen necessities. For three years the strange expedition had wandered through the bush, George riding ahead with the cattle, finding suitable places for camping and routes by which the clumsy waggons could follow, up to the almost unknown northern tableland of New England, down again to the northern coastal plain and to the Richmond River, where Margaret had been perhaps the first white woman to travel, and where the blacks had driven off the cattle; so that Margaret and the children had hidden for days in the waggons, while George and the men rode in search of them and brought back the cattle at last in triumph.

They had taken up land here and there for new stations—worthless land, it seemed at the time—on the Richmond, and had travelled inland again to the fringe of the western blacksoil plains, where on a newly taken up run he had built a hut for Margaret to bear her eighth son, and had marked out land for vineyards. The cattle had done well, the ventures had proved good, and the years of wandering had successfully tided over the bad times. England came out of the trough of depression that had struck her in 1840; wine, wool and hides rose again in price. Unlike many of his neighbours, who were now bankrupt and ruined, vanished forever from the life of the valley, George had triumphantly saved his fortunes; and with the new northern runs, and Dalwood still his own, he now owned a valuable property.

So the waggons had at last returned to Dalwood's columned entrance, and he and Margaret had walked inside, into the house their younger children had almost forgotten. The overgrown garden, the neglected musty-smelling rooms, the vineyard run wild, seemed yet after years of hard living like a dream regained.

Since then everything had come easily. Prosperity had continued, there had been no lack of money, roads had been built, the valley was filling with settlers, there was talk of a railway to run all through it. The northern run, Bukkulla, where his elder sons now were, was doing well, and the wine from its vineyards, though heavy, was good. He was trying now to blend from the Bukkulla and Dalwood vintages a good light red wine, a *vin du pays* that would be popular. He had taken two medals at the Paris judging last year. . . .

To May, free in Dalwood's spacious and disciplined ease, no doubts were possible. The great cool house ruled by Grandmama with her strict kindliness and her French orderliness of housekeeping, was the source of one part of her happiness; the rest she found outside, in the life of the open air, in the equal discipline of the routine of the stables, wine-vaults, and vineyards, and the management of the cattle. The whole routine life of Dalwood was made up of a series of seasonal rituals, gravely carried out and annually recurring— providing a background to Dalwood's other life, in which her gay young uncles and aunts entertained, drove out visiting or on great riding picnics, danced, sang and played in the evenings, knelt in family prayers in the long stone dining-room.

As many as thirty of the family might be staying in the house at one time: sons, wives and children, cousins and relations. Dalwood thus made its own world and imposed its own rules; presided over by George and Margaret, those apparently serene figures of achieve- ment, it left no room for question. When she was back at the little cottage she fretted and felt cramped by the pressure of too close association and supervision; at Dalwood her world grew larger and allowed her freedom.

Nevertheless, return to Richmond Vale always had one compen- sation, for it meant that Papa had come back. Then for a little while there would be gaiety and concord. May loved her father, particularly for something in him that stood, to her, for the adventurous part of the Dalwood story. His dashing air, his horsemanship, his stories of distant places and of long vague inland wanderings seemed to her dangerous and exciting.

But Mama did not like or applaud these tales as the children did,

May soon noticed. She would bite off a thread of her sewing and interrupt them, or droop her head pretending not to listen.

'Now that you *are* back, Arthur, would you please show Harrington how to mend the gig-harness? It's getting really unsafe. I am quite tied to the house for fear of going out.' Or, 'Arthur, do please speak to Harrington about the way the garden is looking. I do my best to show him; but it is so difficult to give orders for the outside work and see that they are carried out. I find the housekeeping and management keeps me quite busy enough, when you are away.'

But her handsome young father remained as splendid as ever, in May's imagination. She told her brothers and sisters—since, though she was only the second eldest, she was the family's accepted leader—that one day Papa would do something remarkable on one of these trips of his, find gold, perhaps, or a great river like the Hunter where they would all go to live, and establish a second Dalwood; or become a famous discoverer. Her faith in him was the more demonstrative for being occasionally shaken.

But Arthur Mackenzie did not seem, to his wife and her parents at any rate, likely to do any such thing. That he was handsome and charming none of the Wyndhams could deny; but it was equally certain that he was too easily attracted away from the solidly profitable venture to the merely alluring. His long absences distressed them for Weeta's sake—indeed, sometimes it seemed quite uncertain whether he would ever come back; and the lack of any tangible result caused them to shake their heads.

And when, sometimes, he returned with news of some speculation or purchase, of some far-off run, or of a splendid mob of horses, or a stallion that was really something out of the common, George, on enquiring into it in his meticulous way, always found material for vague alarm, and for conversations with Weeta or Margaret which ended in sighs and reiterated hopes for the best.

May was ten years old now; between her and her father the bond was perhaps drawn closer by her outgrowing of the close atmosphere of Richmond Vale and by her unwavering faith in the father whose achievement in life had never quite come up to his own expectations. It was to her, then, that, returning home from one of his mysterious expeditions, he first gave the dramatic news of his latest venture.

'How should you like to see the Tropic of Capricorn, Miss Mac-kenzie?'

Mama, combing the twins' hair into ringlets beside the fire, looked up sharply. 'Arthur, what do you mean by that?'

'We've burned our boats, my dear girl. Everything's up for sale that can be sold—the New England country, the horses, and I've just put this cottage up for sale too. We're going where fortunes are to be made. There are thousands of miles of new country opened up for settlement, north of Rockhampton—splendid cattle country, everyone is off their heads about it. All one needs to set oneself up for life is a little enterprise and a good mob of cattle. Well, I have the cattle—they cost money, of course; everyone's after cattle, naturally, with such a chance waiting up there. But they're good cattle—ask Regi, he'll tell you so. And I know of three men who'll come in with me. We'll overland the cattle, up to the Isaacs River or there-abouts, take up as much land as we like, build you a house to any plan you suggest—then there we are, rich landowners, living happily ever after, in a perfect climate. Now, Weeta my dear, do look a little more cheerful. After all, haven't you been at me for years to find something safe and profitable?'

Well, his wife thought, nothing could be done about it now. And perhaps, perhaps it might turn out well. For it was true that reports of the northern country were enthusiastic; and, as Arthur said, everyone was talking of the possibilities of the land just opened for settlement.

The inevitable Wyndham conclave was held. George and Margaret were alarmed over the probable climate of the new district. A con-troversy was going on over the question of the ability of Europeans to live and work in tropical conditions; it was forecast by many that women and children would droop and die, subjected to the northern summers with their high monsoonal rainfall and their bad reputation for fevers. The land that Arthur Mackenzie had taken up was well within the tropics, and in addition it lay many miles inland from the few coastal ports which formed its only access, except that offered by many weeks of hard and trackless riding among treacherous tribes.

But Weeta Mackenzie had gradually come round to her husband's way of thinking. Perhaps she was, after all, a little irked by those frequent visits to Dalwood in search of sympathy and companionship; perhaps she hoped that the possession of this northern country would steady her husband and keep him at work; and perhaps, too, she remembered those adventurous days of her girlhood when, riding with the waggons and the cattle, she had been excited by the breadth and freedom of her unknown country. The little cottage, the care of five children, the comparative poverty and loneliness of her life since her marriage, combined to make her look favourably now on such a prospect of change.

But she agreed with her parents in their concern for the possible effect of the climate on the children's health. She would take every care, she promised. Yes, they would return to Dalwood if it seemed wiser to do so. She was secretly a little alarmed at the thought that so many hundreds of miles would now intervene between her and her large protecting clan; and, too, the thought that she would probably be the only white woman for many miles around, perhaps the first in that district, troubled her as she considered her responsibility to the children. She would, at least, engage a governess to go with them.

Arthur Mackenzie was, as usual, untroubled by doubts. He was already riding round the district with the few men he had persuaded to help him with the overlanding; he had bought cattle enough to stock the run, and he was busy and happy in the work of collecting and drafting them for the long journey.

His wife and children, and Miss Foy, the newly-acquired English governess, removed to Dalwood, for the cottage had been sold to help pay for the cattle. Here they were to spend the remaining month of preparation, sewing, filling and nailing down the cases of stores and clothing that they would need in the north, and packing trunks for the sea-trip to Rockhampton. Arthur had arranged that they were to wait at the port for letters, and to acclimatize the children, while he settled the cattle on the run and put up a house of slabs and bark that would accommodate the family for the time being. When all was ready, he was to ride to Rockhampton to meet them, and to buy waggons and teams to carry them inland to their new home.

2   MAY DOWNS

ARTHUR MACKENZIE, and the few men he took with him to help in droving the cattle, had a hard seven hundred miles of it. Through the better-known country of the southern settlements, things went comparatively easily; travellers coming southwards, drovers on their way to pick up mobs for the northern country, pulled up their horses or teams to yarn awhile, told him where the feed and water were best, and passed on what news they had of the far-off Isaacs and Suttor River country. Passing through stations owned by men he knew, he was welcomed and entertained, farewelled with wishes for good luck, for his easy charm had made him plenty of fair-weather friends.

He stayed a few days, spelling the horses, on Bukkulla Station, where Weeta's brothers managing the cattle and the vineyard of the northern offshoot of Dalwood greeted him with unusual respect and envy. Here he hitched his horse to the old hitching-post that Ludwig Leichhardt had used on his last trip northwards; Leichhardt had passed through the country that Arthur Mackenzie was now heading for, but Mackenzie hoped for better luck from it than Leichhardt had had.

But once past the settled areas, the cattle, which had so far done fairly well, began to cause trouble. He no longer knew the country, and travellers were scarce from whom he could find out the state of the route ahead. Hovering tribes of blacks grew more troublesome; a few cattle were speared, and there was some open hostility.

The tribes presented a problem to the many men then pushing northwards with their mobs. It was best, as far as possible, to keep at a distance from their camps, for there was no way of telling their temper beforehand. This new invasion of men, dogs and cattle on their hunting-grounds had roused them, peaceable as they might be, to opposition.

Perhaps they might take fright at the cattle, vanishing to hide in the bush and watch with spears ready for too close an encounter;

perhaps they would be curious and covetous, coming boldly round the men and begging tobacco and flour and sugar that could not be spared from the dwindling packs, fingering their spears ominously when refused. And at night, the man riding on watch might hear on the other side of the mob a choked bellow and a scuffle, and galloping around might find a few broken bushes and a smear of blood where a calf had been dragged off into the night; or if he were in time, might rescue a beast with a spear or two sticking in its side, before the frightened mob rushed and scattered. Then the men off watch, wakened and running for their horses, would have a wild ride to get the mob together again, galloping often through the dark in unknown country, half-clad and without their saddles.

Old hands said that it was always better to keep the aboriginals at a distance, however friendly they might seem. It was impossible to know what grudges might be rankling among the tribes, now that men and cattle were moving everywhere through their traditional hunting-grounds, while neither law nor settled policy dictated the white men's behaviour to the country's original owners. Thus the men who had gone through ahead a week or a month before might have left a hitherto quiet tribe seething under any kind of grievance. No one could know how the matter stood, until perhaps it was too late for conciliation, and a spear had taken their revenge.

And, too, the whites knew that from the tribesmen's point of view they were trespassing on country where they had no rights. This knowledge did not make for good relations. If they shot a turkey or kangaroo for food, it might prove to be a sacred animal to the people who were almost certainly watching unseen from the bush; or perhaps the lagoon beside which they camped held for the local tribe some incomprehensible significance, making their presence there sacrilege. Not that this would have troubled them. But it was a continual stress upon them; they could not forget that they were under perpetual observation by hidden eyes. It was hard to keep from stealing glances over the shoulder, in hostile country, or to forget the tingling between the shoulder-blades, where a spear might lodge at any time without warning.

It was seldom, in fact, that the blacks attacked travellers, but news of any such incident travelled very quickly, and the provocation given was seldom taken into account in the white man's resultant rage and fear. Distrust quickly led to hatred, even among those who had as yet suffered no losses. The men behind the mobs of precious cattle were disposed to mistake the curiosity even of friendly tribes for a threat; those who had already lost cattle or mates to the blacks' spears were relentless in their revenge. Many bodies, therefore, marked the tracks the cattle took as the new country was settled; and an unwritten law made men keep silence on such happenings.

Many of Mackenzie's cattle died on the long journey. There were long dry stages where they had grown weak and poor from lack of grass, or had moved round restless and unhappy at nights on waterless camps. Some had died of poisoning from eating plants strange to the drovers, who had no knowledge of the country; others had been drowned in the currents of the deeper rivers that had to be forded. But enough remained to stock the big run on the Isaacs River which Arthur Mackenzie now took up.

Two small groups of settlement existed already in this wild and isolated country; they centred on the mining township of Copperfield, where a few tents, waggons and shanties testified to a thriving small population, and on the tiny township of Marlborough, a hundred miles or more towards the coast. Rockhampton, the port nearest to the new run, lay a week's hard riding to the south-east. As Queensland runs went, this one was not too isolated; and the country, lightly timbered downland with much tall grass, seemed likely to suit cattle.

The heat was worse than the men had expected, for summer was now at its height. But Mackenzie set to work in a sanguine mood to build the long earth-floored hut where he and his family were to live; and he named the run May Downs, for the pretty daughter whose enthusiasm over this new venture had helped to keep him in heart during the long northward journey.

The work of cutting timber, stripping bark for the roof and carrying clay from the strange peak-like ant-beds, to be puddled for the floor, was hard, and the unaccustomed heat tired him. The two men who had remained with him to help with the cattle-work were kept busy, for the tribes hereabouts were warlike and resentful, since the population of rough and unconciliatory men at the Copperfield mines kept the situation between the black and white occupiers of the land at simmering point. Cattle were speared and run off at nights, and the constant diet of weevily flour and salt beef, and the continuous work, did not conduce to hopefulness and health.

When the wet season set in January brought new problems of heavy floods. The Isaacs was uncrossable, May Downs was cut off from supplies, cattle were marooned and drowned, and the difficulties were increased by the heavy black soil which bogged horses to the knees.

Arthur Mackenzie was unnerved by these unexpected problems. This was, in fact, the wettest season known in the early days of northern settlement: continual rain, and the steamy heat that went with it, lasted for months. Then the few men on the run were stricken with sickness.

Two illnesses seemed endemic in the north: the dreaded spue, caused probably by monotonous diet and malnutrition, which prevented men from eating even the beef and the poor ration-flour dampers that they lived on, and brought with it the tormenting pus-filled sores of the Barcoo rot; and the malaria-like illness called fever-and-ague, which seemed born of the steamy wet season. Arthur Mackenzie and his men, ill and overworked, found that an additional torture came with the clouds of sandflies and mosquitoes that rose from the swamps and bogs of the flats along the Isaacs River. Men, horses and cattle suffered alike from the sandflies, which stung day and night and could be baffled only by the smoke of smudge-fires, which had to be kept perpetually alight.

It so happened that May Downs lay in the worst of the fever-country; and Arthur Mackenzie, inexperienced in the problems of this country, had built his hut near the Isaacs where the sandflies were at their fiercest. Illness, worry and sleepless nights riding after the cattle or fighting the sandflies began to take their toll of him. When at last the wet season seemed over, and the floods had subsided, he finished his hut-building in no very cheerful mood. He was tired, dispirited and still subject to bad attacks of fever when he set out on the long week's ride to Rockhampton, to meet Weeta and the children.

The family party had left Dalwood at last, after all the bustle of packing and preparation, the farewells, and the anxieties about the children's health and about the northern climate that had led Grandmama to include in the cases such a variety of medicines and instructions. Their moods varied from Miss Foy's open alarms and regrets to May's no less open exultation.

When at last they were actually stowed in the big Dalwood waggonette (the heavy luggage had gone to Newcastle ahead of them, by bullock-dray), and were driving, escorted by two of the young uncles, down the Newcastle road to take ship for Rockhampton, May gazed out with the elation of adventure at the landscape of the valley through which they passed. Mills and houses, green paddocks of wheat and corn, the great slow river itself dotted with its boats and barges, all seemed in a way to belong to her. She was deeply conscious that she belonged to a family that had shared in the subduing of this country into its industrious placidity, and that she herself was now setting out on another such enterprise.

Accordingly, she felt her own importance, helping Mama to quieten the twins, who had burst into impulsive tears at the emotional farewells on Dalwood's carriage-drive, and were still fractious and sobbing. George was absorbed in helping Paddy to drive the waggonette, and Arundel in watching the horses. Miss Foy ('Poor Miss Foy' she had already been named, a name which was to stick) was tearfully recalling her own recent farewells to England. 'It does so bring back the loss of dearer scenes, Mrs Mackenzie!' As for Mama, pale and determined, she divided her attention between the twins and the lastminute lists which needed checking before the voyage was begun. May, efficiently calming Lilla with a nursery-rhyme, felt grown-up and full of responsibility, almost like the leader of an exploringparty.

Seasickness, on this coastal trip, was notoriously unavoidable. The small sailing-ship on which they travelled had few amenities, and below decks it was stiflingly hot and airless. Poor Miss Foy gave way at once; Mama attended to the children's troubles, though dreadfully war herself. But May soon recovered from the effect of the coastwise swell, which sent the little ship lurching and pitching in a continual motion exasperating in its irregularity. When Mama and the twins did not need attention, she was continually up on deck, wildly excited by the new life and the glimpses of strange shores moving past.

The imprisoned air in the stuffy cabin grew hotter and hotter as the ship moved northward, and the sea grew bluer and bluer. At last they passed through the entrance to the Barrier Reef passage; and in its calmer sheltered waters, the seasick revived and came pallidly on deck, to admire the islands and watch porpoises and occasional flying-fish.

When at last they landed in Rockhampton, May stared about her in wonder at the unfamiliar town. Shacks and houses, made for the most part of split palings, were scattered along wide roads which resembled rivers of stagnant mud; the floods of the wet season that almost drowned the town that summer had left pools of putrid irised water by the houses and in the paddocks. Mosquitoes hummed everywhere in clouds. Men down for a brief respite from the harsh life of the inland mines, or from droving trips to the new inland stations, shouted to each other or fought in drunken joy outside the grog-shops.

An immigrant ship had not long reached the town, and bare-footed Irishmen and women walked the streets bewildered; soon they would be hired, or would find transport to the copper-mines and the inland runs. Kanakas wandered here and there in groups, with flowers stuck in their woolly hair, shepherded by men with guns. They had been brought from their islands, willingly or unwillingly, to work on the sugar-plantations of the coast, and they stared round sullenly and afraid at the unknown town, meeting eyes often as hostile as their own.

Poor Miss Foy was filled with alarm at the garish ugliness of the streets and at the goats that trotted boldly wherever they wished and even came sniffing at the hems of her decent English skirts, glancing up with sly bland eyes. As for Mama, she had little time to look at the strange sights, being fully occupied calming Miss Foy's fears, keeping the twins and the two boys under control, and managing interviews with bankers, cabmen and postal officials.

But May could have stood staring for hours at the strange coloured people she saw: the yellow Chinese children tumbling at the door-ways of little shops and stalls with bamboo curtains, the pig-tailed market-gardeners jogging with their poles and baskets, the smiling or sullen half-caste women at their doorways, the groups of aboriginals wandering here and there, already depraved with rum and opium.

Then the children were packed into the cab; Mama had rented a cottage a mile or so from the town, and here they were to wait until Papa should come for them. Letters were waiting at the post-office, which Mama looked grave over; but though she folded them away with an anxious air she did not say very much. The children were disappointed to hear that Papa had not started for Rockhampton yet.

'Papa hasn't been very well; but he is building the house as fast as he can. So we must wait for him here, until the weather is a little cooler.'

It was certainly too hot to think with much pleasure even of a short journey, let alone one of three weeks or more in a jolting dray: so hot that Weeta Mackenzie, when she heard of a cottage to let not far from the town, had taken it with alacrity because it stood near the famous lagoon. A cottage so near water held out the promise of a little coolness, at least at nights.

And the lagoon, when the cab reached its shores, was a sight that made the children call out in delight, covered as it was with the pink and blue flowers of native water-lilies, and crowded with water-birds, wading, diving, floating everywhere. But, as inexperienced as her husband, Weeta Mackenzie too had chosen badly, for the cottage was full of mosquitoes, and the lagoon's banks were notorious for snakes and for the dreadful fever-and-ague that was causing Arthur Mackenzie's own troubles.

When May thought of the cottage in later years, it seemed to her that trees and vines had crowded round the house, in continual flower, that orchids plumed the tree-trunks, snakes of extraordinary colours gestured from the branches, and small bright birds flew everywhere. Poor Miss Foy was afraid—of the insects that crawled and flew and ambushed her in cupboards and corners and even hid in her shoes, of the snakes and lizards that oppressed the walks she had to take with the children, of the Chinese and the blacks and the Kanakas, and of the children too. The children knew this very well, and their tempers were made fretful by mosquito-bites and hot weather. They teased her all the more, putting dead snakes on the paths for her to come upon, picking up spiders and unfamiliar insects to hide in her gloves, those gloves which she wore, as an English lady should, even in this uncompromising climate. Miss Foy, it was clear, would not take very kindly to the inland life that awaited her.

The stings of the mosquitoes and sandflies that haun.ed the lagoon covered their skins with pink blotches the colour of the curious pink bandy-snakes that scuttled in and out of the bushes in the garden. The children began to fall victim to attacks of fever. The rainy season went on and on, the lagoon filled and overflowed its banks, and the river flooded Rockhampton's odorous streets again. Weeta Mackenzie was at her wits' end to keep the household goods and the packed cases of clothes and blankets from mildewing in the damp air. Everyone grew pale and irritable.

It was at this unlucky time of year that Arthur Mackenzie at last set out for Rockhampton to meet his family. He had scarcely finished the work of putting up his house. Like most of the early station homesteads, it was floorless, for there was no means of sawing and levelling boards; the timber of which it was built was all axe-cut, the roof of the thick slabs of rain-impervious bark cut from the stringybark trees. Windows cut in the unlined timber walls were closed with wooden squares cut to fit and hinged from the top with strips of greenhide. It did not look a very inviting dwelling, and the hard work of cutting the timber and building the house in the rainy heat of that season had left him tired and easily depressed.

Two weeks' riding to Rockhampton, with many detours to avoid rivers and creeks made unfordable by floods, and a difficult crossing of the Fitzroy River, on a diet even sparser than usual, did not tend to raise his spirits. He had already begun to be doubtful whether this country would ever be suitable for his wife and children, and when he reached Rockhampton and found them ill with fever, too, he began to despair of his whole venture. Weeta found no opposition to her declaration that she was taking the children back to Dalwood on the first available ship.

May was disappointed and indignant to learn that they were not, after all, to set out for the new home on which she had built her dreams. She had no sympathy with Miss Foy's evident rejoicing over the decision; it seemed to her a confession of failure. But Mama was not to be moved. She was anxious for the twins, and her husband's pallor and dejection alarmed her the more. She longed now only to get the children out of this wretched climate and back to her beloved Dalwood.

Arthur Mackenzie saw them on to the ship, and turned back to May Downs again. It was arranged that he would get the run in order and put it up for sale. If a good price could be got, he would return to Dalwood and buy more country in a less forbidding climate.

But the Queensland speculation turned out to be his worst and last. The great Queensland slump of the sixties had already begun. Prices of cattle and sheep, and land values, inflated by the rush to take up new country, began to fall; the banks, which had advanced vast sums during the land boom, grew anxious and began to call in their capital. A panic began. Then the Bank of Queensland put up its shutters.

Almost all the new stations were working under heavy mortgages for money had been freely offered and accepted during the days of expansion. Now that the interest payments were falling due, there was little coming in to pay them with. Arthur Mackenzie, who had been a carefree borrower, was one of the earliest in trouble. The mortgage on May Downs was foreclosed, the run passed out of his hands, was stripped of stock and abandoned, and Mackenzie found himself bankrupt and ruined.

When he returned from Queensland to Dalwood, the shock of his financial disaster had completed what fever, hard work and malnutrition had begun. He was no longer the carefree optimistic man who had ridden the countryside, keeping the Wyndhams talking with his fantastic journeys and his deals in horses. Ill and broken, he had lost all heart for his old life of bargaining and travelling, and Weeta Mackenzie, when she met the ship that brought him back to Newcastle, was horrified at the change in him.

Long nursing at Dalwood helped him little. It was clear to George and Margaret that they must accept the Mackenzie family as a charge on their own estate. It was fortunate that the Wyndhams were moderately prosperous, and that Dalwood, together with their northern run, Bukkulla, brought in enough not only to support their own large family of sons, many now married and with families of their own, but to allow a considerable margin.

Accordingly, George offered his son-in-law a cottage on the Dalwood property, one built as a foreman's dwelling-place in the old days of assigned labour, and now unoccupied. Mackenzie was too ill and listless to do other than accept; he did not relish the idea of dependence but it seemed there was no alternative. Such small income as he had would barely suffice to keep his family alive, and without Dalwood's bounty he had no prospects.

The Mackenzies moved into their new home without joy, but their eldest daughter rejoiced that, if she was deprived of the pioneering venture she had set her heart on, she was at least to live at her beloved Dalwood. The smallness of the cottage did not dishearten her. Convict-built of stone, it was cramped but not uncomfortable; Margaret, full of sympathy for her daughter's plight, had given them all she could spare of Dalwood's furniture. And over the hill lay Dalwood itself, always ready to welcome the children. There were plans for their education. Margaret herself would teach them; she was secretly pleased to have these grandchildren near.

It was a commonplace of May's life thereafter that her family was poor, even desperately poor; yet poverty seemed no more than a skeleton in the cupboard, whose bones rattled seldom and half-heartedly. It did not seem to matter much that her clothes were patched and turned and patched again, for she knew that if she really needed anything, Grandpapa was at hand to give it to her. And at Dalwood she and George and Arundel and the twins, Lilla and Teenie, spent much of their time; for the cottage, which they had named Wouillah, was not large enough to allow the sick man much quiet with five noisy children near, and they escaped with thankfulness, whenever they could, to the big house where they were not continually hushed and where, now that the family was grown and scattered, there were so many rooms in which they might play.

3   *ALBERT*

IN 1840, ten years after the establishment of Dalwood, there had come to the Hunter Valley a young Cornishman and his wife, equipped with a little money and hoping to make their fortunes by farming.

Philip Wright had brought from England only as much money as was appropriate to launch a younger son from a not particularly wealthy family. This he lost almost at once, being unwise in the ways of the world, to a confidence trickster. He was left almost destitute, stranded in a strange country which was itself passing through difficult times, and his young wife was about to bear her first child.

The child so unpromisingly circumstanced turned out to be a boy, and they named him Albert Andrew. In his solemn unsmiling face his mother always traced her own despair before his birth. His thick black hair, too, was marked by one white lock, and this curious mark he never lost.

Philip Wright, faced with the prospect of becoming a farm-labourer in a country in which farms and runs were daily being abandoned by their owners, wrote home for assistance, and somehow managed to support his wife and child by various means until the months had brought back the sailing-ship which carried the money.

He had had time, meanwhile, to look about him and learn something of the ways of his new country and the farm which he bought, at Blandford on the upper Hunter, was a good one. Times were hard, but his luck began to turn, and by hard work he managed to keep afloat until the slump was over.

Then he grew prosperous, and when his eldest son came of school age, he was sent to Sydney, to the King's School at Parramatta, which was said to be the best school in the Colony. Here Albert remained until he had turned fourteen.

But then the gold-rush of the 'fifties began. So great was the rush of men from town and country that the inland properties were in many cases left without labour, without communications and hence without a market. Philip Wright had two isolated and undeveloped properties in the north-west, a considerable distance from the Hunter, which were deserted by his shepherds and stockmen; and he faced considerable difficulties at home, with a lengthening family and the Blandford property to be looked after single-handed. He had no alternative but to take Albert from school and send him out to take charge of the two runs, for he could not spare time to look after them himself, and as for selling, there was no chance of that, with almost every able-bodied man in the country swarming to the gold-fields and the value of pastoral properties sinking daily.

Albert was then a shy, quiet boy, said by his masters to be a brilliant scholar, but in many ways undeveloped for his age. The responsibility suddenly thrust on his shoulders was great enough for a boy so young, but his own inexperience of life and lack of self-confidence made him feel it as even more crushing than it actually was. He had never taken very much interest in the work of the land, for his taste and his abilities lay more in the direction of study; in practical matters he distrusted his own capacity. He had been naturally slow to make friends, yet he was an affectionate boy and suffered much from lone-liness and homesickness. Now he was forcibly separated from school-life and home-life, and leagues of unpeopled bush lay between him and anyone he cared for.

Albert had always taken life, and himself, too seriously. Now he lay awake at nights in the stringybark bunk of the lonely hut, and tortured himself with vivid pictures of his family ruined and of his

own incapacity contributing to their disaster, of fatal mistakes he
had perhaps made, of everything that had gone or might go wrong.
There was little to interrupt these black dreams; the work he had to
do was hard and unaccustomed, and his life was solitary except for
the one old half-mad shepherd who had stayed with his flock because
his half-witted brain could not grasp the news of the gold-rush.
Sometimes the local tribe of blacks camped on the run in the course
of their wanderings, and contributed a few men to the work of the
place for a time; otherwise he saw few people, and indeed there
were few to see.

The runs were far out, and seemed lost and forgotten in the distances
of trees that separated them from the world. Albert was dreadfully
homesick for the reassuring crowd of children who now filled the
house at Bickham, far off in the valley. He would lie awake and listen
to the weird rising cry of the curlews and the howl of dingoes (were
they at Bennett's fold? Had the old man gone on the grog again?)
or to the beating of his own heart, a lonely rustling in his ears, and
imagine that it was irregular, louder than usual, slower than it should
be. If he died up here, would old Bennett find and bury him? How
would Father discover it—and what would they all do then?

Gradually he began to grow more accustomed to his new life,
and though he did not greatly care for his work he became easier in
it and less anxious. The years passed, and only an occasional brief
visit to the valley formed his holidays. The box of school-books he
had taken with him was more and more neglected: white-ants had
eaten the bindings; floods and summer heat, that alternately soaked
and cracked open the stringybark roof and walls of the hut, had
spoiled them. At first he had tried to keep at his studies, at nights, by
the light of the slush-lamp that flickered weakly in its tallow, but
it was an unequal struggle. The fatigue of a day begun at dawn and
overfull of work and responsibility kept him from understanding
more than a few pages at a time. Sometimes he woke shivering late
at night with his head on the rough table beside a book, the slush-
lamp long since gone out. But later he accepted without rebellion
the fact that he would never learn much more, as long as his fate
kept him on the inland runs. Soon the school-books remained in their
box.

He had remained on the western runs for six years, and was a young man of twenty, when at last his father managed to sell the land, and he was free to go back to Bickham. Prosperity had returned to the family, and now that they were growing up, his brothers were able to share much of the responsibility.

Money was plentiful again in the Colony. The valley, now closely settled and well served with roads, was a gay place: coaches and carriages spun along the roads, fashionable crinolines and bonnets could be seen. Valley society was beginning to pride itself on having a good tone. Fine horses were bred there, and it was a point of importance to have something out of the way to ride or drive. The townships were growing, little churches and big houses sprang up everywhere. The family at Bickham, young and cheerful, were quite in the whirl, and invitations to balls, picnics and riding-parties crossed and re-crossed.

In a way, Albert began to enjoy himself. He lacked conversation, but he was sufficiently good-looking to be regarded as reserved rather than unmannerly, he enjoyed dancing, had a tolerable voice and ear, and could copy music for young ladies. He took various jobs managing properties in the valley and on the Liverpool Plains beyond, and in the intervals fell in love several times, had ill luck with the young ladies, broke his heart and mended it. He had never got over his melancholy, his look of strain and anxiety; he still took himself too seriously.

In fact, perhaps, he was never really to reconcile the two worlds that existed side by side within him: this world in which he now found himself, in which a man must be respectable and successful, a good hand at a bargain, with a shrewd eye for horses and cattle, and the dark lonely world in which he was still haunted by the dingoes' howling and the last struggles of the child he had had to disown and crush in himself too early.

It was from this undeveloped part of himself that his bitter melancholy moods welled up, in which the struggle of living seemed not worth while; in which he doubted himself, and the gaiety which had suddenly superimposed itself upon him seemed a kind of bright bubble enclosing nothing. At such times, the real world seemed to him to lie hidden under the surface of things, a perpetual three o'clock in the morning, with curlews weeping in the dark and dingoes waiting to slip into the sheepfold.

At last he was offered, and accepted, the job of managing a big western station, whose owner was a friend of the family. Albert had acquired a reputation as a good and careful stockman and manager; his very doubts of himself made him so. He would lie awake to plan and worry where a more sanguine man would have left the job to luck and slept soundly; hence, for he was really able, he foresaw and provided against difficulties earlier than most. The Collymongool job carried a salary of three hundred pounds a year, which was very good pay; and he set out (being in love again—with a girl called Sallie Dickinson) determined to do well, save money, and buy a run for himself at the end of his three-year contract.

It was a flood year. The slab hut that was the station headquarters stood beside a great lagoon; behind it the creek took a big curve, and in flood the two met and the hut was left cut off on an island. Rain began soon after his arrival. The men should have been out gathering fat cattle, the autumn work of the run, but the ground was too heavy, horses began to bog, the cattle were sheltering in the scrub and not to be seen. The creeks began to rise, and all work stopped; there was nothing at all to do for long stretches at a time.

He sat in the parlour of the manager's hut and read the few novels in the shelves over and over: Thackeray, Wilkie Collins, and old paper-backs and magazines. In their quarters the men finished their private supply of grog and tried to break into the ration store. They fought, sulked in their bunks, became dangerous or melancholy according to their natures, played cards incessantly and gambled away their wages for years to come, their clothes, even their black gins. At the end of the lagoon, the blacks crouched sullenly in their sodden wurlies; their fires would not burn, and they sent the fattest and most attractive of the young gins to the kitchen to beg or steal food from the Chinese cook.

Rations were low enough at the homestead, for the drays were belated by the floods. The damp steamy air sent the flour mouldy, and tea tasted muddy as swamp-water. There was no colza-oil or kerosene for the lamps, and it was impossible to work or read by the dull yellow flicker of the slush-lamp. The shingle roofs, soaked through with the continual rain, at last began to drip; water splashed on Albert's locket with Mama's picture, on Sallie Dickinson's letters, on the damp blue blankets of the bunk and on the perpetual corned beef at meals.

Albert, racked with homesickness, wrote endless letters, but it was seldom possible to ride to Collarenebri, two days away, to meet the mail, and the letters accumulated in the box beside his bed and got no answer. Where was Sallie and what was she doing? What was happening at home? What day was it? He went to look at his diary, his only means of marking the time. It was Sunday morning, and he sat down at the rough adzed table and stared at the rain-pitted lagoon, seeing instead his family setting out for the village church. Mama would be wearing her black silk, Papa his grey stove-pipe hat, Mary something new from Sydney. . . . But a squabble broke out at the men's quarters: he could hear angry voices, someone fell heavily, something broke with a clatter. The rain went on.

It was a bad year altogether. When at last the rain held off long enough for the fats to be gathered and sent east, he had a bad fall, galloping after a dingo to ride it down, and had to go back to his bunk with a couple of broken ribs, and chafe at lying passive with the sun shining outside. Then the rain began again, with the cattle still on the road; he worried whether they would get across the river before the flats flooded again, or whether they would bog and drown.

The drays made their way through at last, and he was able to have a kerosene light again, instead of the slush-lamp; summer began in earnest and dried out the steaming country. But by this time he had taken an ineradicable dislike to the place.

His first year there was drawing to an end, and the place had settled into a monotonous routine. He began to feel buried alive, as he had felt in his youth alone with his responsibilities. The long wet months had left bad blood among the men, and open quarrels often broke out; the atmosphere was never a happy one. The blacks' camp so near was a nuisance; they were getting grog secretly from the men in exchange for various shady transactions in women, which he preferred to know as little of as possible, since it seemed impossible to prevent them. The whole camp sometimes got roaring drunk, since it did not take much liquor to intoxicate men not used to it; fights would begin and go on, it seemed, all night, high screeching trebles of defiance and challenge piercing through all attempts at sleep.

The lagoon was still high, and the house isolated by water, but the bark canoe was almost always on the other side because a gin had gone over to look for mully-grubs in the bush: he was always having to strip and swim across for it. Thunderbolt, the bushranger, was rumoured to be somewhere near; he had robbed the Wallabadah coach and was supposed to have come this way with the loot. Albert would have liked an encounter with him, for life at Collymongool was growing more and more boring and petty, and he longed for some kind of excitement. But though two constables rode through looking for tracks, they found none, and rode on.

At the end of the year, he was offered a new job. Old Eales, a wealthy acquaintance of his father, had bought up a number of mortgages on Queensland stations. The slump which had ruined Arthur Mackenzie was not yet at an end; stations which had held out for years were falling at last, and among them were two for which Eales held the mortgages. Now he wanted a couple of active and experienced men to go north and take over the stations for him. When the transactions were completed and the inventories taken, the cattle and sheep were to be sent to fetch what price they could, either in the southern markets or nearer home, and the stations were to be abandoned.

Albert and his younger brother Fred were offered the jobs. The two stations were inland from Rockhampton: one not far from the Isaacs River country, one just south of the tropic, in the Dawson Valley. Fred wrote that he was accepting, and would leave shortly for Avon Downs, near the Isaacs; if Albert wanted to go, the job at Nulalbin on the Dawson was being kept open for him.

Albert wrote to Eales and accepted eagerly. He was tired of Collymongool and its quarrels; the trip north sounded attractive and he was anxious to see Queensland. And though the job would not last long, the pay was good. He packed his saddle-bags with relief.

Still, when the time came to set out, his valise strapped to the saddle and the packhorse loaded, he felt an inexplicable regret. Last

year, he had set out like this for Collymongool, all his hopes set on
the future. Now all was changed; the perspectives slid and altered
in front of him. And Sallie's letters were now so few and formal
that he hardly dared to hope for her any longer. Thinking of this,
he rode off towards the valley again, and by the campfire that night
he ended his diary entries with the words, 'Melancholy, I scarcely
know why.'

He must go to Sydney to catch the steamer for Rockhampton.
He wrote to Sallie, asking to see her while he was there, for the
Dickinsons were now living at George's River. Frightened, he dallied
in his lodgings in Macquarie Street, putting off the visit on various
excuses—today he must buy a new saddle; tomorrow he must make
arrangements with the shipping company. At last he took courage
and went, feeling stiffly unfamiliar in his new suit and his mirror-
polished boots.

His two days at George's River, which must serve him for a year's
emotional nourishment, were enigmatical. Remembering them
many times later, he was never able to decide whether Sallie had
been kind or indifferent, whether the gaiety of her welcome had
meant that he was regarded as a likely suitor or only as an old friend.
Sallie was eighteen now, surely old enough to be asked . . . but Mrs
Dickinson had advised him against venturing to speak to her seriously,
saying she was a child yet and did not know her own mind; he must
leave it for a year or two, and then perhaps . . .

At least, she had given him a locket with her picture; and that
day on the river she had promised to answer his letters. He had this
much to comfort him as he went on board the *Balclutha*. But another
year lay ahead, in which he could not see her. He was almost twenty-
eight now. Reserved and quiet, he did not make friends easily, and
the time ahead seemed lonely to him.

There were not many passengers aboard who were travelling
farther than Brisbane, except a few miners hoping to get a living
at the copper-mines and gold-mines near Rockhampton. He talked to
some of them, trying to get some information as to the kind of
country he was going to, for the two runs that Eales had put in his
and Fred's charge both lay inland from Rockhampton, one south of
the tropic and the other to the north of it. They had tales of heat,

floods and fever, and did not have much good to say of the country's prospects, apart from mining. The officers told him that the boat would be crowded enough on the backward journey; for the inland stations were still falling like card houses. The trouble was to get the fares for the journey from the broken men who came on board with little left from their hard years. The shipping company would do well if half the promissory notes it held were cashed in the end.

But it was late June weather, windy and bright, and as the little steamer forged northwards the weather grew warmer, and Albert felt the pleasant weather raise his spirits. The sky was blue and the sea calm, and reading on deck and watching blue headlands and islands slip by, he enjoyed his holiday. He had never been so far from home before, and it was like starting a new life; he was conscious of the good new saddle sewn in hessian in his cabin, and of the trunk full of new working clothes, stiff as boards, and the smell of the harsh blue blanket he had bought in Sydney. And in Brisbane, where the ship waited over for a day or two, he had money to spend, and was pleased with the little city and its palms and plants and flowers that were new to him.

As the steamer travelled north again to Rockhampton, almost empty of passengers save himself and the miners, the atmosphere was easy and intimate. Once a strange thing happened: something which Albert remembered afterwards as one might remember a truce in a long and unrelenting war. The steamer had turned into the narrow channel between a long island and the mainland, and with a few of the other men he was leaning over the rail and watching the island's low timbered shores slip by a few hundred yards away. A crowd of naked black figures ran down a headland, dancing and waving at the ship, and shouting half-intelligible words. 'Sugarbag, bacca, sugarbag,' they cried, begging from the strange white men.

The long lazy days had made the white men tolerant; they felt the need of entertainment. They waved and shouted back, holding up their tobacco-plugs. 'Bacca here, come and get it!' The cook emerged from the galley and held up handfuls of biscuits; the crew idled to watch.

The blacks danced hesitantly on the shore for a moment, then a big bearded man dived in and the rest followed. It was a long swim, for the ship was still moving fast, but as the crowd of black heads drew closer the captain rang down the speed. Men began betting on their favourites; someone threw a rope net down for a ladder. The shining faces, the shining grins drew nearer—the big man who had jumped first seized the net and climbed up, jumping to the deck with a lithe motion. He dropped, panting with laughter, while men crowded to shake his hand. 'Bloody good swim, Jacky; you strong fella all right!' Wet and glittering, grinning shyly, he took the plugs they gave him as the others crowded up the net behind him, shouting with excitement, for their share.

Just for a moment, it seemed, the two races merged; the blacks for once were equals and comrades and there was no ill-will. Young warriors on a hunting-party, muscular and beautifully-modelled, they clowned and danced on the wet deck, streaming water.

But it could not last long. On the bridge the captain rang the bell again impatiently, the ship began to gather way; with cries of consternation the blacks ran to the side, balanced a moment, pushing plugs and biscuits into their wild hair, dived and began to swim back again.

The white men, now that the incident was over, chuckled and looked at each other, half-ashamed; it was as though they had been caught in some act of self-betrayal. 'Good swimmers,' said one, apologetically; another answered, 'It's an instinct, like snakes and dogs.' They dispersed again, the crew back to their work and the miners to their endless card-games, yarning and squabbling. The steamer hurried on up the channel.

But Albert stayed watching by the rail until the dark figures on the shore were out of sight. The incident had troubled him, reviving in him certain questions of conscience which most of the men he knew had long since ceased to ask or perhaps had never asked. Like all these men, he had seen things done that were not afterwards mentioned, or had known of matters best kept quiet except among intimates, in the long unacknowledged business of pushing out the tribes in favour of sheep and cattle. Massacres, drives, the taking of women, traffic in grog and opium, were matters of everyday among the men who had pushed farthest with their cattle, or gone prospecting in tribal country. Such things were not regarded: to the white men the blacks were not human, and as such not to be included in the code of moral prohibitions; the ten commandments did not hold where niggers were concerned.

But Albert had found himself wondering; and staring now at the island's wild shores he remembered the moment of fellowship he had felt, and promised himself further exploration. He would learn more of these people, their language, their stories. Perhaps there was more in them than he knew. He might have time, some day, to find out.

When the steamer drew in at Rockhampton, Albert was first ashore, eager for news of Fred and the work to be done, and eager to see this northern town. But first he must go through the Customs; and he found he had to pay a heavy fee for those new clothes. It disgusted him with the run-down little port. Rockhampton had changed since those roaring days of which he had heard garbled tales, the days when the big land-rush was on and the mines were being opened up, when miners spun sovereigns at street-corners for the favours of half-caste and Chinese girls, and when young men rode in, drunk with ownership of great tracts of country, to lose their money at roulette or with the girls who danced in tights at the Alhambra. There was a sullen air, nowadays, about the half-deserted dusty streets, and vacant shops, boarded up, looked like closed and leprous eyelids.

Letters waited for him at the agent's office. Fred was already out at the northern station on the Isaacs, Avon Downs; he was mustering and counting the stock and preparing to take delivery of the run on Eales's behalf. Albert was to go to the southern station, Nulalbin, in the Dawson Valley, seventy miles inland, where the previous owner had died of fever and worry, and where his wife and the agent whom Eales had appointed were waiting for him to arrive before the business of handing over the run could be completed.

He boarded the train which would take him as far as Westwood, the terminus of a line planned in more prosperous days, which had run only thirty miles inland before it had been abandoned. At Westwood, a black stockman waited for him with horses, for a two-day ride lay ahead. They camped that night at a creek that widened into little swamps here and there, and sang with mosquitoes even now, in the cool season.

The first view of the country, dried by drought, did not much please him. The dry grass looked coarse and rank, and the flat plains reminded him of his dreary year at Collymongool. The first settlers had brought in sheep; at first they had done well, but now they had eaten out the finer of the native grasses, and a coarse spear-grass flourished. The sheep grew thin on it, and their fleeces were lighter at each year's shearing, and full of the spear-grass seed that spoilt their value. It seemed that, as sheep-country at any rate, this inhospitable land was a failure.

The homestead at Nulalbin, a bark-roofed, slab-walled hut with an earthen verandah, looked downcast and already half-deserted when he rode up to it next day. Sheds and yards were neglected; one wall of the house was half-dismantled where a piano had been carried out to the drays. Meeting poor Mrs Glen, the owner's widow, Albert felt awkward and unhappy, though he reminded himself that after all he was not old Eales, but only an employee with a job to do.

He was introduced to the young English storekeeper and 'colonial-experiencer', a pleasant young man with a weak face and anxious eyes. It was a relief to go off with him to the men's quarters and put down his swag and blankets at last on his bunk. Hanks lingered round to talk; he was the only white employee left on the station now that the agent had paid off the stockmen.

Hanks had stayed to help with the stock-taking and handing over of the run, at Mrs Glen's appeal, for she knew little of her husband's business and was helpless to answer the agent's questions. But he was lonely and eager for company. He and Albert sat yarning on their bunks in the deserted quarters, until late that night, and Albert was pleased to think he had made a friend here already.

The two of them rode out next day; Hanks was to show Albert the boundaries of the run, and help him to look over the cattle. They went out eastwards, over the line of low hills known as the Dawson Range, for fifteen or twenty miles. It was a pleasant mid-winter day; there had been a little frost, and the coarse grass snapped drily under the hoofs of the horses.

Hanks carried a revolver, for the range of hills harboured mobs of scrubber cattle, inbred years before from stragglers left behind when the first mobs went through this country, and there were old bulls with bad reputations. As they talked, Albert found out more of Hanks's history. It was a familiar story; the story of the 'broken-down Englishman', as he was tolerantly called, who came to Australia after trouble at home, intending to make good and return in a few years, but who stayed on from year to year, too weak to break away from the year-long round of work followed by a cheque and a spree in town. Last year Hanks had summoned up his courage and taken ship to Brisbane to catch the English steamer there, but the delay in Brisbane had undermined his resolution and he had spent his cheque there and had no money left for the journey.

Hanks's sad confidences warmed Albert's feeling for him, and he began to take up a protective attitude towards him. It was new for him to have a friend, especially one who, like Hanks, had what Albert respected and envied, a University education, and who could talk of other things than the hard bush life that was all Albert had known for so many years. In his turn, perhaps, Hanks found pleasure in a confidant who was willing to respect the English background that he still took pride in and to which he yearned futilely to return.

At last he asked Albert the question he had not yet dared to ask the agent, about his own future. 'Who's going to pay me, now that Glen's dead? I can't walk out and leave without money, and Mrs Glen can't pay me. I suppose when this mustering job's done and the run is handed over, I'm out of a job, and there's nothing else going round here. I don't know what I'll do, and that's the truth.'

Albert promised that he would do what he could. Secretly he determined to write to Eales and somehow get Hanks taken on as his assistant, until his own work came to an end. He did not want to lose Hanks's company now; and he planned that, when the work was done, he would shepherd Hanks on to his homeward journey and see that he bought that steamer ticket. It was the least he could do for a friend; he had seen and heard of too many other men who, like Hanks, could not get past the grog-shops with their cheques and ended their days as hatters and shepherds, broken alcoholic wrecks. He was too shy to sermonize on these dangers, but he felt

a warm glow of resolution that Hanks, at least, must not finally
succumb to them.

The days passed, with Hanks and Albert and the black-boys
gathering the cattle, counting and recording them in bang-tail musters,
where the counted cattle had the hair of their tails cut short so that
they would be known again. It surprised Albert that the cattle looked
so well, though the winter had been dry. Evidently this was good
cattle-country, in spite of his first estimate; and many of the cows
were in calf.

Spring drew on and the days began to grow hotter. A few shearers
began to straggle in and make camp on the river, for it had been
decided that the sheep were to be shorn before they were cleared
from the run by Eales's drovers for southern markets.

When the shearers were ready the flocks came in, day after day,
and the shepherds came with them. Each shepherd was in charge of
his own flock of a couple of hundred, or sometimes more, which
it was his responsibility to look after during the year, folding them at
night and keeping them safe from dingoes. Now they were to be
paid off and sent away, workless; the money was waiting in the little
iron safe of which Albert was in charge, but no one had asked where
the old shepherds were to go or what they would do.

Shepherds were always a problem, Albert reflected. No one took
on that despised work except the very old, the weak-witted, the
worn-out men whom the bush had dried and sent half-crazy. Sometimes after the teamsters had been through with stores, or an itinerant
grog-pedlar had visited the run, they would sit for days in their
smoky bark lean-to huts, drinking rot-gut rum and muttering long
rehearsals of the past; sometimes they lost their minds and memories,
went wandering in the bush and disappeared, causing much time
and trouble in looking for them and much loss in their neglected
flocks, and perhaps were never found or were found dead or raving;
sometimes they forgot the sheep and let the dingoes get amongst
them, or lost them in the bush instead of shepherding them in the
clearings where they could be watched and counted.

They were too weary of life, too self-neglectful, to keep a few
vegetables growing in their garden patches, but lived on their weekly
rations of flour, tea and sugar, and meat, so that they often went

down with scurvy and were found by the ration-men on their rounds, swollen and ill past recovery.

Albert looked at them as they came in with their mobs, dirty and grey-bearded, their torn moleskin trousers full of ragged holes and incredibly greasy with wool-grease from the sheep, their plaited cabbage-tree hats broken and drooping, and thought of Hanks and his inevitable future, if nothing happened to save him from it. He wondered if some day he too—but the thought put him in too melancholy a mood. To protect himself against his pity, he paid them off almost brusquely, but he made sure that they were given double rations for their journey.

They hung around the place for a few days, lost and bewildered; they begged meals from the Chinese cook and slept on the earth-floored verandah of the quarters; then one by one they drifted away on the track to Rockhampton, or inland, or towards the mines, derelicts carried by the wind.

The sheep were shorn and counted, the numbers compared with the station books, the deficiencies accounted for as far as possible. Drovers came, and the mobs one by one were set on the way south for sale. Every night Albert wrestled with the books, which poor Glen had been too ill and dispirited to keep, while Mrs Glen sat sewing by the flickering moth-haunted colza lamp, or raised her head to answer the agent's fussy questions. Everything must be accounted for: harness, stores, household goods and furniture as well as cattle, sheep and horses.

The sheep-work done, the cattle must be gathered finally, and cleanskins branded. All the stockmen in the blacks' camp on the creek were recruited and these extra black-boys were outfitted with moleskins, spurs and saddles. Albert had to watch narrowly to make sure that the boys did not barter their equipment with passing tribes for knives, wives or possum-rugs.

Riding every day, he came to know the country. The run covered perhaps seventy square miles: east to the Dawson River, to Tearaway, Benleith, the Brigalow Hole, the Island and Native Dog; up the range to Bottle-tree and Sandy Camp; west to Mimosa, Denby, Saline Creek. . . . The dry winter had broken in spring storms, and the country had brightened into unexpected beauty. Bauhinia-trees whitened with sweet-scented flowers like moths, pink lotus bloomed in the waterholes, beside the blue lilies whose stems and roots the blacks dived for and ate; the big white crinum lilies, poisonous to stock in dry seasons, were breaking into bud. The cattle, he noticed, had picked up wonderfully on the good grass, and calving had been heavy. It looked like a good season ahead.

He wrote to Eales again, and suggested that the cattle might be left until autumn, in the hope of a price for fats. Eales replied, agreeing to hold the place a little longer, and agreeing too, that Hanks might stay on and help Albert with the run, and with the mustering north at Avon Downs when he should go up to help Fred. Albert was triumphant, and Hanks deeply relieved at the prospect of another six months' work at least and a good cheque at the end of it.

When branding was over, they set off together. The ride northward to Avon Downs was reckoned to take ten days, if the rivers were not in flood. Both of them were relieved to be going, for the sorrowful atmosphere of the homestead at Nulalbin had depressed their spirits. They set off almost hilariously after their months of hard work by day and silent evenings over the account-books. Mrs Glen was packed and ready to leave; she would be gone when they returned, and the worst of the strain would be over.

They did the ride north in nine days. At Avon Downs, things were more stirring. It was a very big run; twenty men were still on the pay-roll, the station books were in hopeless confusion, and Fred was busy, with the flocks lambing and rations short. The teams had not come through at their scheduled time—contractors, too, were going bankrupt, and teams being taken for debt, so that carriers were hard to come by. Albert found that the stores were dangerously low, and the stockmen growing restive at the short commons of weevily flour and sugarless tea.

Albert went off with packhorses to the nearest run, two days' ride away, to buy stores, but he could get nothing except half a ton of flour at an exorbitant price. Fred was ill with ague and nervous, at the responsibility of the muddled books, for which he feared he might be blamed. Work was hard, for even with Hanks and Albert added to the number the station was still short-handed. Albert went back to the old routine of riding all day and working at the accounts by night, by such light as the mutton-fat lamps afforded, since oil had long run out in the store. Hanks, grateful and affectionate, gave him as much help as he could; the two were fast friends now.

When the work was at its most exacting, the local tribe of blacks suddenly returned from their annual walkabout. They were a large and strong tribe, and among the white settlers around they had achieved an alarming reputation. Years ago a number of their young warriors had been recruited for the notorious Native Police; now they had either been discharged or had run away and returned to their people. During their time in the Native Police they had learned much, and none of it was good. The tribe was now addicted to grog, gambling and cattle-raids, and the deserters, intelligent and adept at stealing, had brought back with them rifles and ammunition which were now common property, and carefully concealed from the occasional inspections of the police.

Now they seemed defiantly disposed. They had been allotted a camping-place at a safe distance on the other side of the Isaacs River from the run's headquarters, but, still resentful of the intruding white men, they did not stay there. They could be heard at night, too close for comfort, holding long corroborees at which they boasted in song of the bullocks they had killed. Albert, in accordance with his resolution, had picked up a good deal of the Dawson dialect from the native stockmen during his time at Nulalbin, and felt uneasy at what he could understand of the songs, though here the dialect was confusingly different. Some of the men reported that the young warriors had begun to threaten them, and it was no use trying to get the tribe to provide men to help with the cattle-work.

The whole station began to feel uneasy. Guns were cleaned and hung in reach; men lay awake at night. The Hornet Bank massacre, too recent for comfort, kept cropping up in conversation; the details of that attack which had wiped out almost the whole of the Frazer family, southward in the Dawson Valley, were gone over again and again. Stock-riders did not care to go alone.

Albert felt his responsibility. At last he decided that the local detachment of the Native Police had better be called in. It was a step he was not anxious to take, for the stories current in the district did not show the police in any pleasant light; and when they arrived

D

he was little reassured by their methods. However, at least they had broken up the blacks' camp and driven them across the river to their allotted camping-ground. Their yells of defiance and threats of vengeance were too much muted by distance, henceforth, to trouble the men's sleep, but Fred and Albert were kept busy pacifying a minor rebellion among the few station black-boys who were not with the tribe. They were more than inclined to desert, and since they could not be spared, they had to be bribed with extra rations, scarce as food was, and given new blankets. The air was menacing, and the heat of full summer, now closing in, did nothing to help men's tempers.

One day, after the teams had at last brought in a load or two of long-overdue supplies, one of the shepherds, a Kanaka lad who had somehow escaped from the forced-labour gangs on the coastal cane-fields and strayed inland, came in to get his rations from the store, since no one could be spared from cattle-work to go on the usual ration-round. He had to cross the lagoon in a bark canoe to reach the run headquarters, and as he returned with his load the canoe capsized and the boy vanished under water. Six men were hastily called in from their work to help in the search for his body which had never risen, and Albert stripped and dived again and again, in the blood-warm water, searching in the mud among weeds and thick-growing lily-stems. But the corpse was evidently caught some-where among the weeds and snags, and could not be found. They gave up the search at sunset.

That night, Hanks had a touch of fever, and Albert stayed up until late, dosing him with makeshift medicines and cooling him with wet cloths in the night's still heat. The day's tragedy had brought on his old depression of spirits; with his incurable habit of looking for a meaning in his life, he was restless and questioning. As he wandered up and down the moonlit earth floor of the hut verandah, he could hear snatches of a wailing chant from the camp over the river. They were holding yet another corroboree over there, apparently; he listened to catch the words they sang. Whether this was part of some usual ritual ceremony, or something more sinister, or whether it had some connection with the drowning of the Kanaka boy, he did not know.

The long repeated chant began to wreathe itself around his mind, mingling with the warm muddy smell of the lagoon-water and his memory of the slime among the lily-stems. At last he brought out his diary again and wrote it down in the moonlight.

'Woombareendah-ah,' they cried, the high shrieking treble of their voices clear against a background of rhythmic clapping.

'Woombareendah-ah . . . . . woombarecndah-ah
woombareendah—bullyina—ngullina
woombareendah-ah . . . . .'

It was a fierce country. He looked out at the moonlight flooding the clearing round the huts; beyond, he could see the faraway glow of the fires over the river. The faint wailing cry possessed the night, mournful as the cry of curlews in the scrub. He wished he knew its meaning.

4   *NULALBIN*

THE WORK AT Avon Downs went on beyond the New Year of 1869, and until late February. Both Hanks and Albert were glad when it was over, and they were free to leave again for Nulalbin. The cattle at Nulalbin should be fat now, and ready for market, for the wet season had been long and the rains good this year, and feed was high everywhere. They would finish the Nulalbin work, close the books and abandon the station, this time for good. Old Captain, the aboriginal who was now Nulalbin's head stockman and could be trusted, would help them until they left. Then the run would pass again into his hands and those of his tribe until perhaps, some day, prices might rise and Eales find it worth while to re-open the run and send up a new manager.

Avon Downs, too, was to be abandoned. Albert would ride back in April to help Fred with the final stock-taking and clearing away of the cattle. Then their job would be done and they would be free to return home.

There was plenty of hard riding awaiting them at Nulalbin. All the cattle had to be gathered, and handed over mob by mob to the drovers who would take them to market, and there were few men to do the work. The cattle, too, were wild and shy, for they had been little handled and were unaccustomed to the horsemen and dogs who disturbed them from their fenceless scrubs and hills. Several times the mobs, gathered together with days of labour, rushed at night when camp was made, and sometimes got away from the stockmen in spite of the men on watch, so that the work of days was undone. When autumn ended, most of the mobs were gone, but a few wild scrubber cattle still remained in the range hills and the heavily-timbered Benleith and Island country, which Albert after fruitless search decided were not worth knocking up the horses over.

The horses, such as remained now that the drovers had taken a number to market, were certainly in bad shape, for they had been overworked and the wet season had lasted far into autumn, so that the ground was always boggy and slippery. The sandflies, too, had been particularly bad that year. The Dawson sandflies were the subject of many district tales. As soon as the wet set in, the sandfly season began; great clouds of them would rise from every swamp and creek, each almost too small to see, but together a formidable army. They would gather round each horse and man, each beast in a mob, and sting them almost mad, leaving big suppurating swellings. But the old-timers pointed out that the sandflies had their uses, for the cattle, hard to find in the thick scrubs during the rest of the year, were driven by them into clearer country away from the swamps and creek-beds. Even the wildest scrubber cattle sometimes came in to huddle in the smoke of the fires when the sandflies were at their worst, so that mustering was easier in that season.

Still, Albert winced every evening, when he took the saddle off his horse, at the sight of the raw flesh under the saddle-cloth, where sandfly-bites had turned to great sores. The brumby mobs were tormented by them, too. Sleeping among campfires piled with dry cattle-dung to thicken the smoke, Albert would often wake in the moonlight to see groups of horses, all strange to him, stamping and twitching in the firelight, and he would waken Hanks or Captain to identify them. 'The bay filly must be out of that old bay mare the Rio men lost when they went through three years ago; I don't know that chestnut—he might be out of the old Cat.' But after the sandflies had passed, there was not much hope of seeing such horses again, unless the men came on the brumby mob by accident when the wind was right. The run might have more than a hundred horses left on it, but not more than half of them had ever felt a saddle.

At last the final mob of cattle had left the station; the agent had come out from Rockhampton again, checked all the books and accounts for the last time, and signed the documents. Albert was relieved that this part of the job was done with, for he detested the figures over which he had to spend so much of his scanty spare time after the day's work was done. Now nothing was left on the run except the tumbledown huts and buildings, the few cattle unaccounted for, the brumby mob, and a few weak old cows with calves which the drovers had left behind.

Albert felt rather pleased with his year's work. There was no doubt he had given Eales good advice over holding the cattle, for his estimate of the season had been fulfilled, and the mobs the drovers had taken were in much better condition than they had been the previous spring, and should fetch a higher price. He hoped for a little praise from the old man for his services, and perhaps something extra on his cheque.

He paid old Captain and the other black-boys, and the gins who had helped in the kitchen and the huts, and gave the tribe the remaining rations in the store and such blankets and clothes as remained. He had developed a kind of affection for the blacks, and for Captain in particular. The old aboriginal's wisdom and knowledge had impressed him, and in turn, he felt, Captain liked and trusted him. He was sorry to leave him now, perhaps forever.

Nevertheless, the day before they were to leave, Hanks was surprised and a little amused to see how carefully Albert went over the buildings, replacing a sheet of bark on the roof here and barring doors and windows there. It seemed scarcely worth while to take so much trouble, since the place was to be abandoned and nothing remained worth the trouble of stealing.

But Albert had begun to nourish an idea. He had come to respect this country, which at first had seemed to him so uninviting. And he had the contours of the run clear in his head; he could see how it should be worked and what its virtues were. It had become a unit to him: the spread of country along the creeks, to the range and beyond, out to the Island and back to Mimosa. He felt it as a piece of knowledge that ought not to be wasted, the map in his head, the experience he had gained of the seasons, the rainfall and the distribution of feed and water. It was good cattle country, he knew now, though hard and uncompromising. He did not like the idea of raping and leaving it.

Some day, things would look up. And meanwhile, he nailed a sapling over the door of the quarters, just in case. He would talk this over with Fred at Avon Downs.

It was a hard ride to Avon Downs this time, for rain had set in again. The soft heavy ground pulled at the horses' hoofs. Albert and Hanks had to make several detours to find better fords at the creeks and rivers, for every creek meant a swim for horses and men. The trip took longer than it had done before. They did not reach the huts of Avon Downs headquarters until the end of the eleventh day.

As they dismounted at the yards, Fred came across to greet them. He was startlingly thin, and trembling with uncontrollable ague. Four of the men were down with sickness, he told them. It was some kind of fever, but worse than usual; he had already had one go of it, though not badly. Quinine was very short, for the whole district was full of fever, and at the mines at Copperfield a single bottle was now selling for more than a good horse would fetch. The work had been held up for days, since few men were fit to ride.

Albert hung up his saddle and went to look at the sick men. They were in very high fever. Their blank bright stare and the burning heat of their skins worried him. It might be something really serious. But there was nothing to be done, except to look after them as well as possible with the rations they had, and wait for the thing to burn itself out. He went to the kitchen hut, since the cook was one of those down with fever, and concocted a thin gruel of flour and some kind of beef-tea that might tempt them to eat. He and Hanks took over the job of nursing, that night, to allow the other men some sleep.

But by next morning Fred had relapsed; he lay shaking and muttering in his bunk, throwing off the blanket at one moment and crying out the moment after that he was dying of cold. Next, Hanks began to complain of feeling ill and stayed in his bunk, another victim. The day after, Albert, tired with nursing more than half the men on the run, felt the thing seize on him too.

It was not until more than a month had passed that the sickness began to recede from him. He could not remember much of that month afterwards; it stayed with him only as a confused memory of endless nightmare. He did not remember having eaten or drunk anything during that time, and he had no idea who had looked after him. In fact, those of the men who were able to walk had nursed the others until they themselves had fallen ill or relapsed in turn, and their recovering mates had taken over the work of nursing.

Albert's illness had been particularly severe. It left him with violent attacks of ague which made him powerless to move or speak while they lasted, and a desperate weakness. For two weeks more he could scarcely hold a pen to write; if he tried, the ague played him tricks, jerking the pen up and down suddenly on the page until the word was illegible, and he had to cross it out and begin it painfully over again. It was not for another week that he dared trust himself in the saddle, and then, after a mile or two of riding, he had to dismount and lie in the shade until he was able to stand again.

He was deadly homesick. What he had wanted most of all, during his illness, had been to lie in a bed again, with sheets and blankets, instead of on a hard bunk of bark and saplings, with a harsh sweat-soaked and mildewed blanket, that gave his aching weakness no comfort. He sat in the winter sunshine—for it was mid-winter now, and the winds were chilly—and read the accumulation of letters that had at last come with the supply waggons.

The railway had been opened as far as Muswellbrook, in the valley, he read; there had been a grand ball to celebrate the occasion. His sister Mary and his mother gave him all the gossip of the event, and his mother added that a young Englishman who had been there had been very attentive to Mary. People had come from many miles around to the ball and the other festivities, for the railway was a great thing, and new prosperity was hoped from it. When he returned he would be able to come all the way from Sydney or Newcastle by train, and they hoped that it would not be long before he was back. There was a letter or two from Sallie, as well, though this was a scanty return for his own long letters written before his return to Avon Downs. She sounded very far away, and most of the letter was taken up with accounts of her own gay doings and the society of George's River. But it was an effort for him even to read.

Now that most of the men were well again, the long-overdue mustering for fat cattle for the market could begin. Eales had written, impatient for news. He had decided to keep Avon Downs in work for a year or two, since the Nulalbin cattle had sold well, and Fred was to stay on as manager.

Albert went out with a couple of other men to camp over the run, moonlighting for wild mobs which were easier to bring in by night than in daylight. This was the hardest and most dangerous work of the station; even at full moon the light among the thickly-growing trees of the scrubs where the cattle sheltered was sparse and treacherous. Only good and trustworthy horses were suitable for the job, horses that would not lose their heads with excitement in a close gallop, that would be clever-footed and wise among the swamps and logs, and fast enough to keep the cattle from breaking back from the clearings into which they were being manoeuvred.

Sometimes it was necessary to race to head a mob by sound alone. The deceiving bars of light that marked the ground under the trees would vanish altogether as a cloud covered the moon, and then horse and rider must run blind through the timber until the light came back. It was seldom that the cattle were yarded without a horse or two lamed, a saddle ripped, and men bruised and bleeding if no worse.

At first Albert was afraid that during one of these dangerous gallops his ague might return—as now and then it did for months to come—to make him powerless, but after a night or two his confidence came back, and he was able to laugh at Hanks, who kept close to his horse in concern for him. They finished the moonlighting without serious mishap.

He had begun to discuss with Fred the question of borrowing money to take over the Nulalbin mortgage from Eales. Fred, who had not seen the country, was dubious, but Albert insisted that it was a good run, and if money could be got cheaply, and Eales did not ask too much, it would be worth the risk. Secretly he hoped that, if he had at least this much to offer Sallie, her parents would not object too much to the match. He had no money and hence no chance of buying one of the more expensive southern properties, but a run-down mortgaged Queensland property like Nulalbin, for which there would certainly be no other bidder, might be within his reach, given hard work and good luck.

Finally Fred agreed that, if Albert could arrange a satisfactory price with Eales, he might come in on a partnership basis. The worst of the crisis seemed over now, and they had heard of a few men who were straggling back to their deserted runs and beginning to build up herds again. Eales might even be willing to finance the purchase himself; he might be glad to find a buyer at any price for a place so remote and difficult of access.

Albert was to help at Avon Downs over shearing, which would soon begin. Then his work would be over, and with Hanks, who was then to be paid off, he would set out for Rockhampton. Albert had made enquiries and found out that the *Balclutha* would sail from there on a date that would suit them; he decided that he would book his own passage right through to Sydney, instead of getting off at New-castle, as he would otherwise have done. In this way, he could keep an eye on Hanks, make sure that this time his steamer-fares to England were paid and that he was put on board sober.

Another reason was his nagging desire to see Sallie and have things settled one way or another; but perhaps, in the end, he would not be brave enough for that—not, at least, until he had seen Eales and found out what his future might be.

Spring was well begun, and now the shearers began to come in to the run. All along the river-bank their camps sprang up, with carts and jinkers, waggons and ragged tents. There were even a few women and children travelling with them, a sight so unusual on the inland runs, where white women had as yet seldom ventured, as to frighten into speechlessness the old shepherds who came in with their flocks.

The drays came with shearing-supplies, and for a while there would be plenty of fresh rations, and a change of diet from the ever-lasting salt meat and damper and duff. Some of the drays had brought onions, potatoes and even cabbages for sale as a sideline, at an ex-orbitant price. There was rum in plenty, and various other kinds of raw spirit. An Indian hawker came with his covered cart, selling shirts, knives, hats, long ornate sets of spurs, gay handkerchiefs and cummerbunds. The stockmen, who seldom saw a town, spent their money freely. At night, guitars and concertinas sounded from the river camps, and men sang round the fires.

The men of the inland runs looked on the shearing as the best time of the year, making up for the long loneliness and hard work of the autumn and winter. Every Saturday night, when the stockmen were in from their work, they joined camps with the shearers for songs, card-games and concerts, and the evening usually ended with a fight or a wrestling-match. Only the old hatter-shepherds, in from the out-stations with their flocks for shearing, were disturbed and made unhappy by the world's irruption into their vegetable lives; they skulked outside the homestead clearing, camping in the scrub, until their flocks were shorn. There was no message or news from the outer world that could touch them any longer.

This shearing-time brought Albert a problem with which he had to wrestle alone. A trooper, riding in one day, brought news that two men had been killed by blacks on the diggings at Mistake Creek, not far away. The shearers' camps and the stockmen's quarters alike were set in a turmoil of anger and excitement. It was always a lurking fear, in the minds of the few Europeans scattered through the inland outpost stations, that the blacks might some day unite and begin a mass slaughter that would wipe out their invaders. Rumours began to fly round at once.

Indeed, it would have been easy enough, if they had ever joined forces, for the tribes to get rid of their oppressors, for they still far outnumbered the white men, and they had learned the use of fire-arms from renegade members of the Native Police. They had many wrongs to avenge, as the white men knew; uneasy consciences bred suspicion.

Early next morning, one of the stockmen, who had gone out to help a shepherd bring in his flock, galloped back to the run and drew Albert aside. He had seen the bodies of four blacks of the Avon Downs tribe lying in the bush on the other side of the lagoon.

Albert rode round at once to investigate. Apart from his position as co-manager of the run, this was especially his business, for he had just been notified of his appointment as a Justice of the Peace for this district, and it was now his duty to keep the peace and see that criminals were apprehended. As he rode, Albert wished very much that the appointment had never been made, for this was going to be a difficult problem and unpleasant choices lay ahead of him.

The bodies were those of three young warriors and one old man. Their spears and throwing-sticks lay nearby, but it was evident they had only been on a peaceful hunting-trip, for they were not wearing the feathers and clay decorations of men going out to war. They had been shot and dragged into the bush, and their bodies half-hidden by branches, perhaps the night before.

Albert was deeply troubled by the sight of the murdered men. He had seen death many times before; it was a commonplace of the inland, where thirst, starvation or scurvy might attack any man, where doctors were few and tracks easily lost. And stories of murder and massacre had been plenty in his life. But here for the first time he found himself face to face with massacre, of men he knew and had talked with, and he was faced with a bitter dilemma.

Any of the shearers or stockmen might have decided to execute a muddled revenge on this tribe for the Mistake Creek killings, though as far as that affair was concerned the tribe was obviously quite innocent, as Mistake Creek was far outside their tribal territory. It was equally possible that, as sometimes happened, one of the renegade Native Police with a grudge against the men of his own tribe had chosen this method of revenge; it was well known that the tribe owned several rifles. But Albert was almost certain in his own mind that this killing was the work of a white man, perhaps several white men.

There was no constable nearer than a hundred miles away. If Albert were to send one of the few stockmen (for the run was always short-handed and over shearing doubly so) to ride to the town of Emerald for the police, the killer would certainly know of his going and disappear at once; the work of the station would be interrupted, shearing would be put back perhaps for weeks, and a first-class scandal would begin. On the other hand, if one of the blacks had done the killing—and, Albert reasoned with himself, it might after all be so—it was certain that the tribe would suffer further, for the Native Police would be sent in and there would be a big hunt. Whatever happened, news of the killings would inflame the blacks' camp and the quarters and the shearers still further. There was no knowing where the thing might end.

If only he had not been given this unlucky appointment! It was, after all, his clear duty to send a man to Emerald, whatever the result might be. Otherwise, he would have done what so many men of his acquaintance had done. He would have buried the bodies and said nothing. These things happened . . . it was the white men's duty to stand by each other. If he reported the deaths, it was certain that he would be shunned by everyone he knew, as a traitor to the white men. Gazing down at the dead men Albert was wrung by his responsibilities.

The stockman who had found the bodies was with him—Albert had prudently brought him in order to be sure that his mouth was kept shut and the news did not spread. The two of them discussed the situation in painful whispers. It was clear that the stockman assumed that Albert, whatever else he might do, would not let the police know.

Albert, torn between his knowledge of what ought to be done and his anticipation of the certain consequences, decided to procrastinate. He swore the stockman to silence and returned home. He would wait and see, and tonight he and Fred would ride over with spades to bury the bodies.

In his heart he knew that this was to take an easy way out of his troubles, for the killers, whoever they might be, would certainly be on the look-out for riders in the direction of the dead bodies, and would have been warned by now. If he wanted the bodies as evidence—and they would be the only evidence that would be accepted, if a white man were accused of murder—he must take them now, and put a guard over them until the constable arrived; mere burial would not be enough. Either the tribe would find their dead and carry them away, or the murderer or murderers would hide them. And Albert knew he himself would not look for them.

Accordingly, when at evening Fred rode in from work, the two of them went across to the lagoon scrub. No trace of the four dead remained, and Albert and Fred looked at each other in unspoken relief. Next day the camp over the river had broken up and the tribe had vanished, flying as they always did from the presence of death.

The four men might never have existed; neither whites nor blacks would ever speak of them again. But on Albert's mind they stayed a heavy load.

Shearing finished at the end of September, and the last of the wool-drays set out for the coast. The shearers' camp broke up, and the string of riders, broken-down buckboards and waggonettes straggled out on the Clermont track.

Albert wrote out the pay-cheques for the year's work, for stockmen, shepherds, shearers, and last of all for himself and Hanks. Part of his own cheque he lent to Hanks to make up his fares to England. Fred would stay on at Avon Downs, but he and Hanks rolled up their belongings in valise-rolls and blankets, packed their horses and set out in the heat of early summer.

On their way to Rockhampton they must pass through Clermont, where the copper-mines supported a shanty township. For six months they had not left Avon Downs, and Albert's fears for Hanks were redoubled by Hanks's eagerness to get to Clermont.

They had to stop in the township, in any case, for the horses to be shod, and to get fresh food-supplies for the ride to Rockhampton; and while Albert was busy at the farrier's, Hanks gave him the slip and disappeared into the bar. He found a red-headed woman serving drinks, pushed his cheque across the counter and began to shout rounds of drinks to all Clermont.

Albert missed him very soon, but by the time he reached the grog-shop Hanks was already too far gone to listen to argument or persuasion. It took a good deal of tact, and a little more than tact, to get the cheque from red-haired Lily among the bottles and exchange it for one of his own; and all Albert could do, having recovered it, was to wait until Hanks had drunk himself stupid, and then half-persuade, half-carry him out to the horses.

The day was almost gone and dark was coming on, but Albert was determined to leave Clermont far behind. They had ridden ten miles in darkness, with Hanks pleading and abusing him, before he consented to make camp, and by now he was very weary. He had had to drink a good deal more than he cared to, at the grog-shop, in order to keep Lily on his side, and when he slept, he slept soundly. He woke at dawn, to find that Hanks had woken first and set out to find his horse for the ride back to Clermont. However, he had got no further than undoing the hobbles and now he was sprawled asleep with the hobbles beside him and the horses gone.

Albert swore at him, but there was no rousing him. The horses' tracks led back towards Clermont, on the back track to Avon Downs, and there was nothing to do but walk after them. Luckily they had not gone farther than a few miles, but he had wasted four or five hours of the day, and was not in a good temper when he brought them back to camp.

Hanks had woken headachy and penitent. He had lit the fire and had tea and johnny-cakes waiting, and was ready to be apologetic about his lapse and grateful for Albert's guardianship. But Albert, who had prided himself that his influence had cured his friend, was hurt and angry. Most of the day he rode without speaking, and it took all Hanks's charm and pleading to smooth down his bad temper.

In Rockhampton, Albert escorted Hanks severely to the bank, and made sure that his money was safely spent, the steamer-fares all booked and paid for, before lending him the extra money for clothes that he still needed. But Hanks, though he looked wistfully at bar-doors, was obedient again, and Albert, pleased by this and by Hanks's gratitude, soon forgave him.

When the *Balclutha* reached Sydney, and the two of them had bought new clothes to replace the ragged shabby outfits, mildew-marked by the wet season, that were all they had left after their two years' work, Albert saw Hanks on to his ship for England, and prudently made him put his money on deposit with the purser at once. He was genuinely grieved to part with his friend. Their two years of companionship was the first real friendship he had known, and he felt lonely and miserable as he waved on the wharf to the departing steamer.

He had given up playing with the idea of going straight to Sallie. He could not help feeling that he might not be entirely welcome. No, he must see Eales first and find out the old man's terms. He must arrange something, so that when he went to Sallie he would not go empty-handed, a bush worker without a future. He caught the Newcastle packet and went on up the Hunter Valley towards Duckenfield.

But when he reached the nearest town he was prudent enough to wait there until he could shave and bathe, and hire a good horse. It would not do to let Eales see him looking like a tramp. For all that, as he turned along the gravel drive to the great barrack of a house, and handed the reins to a groom, he could not help feeling a little shabby and apprehensive.

But his welcome was reassuring. He had finished the Nulalbin job creditably and had made the old man money. The drovers he had engaged to clear the station of stock had luckily had a good trip, and the beasts had sold better than Eales had expected. Even Avon Downs, which Eales was keeping in work rather against his own judgement, had not as yet made him any bad losses. Accordingly, he was disposed to regard Albert as a steady and promising young man; and though he showed signs of balking, at first, at the idea of financing the Nulalbin deal, he gradually came round even to this. Albert left Duckenfield at last with an offer of Nulalbin at a price he thought worth paying, even at the high interest Eales stipulated, and it seemed he would be able to get enough money for re-stocking the run as well.

Nevertheless, as he travelled up the valley for a few weeks' holiday at home, he wondered anxiously whether the load he had taken on was too great. Six thousand pounds at eight per cent seemed a dreadful sum to one who had never yet earned more than two or three hundred pounds in a year. Moreover, the colder climate of the valley had brought on his ague again. He was glad to reach Bickham and resign himself for a few days to being looked after by his mother and his numerous younger sisters.

By the time his holiday drew to an end, he had recovered health and confidence in himself. But there still remained one question that had power to affect his spirits—his long-anticipated visit to Sallie Dickinson. His two years of absence, her friendly but brief letters, and especially the feeling that had gained on him, over the past year, that they were strangers to each other, seemed to raise an unclimbable mountain between him and what had been his dearest hope. The stiff little portrait in the locket she had given him, which he had carried so long in his pocket notebook, had gradually lost all relation to reality for him. His memories of his last visit to her had altered focus in his mind over the years, until he hardly knew whether, in fact, he wanted to marry her now, even if she would have him.

And surely she would not think the prospect of a slab-and-bark house in lonely fever-ridden country, and a husband loaded with debt, a pleasant exchange for her lively home, and the dances and boating parties, the weekly trips to Sydney for theatres and shopping, that had filled her infrequent letters? Yet he must ask her; for to what end would his lonely years of work have been, if his vow to marry Sallie came to nothing now?

He had only a few days left of his holiday when he set out for Sydney again. He went straight to her home at George's River, more determined than eager.

Mrs Dickinson, to whom he spoke first, was kind but not very encouraging. It was for Sallie to decide, but he must not be too much hurt if. . . . At last he manoeuvred Sallie herself away from the party of friends that seemed always in attendance (there was one intrusive young fellow in particular), and in the canoe on the river he managed his proposal.

Just as he had remembered, she was a charming girl. She refused him so kindly that for a moment he hardly knew whether it had been in fact a refusal or an acceptance. Yet it hurt, none the less; he had scarcely known, until then, how much his years had grown round the hope of her, or how empty they would stretch in front of him, now that he was condemned to Nulalbin without her. Lighting his candle before dawn next morning, he found his pen, since he had no confidant now that even Hanks had left him, and wrote the story of his refusal. 'I did not think I should feel it as much as I do. Have hardly slept tonight.'

Nulalbin looked dreary enough as he rode in, the new owner, at the end of November. There was a drought and the waterholes were low; the kitchen, when he opened it, was musty and cobwebbed, and smelt of rats; the dining-hut, which had had a slab of bark pulled away from one side, smelt, on the other hand, of blacks. At night the heat was stifling, as he lay in the narrow bunk and tried not to

E

think of George's River, of his loneliness, or of the fact that he was thirty years old and in debt.

But there was a great deal of work to be done, and in this he lost himself and his pain. He had inspected a thousand young heifers on a station near Gladstone, on his way north, and had decided to buy them and to drove them north himself, to save money. Before he set out to bring them back, he must get the run into some kind of order and hire one or two stockmen to help with the working of the cattle.

The tribe was in from its walkabout, and though they were not too pleased to find the station occupied again, there were certain compensations for them, since the drought had left them short of food. Accordingly they came to beg rations from the store and to offer the services of their young men as stockmen; and of this he was glad. And Captain was with them. He and Albert greeted each other almost with affection, and Albert was warmed by his friendliness.

He found a stockman, Tom Turner, who seemed reliable; his wife would come to the run and act as cook, and this seemed a remarkable piece of luck, for the cooking of the old black gin who had worked in the kitchen in Mrs Glen's day was sketchy and sporadic. Albert began to feel a certain pride of ownership, now that he had a household of a sort. He and Tom Turner rode the run, looking for such cattle as had remained when the drovers cleared the stock away; there were a few calves to be branded with Albert's newly-registered brand, and it was pleasant to him to see the V2V on their flanks.

The station was almost without working horses which could be saddled, and he and Turner ran in a brumby mob from the range, with great difficulty, and broke in a few of the more promising colts and fillies. Captain was his chief helper now, for he knew the run as Albert would never know it. This was his own home country, and every sign and track on it was instantly legible to his eyes.

Albert had to repair the kitchen and the quarters for the Turners, for storms had blown bark from the roofs and the buildings had suffered from their long neglect. The store had to be replenished, books begun afresh, the whole machinery of the run set in motion again, and all this must be done almost singlehanded, for he could not yet afford to hire the men he needed. After Christmas, he and Turner were to ride to Gladstone and bring back the cattle, leaving Captain in charge, but before then he must have everything in running order. He set to work, and worked grimly from early dawn until long after dark, till Christmas came.

It was a blank enough Christmas, one that he might have been celebrating as a man engaged to marry Sallie Dickinson. Just before Christmas Eve, he had a message to say that one of the shepherds on a neighbouring run had gone mad and died. Albert, as a J.P., had to ride over and hold an enquiry on the body, which was not a pleasant task. When this duty was done, he rode on to spend Christmas Day with neighbours on a nearby run, friends of Hanks whom he had met in his company. Like Hanks, they were young Englishmen, 'broken-down swells', as the phrase went, who could not keep off the grog, drinking to drown fever-pains or the pains of memory, to start and finish the day, to keep out the cold in winter or to sicken the sandflies in hot weather.

This Christmas the drays had for once been in good time, and the young men had a plentiful supply of grog; there was whisky as well as the common rot-gut rum from the coastal sugar-plantations, which every hawker carried. A few other lonely and womanless men from the few runs in the district which were not abandoned, rode in to join the party, and each brought his own grog-supply as a contribution. As for food, the young gins in the kitchen would cook the bustards and mix dampers from the flour ration each visitor brought with him, and with so much to drink, no one was disposed to question the cooking.

The old man they called the Madman, who had once owned ninety square miles of country out near the Peaks, but who now owned nothing but his blanket and a broken-winded horse, rode in too from his hopeless prospecting along the Dawson River, and they welcomed him noisily. He would provide entertainment for the party, in return for a share of the grog.

The more glasses they pressed on him, the more amusing he became. He sang them songs, the obscener ditties of the goldfields, songs from Hawaii and the Islands, songs from Italian opera and German *lieder* and Schubert—for he had been a moneyed man and had travelled the world in his time. He danced the can-can and the hula and wilder dances from South America, and they accompanied him on jews' harps, tin whistles and improvised drums. They were a strange and shabby crew, in the worn clothes that were the uniform of the outback stations—Crimean shirts and stiff dungarees and plaited cabbage-tree hats—and they were all bearded to uncouthness.

Albert laughed with the rest and egged the old man on for a time. But the drink he had taken (and for once even Hanks could not have outdone him) gradually cleared from his head and left his stomach sick, and he could no longer believe in the gaiety of the party. The ridiculous old man, with his white hair and beard blowing round his shoulders, and his moustache stained yellow with tobacco, danced bright-eyed among the bottles, singing a song that came from the brothels of Hong Kong, while drunken men clapped time and yelled the chorus in the flickering light of the slush-lamps. Albert sat staring with a fixed smile of which he was no longer conscious except as an ache. The old depression and melancholy of his lonely youth in the bush had swept back to drown him. It seemed dreadful that not even drunkenness could blot it out from him.

5   *THE MEETING, 1871*

BY THE TIME May was sixteen, the life at Dalwood had altered almost out of recognition. First, Margaret Wyndham had died. She had been the central authority and the spirit of the big household, gently as she moved and quietly as she spoke. Now that she was no longer there the whole routine and temper of the place began to halt and change. The sons' wives, formerly quelled by her tactful handling, began to manoeuvre for position. George, bewildered by grief, no longer kept the firm hand he had done over the running of the estate, and other dissensions split the family into factions. Dalwood seemed like a clock in which some wheel has begun to loosen.

It had been a kind of federation of families and of interests. The northern runs, managed by the elder sons, and Dalwood, which was still the home of some of the younger men, had worked in unity: Dalwood had supplied stud cattle for the northern herds, and the wines from Bukkulla had been sent down to be blended under George's expert supervision with the lighter wines that Dalwood itself produced. Now there were quarrels among the sons as to their share in the work and profits.

George was too griefstricken to remain the family's arbiter. He decided to return to England, perhaps to end his days there, where several of his brothers and sisters were still living, though overgrown as he himself was by sons and daughters and old age. But he did not live to board the steamer, dying in Sydney, where he had gone to embark, as quietly and suddenly as Margaret had done.

May understood very well the dimensions of her loss. It was easy to foresee that Dalwood itself might not last much longer than the lives of its founders. The estate was now to be shared among George's sons, with a small legacy to Weeta Mackenzie which would suffice to keep her and her family in moderate comfort, but it was already clear that the brothers would not long pull together in such an irksome harness. Though the cottage at Wouillah now belonged to the Mackenzies, the Dalwood chapter of May's life was in fact over. It was now that poverty really began to press upon her life, and the kind shelter of the big house to recede from it.

But at sixteen May was almost grown up, and she had few of the awkwardnesses and uncertainties of that age. Already she was mistress of herself, and that was as well, since her parents could not now give her much help. Arthur Mackenzie had never recovered from the illness he had brought back from his disastrous northern year. He seemed indeed to grow weaker, his handsome head now quite white and his face lined and sallow with fretfulness and indoor living.

His wife, long devoted to caring for him and for the younger children, had lost her old gaiety and her pretty singing-voice; she never now sat at the piano and sang the old songs May remembered—'Juanita' and 'When the Swallows Homeward Fly', or the Italian songs that her singing-master, in the years before she married, had told her suited her clear contralto. Instead, in the evenings, she would sit casting up accounts under the cheap tallow-candles in the wedding-present chandelier, or making and mending the family's clothes. May had often been called upon to help with the adding of those precariously-balanced accounts. She too was beginning to know the anxieties under which her mother had lived so long.

Nevertheless, poor as the Mackenzies were, they had so many cousins and related families living in the valley that May never lacked for invitations, and now that she was old enough for balls and parties, she was beginning to find herself popular and even sought-after. Men far outnumbered women still, even in the comparative civilization of valley society; and May was now a lively and pretty girl; she had always been quick-tongued and was lately gaining a small reputation for her wit.

As well as these assets of youth, she possessed another quality which was never to leave her, and that gave her, when she wished to exercise it, a certain command over others: a warmth, a charm, that had about it more of strength than of softness. It was a quality which was all her life to make her a centre to whom others turned, for help or for leadership.

She was sufficiently conscious, by now, of her own assets to use them at times with deliberate purpose, but nevertheless this charm that she exercised sprang from her real being. People were the element in which she lived and moved, and though she criticized and even secretly mocked their defects, it was in relationship to others that she found her real world and used her gifts most easily. There were few who were proof against her smile, and though she might rouse jealousy she was never overlooked. Already she had a poise and maturity of judgement that made her turn often to women older than herself for friendship, rather than to girls of her own age.

In this way she met Mary Wright, and struck up a friendship with her, while May was staying with her Uncle and Aunt Mackenzie at Cliffdale, near Bickham. She had been to visit the family at Bickham, too, and had listened for hours to Mary's confidences about her rather nebulous affair with the young Englishman who had gone back to England, last year, without declaring himself.

No one but Mary, now, believed he would come back, for Mary, twenty-eight already, was tipped in the valley as a certainty for the Old Maid Stakes. But, surprising everyone, he had come after all, and now that Mary was to be married, May was invited to the wedding.

There was great bustle at Bickham. The wedding was fixed for the tenth of January. Things were prosperous at present, for the slump was past and prices good, and Mary, as the eldest daughter of the house, was to have a big wedding with many guests. Fred, still at Avon Downs, was not able to leave his work, but Albert had written that he would come; Mary was his favourite sister and he must dance at her wedding.

It would be his first holiday for two years. They had been years of unremitting hard work, but Nulalbin was securely his now, and it seemed that Queensland's hard times were passing. Prices were mounting again for cattle, and he had had good luck with the heifers he had bought. Their first drop of calves would soon be ready for sale and should fetch a good sum, for the last two seasons had been satisfactory and no droughts had come to trouble him. He had bought Fred's share of the partnership, but the two of them were now in partnership again on Avon Downs, which Fred was buying from Eales.

Mary and the younger sisters, for whom he had become a remote figure, had made him bit by bit into a somewhat Byronic legend for the benefit of their friends. His portrait on the sitting-room wall, looking shy and rather stern, with a fine beard and curling black hair, lent itself to this exaggeration; and then, too, he was known to have been disappointed in love and to be, in consequence, rather a recluse. This legend did his sisters no harm, and gave them a certain vicarious glamour in the eyes of their friends.

May, too, had been shown the portrait, and perhaps her memory of her childhood excitement over the thought of pioneering the Queensland station had added something to her curiosity to meet this good-looking young man. Nevertheless, her private opinion was that the rest of the family were certainly a little humdrum. She had no intention of falling at this young man's feet.

She was to stay at Cliffdale with her aunt and uncle for the wedding, and to drive over to Bickham with them. Her aunt would chaperon her to the dance at Bickham afterwards. She travelled up by train, with friends who had also been invited; Mary's wedding was an important social event, and friends of the Wright family were coming from many miles around.

The early January weather was fiercely hot, when with Uncle and Aunt Mackenzie she drove to the Blandford church and sat correctly in the Mackenzie pew between them. She was sorry, as she settled the muslin skirts of the dress that she and her mother had made for the occasion, that she was not yet old enough to wear her hair up; it hung over her shoulders, brown and wavy, tickling through the thin stuff of the dress and making her very hot. The little church was overcrowded; dust blew through its windows as more and more vehicles drove up, and soon May was crushed uncomfortably between the horsehair padding of Aunt's crinoline and the stiff harsh cloth of Uncle's frock-coat.

The Wrights' big waggonette drove up to the church with an attendant cloud of riders—those of the children who had not been able to find a place in it, for of the seven girls and four boys of the Bickham family there were still some not yet grown up. They were soon heard gathering in the porch, with a great whispering, giggling and brushing down of coats and bonnets.

But May noticed, as they all came in and settled into their front seats, that the brother from Queensland was not there. Perhaps he would be on this afternoon's train; otherwise he would not be in time for the dance tonight, and May could not help feeling a little disappointed, for a new young man always provided interest at a dance. But here came Mary up the aisle, flushed with excitement and the hot weather but really quite handsome. May stood up and opened her prayer-book at the right place.

The service ended just as the sun began to sink behind the tall range of hills that closed in this upper glen of the valley. The congregation rose and poured out behind the bridal procession in a rising sound of chatter. There were to be eighty guests at the wedding-breakfast, May was told, and two fiddlers and a pianist were coming from Newcastle in this evening's train—an unheard-of extravagance.

May knew almost everyone among the guests. Indeed, there were members there of most of the families which could be counted in the valley's jealously strict list of 'gentlefolks', for valley society was narrow and exclusive, so soon after the days of transportation, and the line of demarcation, in a district where everyone's history was known, was firmly kept. There was little chance of an outsider's breaking in among the community of the respectable, who felt themselves still islanded in lawlessness and held an anxious solidarity in consequence. There were those whom one knew and those whom one could not know, and May in youthful impatience hoped for a few unfamiliar faces in the congregation but found little to interest her. Accordingly she was disappointed at Albert's absence, as she watched the groups of riders and the gigs and waggonettes begin to move off down the dusty white road that led to Bickham, and waited for Uncle and Aunt Mackenzie to finish gossiping to their cluster of acquaintances.

It was a perfect evening. The sunset light now set the steep forested hills glowing, and a full moon was rising, reddened by the smoke of bushfires in the hills, for heat had dried the country and fires were beginning.

The train from Newcastle was late that night. It had just begun to labour up the steep grade into the little station, sending out a great announcement of whistles, although it was still enough of a novelty for its passage up the valley to be known to all the district.

Albert stood up and lowered the window of his compartment to look out. He knew that he must have missed the wedding; the steamer had been delayed on the trip south and he had been lucky to catch the train at all. In his box lay a new frock-coat hastily bought in the Newcastle shops; he had had time there to have his beard shaved for Dundrearies, the new fashion in whiskers. Nevertheless he felt shy and awkward at the thought of the crowd of people he must meet. He was not at his best among strangers, and his years in the north had cut him off from his family and accentuated his reserve.

His brother Percy was waiting in the station-yard with the gig. Albert hardly knew him, a grown man now. The musicians from Newcastle were on the train; they climbed into the back seat of the gig with their instruments, and clung there in some anxiety as it spun down the road, for Percy had evidently been celebrating the wedding already.

By the time Albert had washed off the grime of the train and put on his frock-coat, the wedding-breakfast had long begun. The Bickham dining-room was not large enough to hold the crowd, and trestle-tables had been put up on the long vine-shaded verandahs for the young people, while the older and more important guests sat at the long main table with the parson and the bride and groom. In a corner of the parlour next door the musicians were settling down, and an occasional squeak of the violin or odd note enquiringly struck on the piano drifted in and was lost among the noise of toasts and speeches.

May was sitting at a side-table with a group of friends. She looked up as Albert came to the door and stood a moment hesitating. Several others looked up too, for Albert, tall and dark in his stiff new clothes, was now a stranger to most of them.

For the rest of her life May maintained the opinion that it was possible to fall in love at first sight. At any rate, when the speeches were over, the turkeys and fowls on the tables reduced to wrecks of bones, the jellies melted to trickles of red and yellow liquid, and when everyone was moving towards the parlour and the verandah cleared for dancing, she contrived matters so that Albert was introduced to her in time for the first dance; yet having succeeded she found herself for once in her life almost tongue-tied as they circled and set to partners. Albert, tall and shy, was silent too; in his lonely years he had almost forgotten how to talk to young women.

But silence was an unusual state with May, and by the end of the dance, when he led her to a seat on the cool verandah and bowed her down among the other girls again, she felt herself confident enough to ally her smile as she looked up at him with a certain look of gay intimacy which was her peculiar gift, and to let her eyes stay in his just that instant longer than was necessary.

After that the evening was made for both of them. It was after midnight when Uncle and Aunt Mackenzie decided finally and firmly that the horses must not be kept waiting a moment longer. May was sent to fetch her cloak and say her goodbyes, but Albert's mother, prompted by a short conversation with Albert, invited her to drive across next afternoon for a little party. Indeed she must come to cheer them all up; they would be feeling so strange without Mary. Should they send the gig across for her?

But May was wise enough to make no promises. Perhaps she would come if she were not too tired, but Mrs Wright must ask Aunt Mackenzie; and Aunt shook her head doubtfully. May was too young for so much excitement; she had better have a day at home and rest. Perhaps they would bring her across later in the week. May was not sorry; she was sure enough of herself to be able to wait.

Albert was not at all so confident. She had left him so coolly, with hardly a glance. Did she like him, or not? He could not be certain, and it was with anguish that he remembered how young she was, how young Sallie had been, how that affair had died in silence and loneliness leaving him with a wound that he had thought would never heal. He returned to the dance, which was going on as energetically as ever in spite of the heat and the lateness of the hour, and helped himself dazedly to hock. It was not worth while dancing again, but he leaned against the wall and watched the narrow-waisted girls and red-faced young men whirl in their sets, listened to the music (how long since he had heard music!) and filled his glass again and then again.

'A very jolly party,' he wrote in his diary next day. 'We kept it up till daylight. I got pretty well stewed,' and at the foot of the entry he added a scribbled note: 'My affairs today totally disarranged and everything thrown out of gear by *her* not coming.' May's confidence in herself had not been misplaced.

For a day or two Albert waited irresolutely. It was hotter and hotter; the fires in the hills were increasing; Bickham was occupied with its own affairs with which Albert had long been out of touch. He did not quite know what to do next. It was Mama who solved the problem for him by suggesting at the dinner-table that little May Mackenzie might be brought over for a day or two from Cliffdale, where she must surely be bored with no young people for company.

Probably Mama had noticed Albert's restlessness and guessed the reason for it. And though May was certainly not likely to be a great match as far as money was concerned, since the Mackenzies were known to be living from hand to mouth, still she was well-connected, lively and pretty, and perhaps would be able to lift Albert out of his melancholy ways; he had lived too much alone up there, and Mama had seen too much of young men living alone in the bush to approve of it.

Accordingly she had the gig put in, took two of the girls as a cover for her plans, and invited Albert to come as driver of the gig. They drove over to Cliffdale through such dust and heat as Mama would not ordinarily have chosen for visiting weather.

May saw the gig as it came over the hill, with the two chestnut horses she remembered as the Bickham pair, and ran upstairs to change her dress, noticing as she went how very loud her heart was beating. She knew that Albert was driving; his tall straight figure and dark hair were unmistakable, and she felt that she had won. But she was both happy and afraid as she greeted him and sat down by Sara on the plush love-seat opposite him and tried to look at him and not to look.

The matter of the visit to Bickham was soon arranged; Sara and Edith helped her pack her little tin trunk and Albert tied it on under the gig seat. The three girls sat side by side on the back seat, so that May's shoulder almost touched Albert's as he drove and the scent of her long brown hair blew across his face.

He was in a bewilderment of contradictory emotions. Sometimes he was almost sure she looked at him in a way that—but how hard it was to get her to talk to him, though she chattered away to the girls fast enough! He did not trust himself or his love. It had been given more than once to a girl and rejected, and when he thought of the hard life which was all he had to offer, and May's youth, he almost resolved to give up all thoughts of her for her own sake as well as his. But she leaned backward a little and almost touched him and a strand of her hair blew across his coat and almost took his breath away with tenderness.

He answered Mama's talk at random. He would have cut that hair off if he could and kept it always; he would at least have something of her then. If she wouldn't have him (and there was every reason, he thought, why she should not) he would sell out of Nulalbin and go to the Islands, where the sooner he got a fever to finish him off, the better.

'Really, Albert,' said Mama, 'you don't hear a word I say.'

He did not know, after that, that the household at Bickham, or at least the feminine side of it, was organized in his behalf. Mama, Edith, Effie, Agnes, Sara, Emily and Constance, as well as May herself, were all perfectly aware of the state of things. It was Albert's wretched lack of confidence in himself that was the only obstacle, they considered. On one excuse or other they prolonged May's visit to a week, then to a fortnight, a fortnight for Albert of transfigured indecision until at last, as he thought, he managed to manoeuvre May away from his far too numerous brothers and sisters and dared to ask her to marry him. She accepted.

Immediately the household, like an ants' nest disturbed by the nuptial flight, sprang into distracted motion. Letters must be written, visits paid, Albert and May must drive to Cliffdale (chaperoned of course by Mama) to break the news to Uncle and Aunt Mackenzie, there must be interminable discussions, small parties of announcement, a visit to Dalwood must be arranged at once.

All this scarcely disturbed the radiance that hung over those hot summer days for Albert. But there was a darkness somewhere in his world, for he knew that his holiday must soon come to an end. The work of Nulalbin could not be put off much longer, and now that at last he had something to work for, after the lonely years (he was thirty-one now), it was doubly necessary that he should get back to the station and begin to save money. He knew that the Mackenzies would not let May marry until she was eighteen, and he could not help a tremor of fear as he remembered what absence and loneliness had done to his love for Sallie and hers for him.

Now May must go home, and he would follow in a day or two for his formal visit of introduction to Dalwood, where he would stay for a few days on his way to Newcastle to catch the northern steamer. The cottage at Wouillah, always overcrowded, had no room for visitors, but since it was so close, he and May would be able to spend the best part of the days together.

He was met at the station, when he got down from the train, by Regi Wyndham with the gig. He had never met any of the Wyndhams before, and Regi's air of the English squire abashed and rather amused him. The family was in force at Dalwood that summer, for Reginald, Hugh, Alex, Guy and their wives were down from the northern stations to escape the heat, and ten Wyndhams and their children were occupying the house.

His long years in the far-away northern country, where for months at a time he might speak to no one but Tom Turner and his wife, the blacks from the Nulalbin camp, and a passing drover or waggoner, made Albert dread these formal meetings and visits, these tea-parties where so much stress was laid on correct behaviour. He had been impressed by the house itself, its pillared entrance, its stone watchtower loopholed against bushrangers, and by the size of the great stables behind where he knew that racehorses were housed. The family were assembled in the drawing-room to meet him.

It seemed an immense room to him, and from all round it, as he entered, young men rose and women smiled. Even May seemed inaccessible here, though he saw her smile from across the room and come almost running to greet him. George had planned the entrance-hall and the great room beside it with a view to the establishment in visitors of a certain awe, a recognition of values which, though they certainly did not prevail elsewhere in this raw new country, he intended his house and his sons to help him to impose upon it. Albert dimly recognized that the place was an anachronism, something too stately to be other than alien in a land which was certainly not lending itself to expression in such terms, but he submitted himself humbly enough to its atmosphere, and tried throughout the difficult afternoon to behave as it dictated. This was May's home—at least in important respects—and he felt himself lucky indeed to be tolerated by it and its inhabitants.

However, May's mother and father were there, and luckily he got on well enough with old Arthur Mackenzie, who talked eagerly of the northern country and of his own days on the Suttor and the Isaacs, not so far from Avon Downs. He began to feel he was acquitting himself quite well. It put him more at his ease, and he handled the tea-cups creditably.

Tea-cups were always an anxiety to him after a long spell in the bush; they felt light and frail as eggshells in his large rough hands, after the big tin mugs in which for years he had stewed his tea on the fire. He only hoped that after three days' stay here he would have done no worse than this.

Wouillah was near, and now, as he was May's accepted suitor and they were officially engaged, it was possible to escape from his hosts and hostesses and spend hour after hour with her, walking through the vineyards where great bunches of grapes—Hermitage, Burgundy, Lambruscat—hung ripening on the long rows of trellises, and where the world shrank to a narrow lane of warm greenery whose inhabitants were May and himself; or wandering through the big orchard where peaches were ripe and apples and pears hung in low clusters on the boughs. The quiet heat of the days, the fruitful stillness of orchard and vineyard, the roses and lavender flowering in the garden's quiet walks, mingled in his mind till each hour of his short time there seemed a world in itself, in which he could wander forever, banishing the old hardship and loneliness and killing work of the life he had known. Everything that he looked at seemed to glow with the colour of his own happiness.

6 *MARRIAGE*

THE THREE DAYS were almost over, and he must leave to meet his steamer and return to Nulalbin for the autumn muster. He would not see May again for a year. So, at least, it had been arranged by the Mackenzies, and he had acquiesced for May's sake, though she would have been willing to marry him offhand, straightaway, and go to Nulalbin at once.

But the Mackenzies and Wyndhams were horrified at such a rash notion; and Albert could not help agreeing with them, when he remembered the house at Nulalbin, or as he looked at May who seemed so lately emerged from childhood. He promised Mrs Mackenzie earnestly that the house would be made as nearly worthy of May as, with his handicaps and lack of money, it could be. And in a year, May would be almost eighteen, and he would come back to marry her.

He went wearing, in the fashion of the time, her likeness in a locket with a tiny plait of her hair clasped opposite it. The journey had never seemed so far to him, nor the thought of a year so long. If, like Sallie, she forgot him? . . . Or if she changed her mind and refused to live in the heat and hardship of his northern country? He winced away from the fear of it but yet he could not help returning to the idea of losing her. His luck would not hold, he was certain.

When he reached the station again, he saw the homestead with new eyes. The run-down old hut, scarcely more than four slab walls and an earthen verandah, had been neglected over the years he had been at Nulalbin. Occupied with the outside work, miserable over his rejection by Sallie, he had been in no mood to trouble with repairs or improvements, and now the bark roof was split and drooping, rain had mildewed the rags that remained of Mrs Glen's attempts to curtain the unglassed windows, cockroaches scuttled everywhere and the dogs regarded the place as their home and dragged bones under the broken-springed sofa and the rough slab table. The swallows had built in the unceiled dining-room that was the hut's main room, and there was no garden, except a little enclosure near the creek where he grew a few vegetables against the ever-threatening scurvy.

Clearly this was no place for May to come to—May who was used to Dalwood's English formalities and luxuries. He must set to work at once to build a new home for her.

He tried to enlist Mrs Turner, the only white woman on the place, or indeed for many miles around, to help him in drawing up plans, but she was obstinately unhelpful. She had not taken the news of his coming marriage with any pleasure, since for the two years she had been on Nulalbin she had had undisputed authority over the homestead, the cooking, the household accounts and the black gins who intermittently helped with the kitchen work and the washing for the men. So Albert spent his evenings drawing plans and writing to May in smoky uncertain lamplight: letters that could not be posted except by the fortnightly mailman who rode past twenty miles away with packhorses, or by some chance drover passing through on the stock-route that crossed Nulalbin.

He sent to Rockhampton for carpenters, rode out to see the two men he had employed on a timber-clearing contract to fulfil the conditions of his leasehold, and set them to cutting wall-slabs and adzing studs and rafters.

Before the carpenters could come out from Rockhampton, the rainy season had set in, and the Dawson was down in flood and could not be crossed. Albert's letters piled up on the table, for the pack-horse mail was held up, and he had no news of May for weeks. He fretted bitterly over this, and fretted, too, over the length of the year ahead which separated him from her. He was lonely; he had been lonely for too long; and there was about May a cheerful certainty, a gaiety of trust in the world, which Albert had already found answered a depth of need in him that he had scarcely known was there.

After all, he had had little or no youth that was not overshadowed by hard work and worry, and even now, black fits of depression would sweep over him if anything went wrong with his plans or expectations. It only needed a long dry spell, a report of smallpox in one of the cities, a rumour of possible falls in prices or a little trouble with the cattle (and pleuro-pneumonia was particularly bad in his herd just now), for that old uncontrollable dark mood to overcome him. It was to May, now, that his thoughts turned for rescue, as though with her near him his troubles would cease to gnaw at him. She was so gay, so reassuring, that even the thought of her had power to calm him. How should he live through this endless year without her?

But then, too, how could he find the money for another long journey south, for all the expenses of a wedding (supposing that the Mackenzies might consent to her marrying before the time they had agreed on), and pay for the new house and the furniture that it would need, so much sooner than he had reckoned on?

Still, he would try his luck. He rode out every day with Captain or Tom Turner, and went through the cattle in every part of the run, looking everywhere for beasts in sale condition. He must get every beast that could possibly fetch a price, from this muster.

He worked both by day and by night, moonlighting for the wild mobs. If he could get together eighty fats, he reckoned, for the autumn sale, and another eighty by September, he might manage both to pay the interest on the run and on the new house, and have enough left over for a trip south before Christmas. He watched the weather and the grass, the water in the creeks, as though his life depended on a good season. Meanwhile, he wrote to May and to the Mackenzies, to ask their consent to a possible wedding in September.

The winter was kind to him until June was half gone. Often the westerly winds that cut up the pasture and stopped the growth of the grass began early in June, but this year they held off. Usually cattle work slowed down after the autumn muster, but this year Albert worked on, searching for possible sale cattle and moving them in towards the water and good grass, moonlighting night after night and putting the young cattle he manoeuvred from the wild mobs into his one fenced paddock until they joined up with the Nulalbin herd and began to graze more peacefully. Meanwhile he waited for the answers to his letters.

Letters took at least two weeks to reach Dalwood, and if the steamer were delayed, or floods blocked the mails, they might take much longer. It was not until mid-June that he got his answer.

The Mackenzies had allowed May to persuade them; the wedding might be in September, since she would give them no peace till they consented. If Albert was sure that the house would be ready and that May would not have to put up with too much hardship over the summer months at Nulalbin, he might take her to Queensland; but Weeta Mackenzie could not help fearing the worst, remembering what the country had done to her husband, and her letter was full of anxiety for her daughter.

Albert read it with his own alarms added to it. Was he asking too much of a child like May? But her own letters restored his confidence in her and he carried them everywhere in the pocket of his shirt and read them over as often as he had solitude.

But the weather had broken at last, and drying winds were beginning to cut up his grass and send the cattle into the shelter of the thick scrubs over the range, where they were hard to reach. At any rate, he got in the mob that he had collected for sale and yarded them overnight, ready to start for Rockhampton next day. They were a good enough mob, for the season had been kind. Prices were still fair, and he should do quite well by them.

That night he and the two black stockmen slept close to the yard, in case of trouble, for the yard timbers were old, and full moon and windy weather made the mob restless. Sure enough, in the small hours he woke with a jump at the crack of splintering wood and the sudden jostle of hooves, as the old fence-rails broke and the cattle thrust their way out.

There was no one on watch, for the weeks of hard work had tired him and his few men out and they had had to trust the yard, but Albert had his horse bridled in a moment, for he had left it in the horse-yard for fear of the break. He was on its back almost as the bridle was on, for there was no time to saddle-up, and away after the cattle at a gallop. He could hear the others close after him, swearing as they pulled on their clothes while they ran for the horses.

It was not unusual for such cattle as Albert still ran on Nulalbin—part-wild scrubbers, many of them brought in as calves after moon-lighting raids on the wild range mob, weaned and branded and joined to Albert's own cattle—to rush and break the yards. They were unused to fences and stockmen; lean, long-legged animals cunning at dodging through the close-growing scrub, lovers of free-dom. Often it might take days to get a mob together again after such a rush; but this time it was doubly urgent to halt their wild rush and quieten them, before they ran off what condition they had. By hard and daring riding, he managed to head the main mob before the men caught him up and took charge of the wings. Gradually they steadied the cattle and brought them back to the yard again, but by this time men and horses were weary and the cattle run to a standstill.

The trip to Rockhampton had to be put off for a day, until the cattle and horses had recovered. Albert fretted himself into a rage of impatience over the delay, for with the frosty dry weather, water on the route to Rockhampton was growing daily scarcer.

At dawn on the second day he set off with the mob, leaving Turner in charge. He had between eighty and ninety cattle. If the price were good enough, he would make enough for his wedding expenses and something over towards the annual interest payments that had to be met, to Eales and to the bank. The trip would take a week, for the cattle must be kept in good condition.

His chief fear now was the dreaded Gogango Scrub, a patch of rain-forest straddling the stock-route, where the trees and vines grew so closely entangled that if, by bad luck, a mob rushed while passing through, it was almost impossible to head them before they scattered and were lost. Tales were told of drovers who had spent weeks there looking for lost cattle without avail. Mobs of wild cattle, descendants of such lost beasts, haunted the scrub, and made the drovers' task harder by occasionally joining a travelling mob and leading a rush towards their own almost inaccessible hiding-places.

There was a cut-road through the scrub, wide enough for waggons and bullock-teams, but narrow for a mob, so that it was not possible to ride on the wings to check the inclination of the cattle should they try to move off into the scrub. The mob had to be strung out and taken slowly and carefully between the walls of scrub, and Albert guided them through with tense nerves, afraid most of all that they might meet a teamster with his waggon, on the way to the mines, or another drover bringing cattle from the coast. One of the stockmen rode ahead to steady the mob, another scouted farther on for wild cattle. Albert had lost cattle here before. He trained ears and eyes, speaking to the dogs almost in whispers as he ordered them here and there to check and turn the straying cattle.

As always, after a day or two with a mob on the road, he and the others knew each animal intimately, especially those with nervous or obstinate tempers: the one that lags and tries to slip back behind the mob and escape notice, the cranky one with a bias to left or right which works its way again and again to the wing and heads away from the mob at the first opportunity, leading the rest, the co-operative leader, the weakling which has to be humoured.

But this time luck was with him. He lost no beasts, and once out again on the open road, his way to Rockhampton was uneventful. At the sale-yards he heard that the market had taken a turn upwards. The drought which had touched Nulalbin lightly was hitting the stations farther north, and few mobs of fats were coming in from that direction. He had struck one of the best markets of the year. And his cattle, nursed so anxiously, had kept their condition.

His cheque from the sale of the cattle was by far the best he had had since he had bought Nulalbin. He felt it a good omen, and took it to the bank with pride and a lifted heart, calculating that he could even afford, now, to take a honeymoon trip before coming back to Nulalbin. Captain and Billy, the black stockmen, had a bonus and a few days' holiday, while Albert scoured Rockhampton for furniture and materials for the new house.

The framework of the house was already going up, back at Nulalbin; there were to be four rooms, divided by a passageway, and a verandah at the front. It would be one of the best houses for many miles around, and now, in his triumphant mood, Albert had no qualms about his extravagance. He ordered ceiling-board to be brought by the next drays, at alarming expense. The house would be ceiled in every room and the sitting-room lined with tin and painted. He bought bamboo mats, the Chinese mats brought down from Hong Kong by trading-ships, to line the bedroom and cover the floor, and lime to whitewash the slab walls of the verandah, and he determined that he would even go to the expense of having the verandah floored instead of leaving the bare earth to be puddled with ant-bed clay, and would pay for this extravagance by finishing the house off himself.

Back at Nulalbin, he spent August, the cool and pleasant month of the northern spring, in feverish work on the house, and in writing to May every evening about its progress. He hung the doors and ceiled and lined the two main rooms. The precious glass windows for the bdroom and sitting-room arrived unharmed, and were a wonder to ethe whole station, for the blacks had never seen anything of the kind before and Albert was at much trouble to prevent them from putting their hands through the panes in their interested examination.

The old kitchen-hut was to be pulled down, and the original homestead, or the Main Hut as it was called, connected to the new house by a wooden passageway, was now to act as kitchen quarters. Mrs Turner moved into her new quarters sourly; the old had been good enough for her, she said. But her hints at extravagance and prophetic undertones foretelling disaster had no effect on Albert. He built a garden fence, and whitewashed the palings; he started a flower-garden with a few bush plants, and any dog jumping in to bury his bone in the new-dug plots found trouble.

All this work and preparation kept his spirits buoyant. He had really begun, now, to believe in his own good fortune, and to believe that his years of loneliness were ending. Neighbours rode across to farewell him and wish him luck, from thirty, fifty, seventy miles away and more. For men were still so few in that country that distance counted for little and any neighbour was a friend. Mostly womanless men (women were a rarity still in the northern back-country), they congratulated him and admired the new house, or commiserated themselves on their own primitive living and harder fortune. Fred rode down from Avon Downs for a look at the house, whose fame had spread, and for a last bachelor yarn. Albert had not seen so many people on Nulalbin since he had first come there.

He wrote to Hanks in England—they kept up an occasional correspondence, but now their interests were grown so far apart that it was hard to find much to write about—and told him of the change that was coming over Nulalbin. For the first time he felt the place to be his home, not only the place from which he must make a living, and, surveying the house and the beginnings of the garden, he tried to look, too, at the country round them with new eyes, seeing the beauty of the low Dawson Range, its hills blue with the cold blue of the spring weather, seeing the long lagoon, the blacks diving for stems and roots of the dusky blue water-lilies, the dark scrub-trees that clustered round it, the flocks of black-duck, cranes, egrets that waded there, the water-hens with their red beaks and purple-blue plumage. Would May like the place? Would she think it beautiful?

The question of its looks had never entered his mind before; it had been simply a good place for cattle; and he wondered at the new questions that rose in his mind. She loved birds—she would ask the name of this one and that, and he realized he did not know them. The clumps of crinum lilies on the flats—he thought of their great white spider-blooms, and how she would admire them; before this, he had looked at them awry, because in certain dry seasons the cattle ate them and were poisoned. And the bauhinia-trees with their small double-curved leaves and butterfly-flowers, so sweetly scented; those too she would like—he had planted one in the garden. On her account, the landscape was coming alive in his mind.

But the weather worried him still. September was beginning, and the house was finished at last. He was due to leave, but the spring storms had not begun. He looked at the sky every morning, with mounting uneasiness. If the creeks failed further and the waterholes began to turn boggy, he could not leave Nulalbin with an easy mind. Suppose in his absence the cattle began to bog and die; suppose Tom Turner should forget to go round Mimosa and Perch Creek waterholes and pull them out; suppose this were the beginning of another drought like the '70 drought!

But the week he was to leave, the clouds began to gather; a good storm broke, and the creeks ran high. He rode to Rockhampton through country already growing green. It would be a fair spring now, whatever happened.

7 COMING TO NULALBIN

IT WAS VERY hot, with a languid heat May had forgotten over the years since she had last known Rockhampton. The sun beat like a hammer through waves of steamy air. But she was thankful to see the town, all the same, after the dreadful little tossing cabin on the *Egmont* —it was most humiliating to be seasick, and only the fact that Albert had been even sicker lessened her shame.

Now they were tying up at last, and she had washed as best she could, in a basin little bigger than a teacup, and put on her blue silk, hoping that the creases of packing would soon come out of it, for she wanted to impress the town. She leaned over the rail of the narrow deck and watched the wharf and its various activities, while Albert saw to the luggage.

On the high bank of the Fitzroy River, above the wharf, some native tree was in bloom. The scent streamed out like honey on the heavy air, mixed with the scents of tar and rum, for the hatch was now off the forward hold and someone had apparently stove in a barrel. She could hear an officer shouting instructions; a group of yellow and black men on the wharf scuttled busily with ropes and trolleys, and the other saloon passengers began to move off down their gangway, calling out greetings to their friends waiting below.

When the gangway to the steerage quarters was in position she watched while the crowd of passengers emerged from their dark cramped hold and began to file down to the wharf with their bundles and baskets. The women drooped, in want of food and sleep; the children looked grimy and pale. Rough-looking men went with them, miners and labourers for the most part. There were a few Chinese, one or two half-caste boys. She watched them rather incuriously as they stood on the wharf a while in bewilderment, or began to trudge wearily up the river-bank towards the town; her mind was occupied with other things, and it scarcely occurred to her to pity them, squalid and incredibly crowded as their journey must have been.

Albert came back; he had arranged about the luggage, and a cab was waiting to take them to their lodgings. He helped her proudly down the narrow gangway, while she managed her blue silk with one hand, and led her delicately across the busy wharf. Until now the sight of the town had always been enough to remind him of his commitments, and set him worrying again. The bank-building near the river, which he had so often entered to ask for another extension or another overdraft, had always had power to set his heart moving unpleasantly. Now he scarcely glanced at it, though the trip and the honeymoon had been expensive. He had never felt so confident, so decisive.

He wore her on his arm like a symbol; she was his link with reality, his guarantee of the future. For the first time in his life, it seemed, he had moved from tension into confidence; the world seemed intimate and friendly, and worked in ways that could be controlled; people were as May saw them, friendly, understandable, sometimes foolish; the world had taken off its mask, its smile was honest and hid nothing. He broke a twig of flowers off the white bauhinia and tucked it in the narrow waist of the blue silk dress; he laughed with her as though he had suddenly entered on the boyhood he had never had.

For her own part, she needed no gift more intimate than the world itself. She leaned eagerly forward in the cab, exclaiming and remembering, noticing faces, the scents of flowers, the articles in the few shops. This tree they must have in the garden at Nulalbin; had Albert a saddle for her, or had they better have one made at this shop? . . .

She took possession of their lodgings, found out enough about the kitchen and the landlady to form her own opinion of both immediately, but decided it was not worth while to move, since the train to Westwood left next morning.

She enjoyed her new position, her little accession of authority as Albert's wife—and Albert was so clever, had such judgement and ability, that he would certainly be rich and important before long. This assumption was to her by now so basic and unquestionable that it never occurred to her that it might perhaps be only the expression of her own intention.

Yet this quality in her love did not detract from the nature of the love itself, which was deep and even humble. It was in the very opposition of his nature to her own that she found completion and security; the difference of his view on life from hers added a depth to life itself. Through his eyes she saw, as it were, a new dimension of the world, as he did through her own. She felt mature and wise, as though she had finished already with her girlhood.

That afternoon, Albert's business being over, they drove out to the lagoon. May wanted to look at the little cottage again, and see the expanse of water-lilies that she remembered, and the walks where poor Miss Foy had trembled so. She remembered the trees and their November flowers, and the thousands of pretty birds. . . . How angry she had been at the hunters who limed and netted them to sell in cages!

She got out of the cab and walked with Albert along the lagoon; but over the low close hills of the Berserker Range across the river a storm suddenly gathered and came up. A fierce wind snatched at the blue silk and began to tear the white butterfly-flowers from the trees, and the last of the violet-coloured bells from the jacaranda in the cottage garden.

They had to run for it, panting up to the impatient cab. The wind was fierce as a hand shaking the torn old blinds of the cab, and the rain blew in violently. They reached their lodgings again, laughing and enjoying the dramatic wind and thunder and the rain that streamed down so thickly that the ground was a wide river. But at night they heard that seven people had been killed by falling trees and flying branches, and the cab next morning took them to the train over a gullied road of mud, scattered with broken boughs and wet flowers, withering in the morning heat. The blossom on the trees was beaten, torn and spoiled.

The train, slow and immensely sooty, took them jolting out to Westwood. It was still the terminus, but there was talk nowadays of the line being extended farther west at last. This was one sign of the gradual increase in prices and optimism. Markets were slowly beginning to rise again, there was already a mild rush inland to take up new western country, and the abandoned pioneer stations were little by little coming back into the market, when the mortgages they still laboured under were not too killing. Through the sooted windows, Albert showed May the overgrown bush tracks that branched off to this run and that, and the lean mobs of scrubber cattle that now and then bolted from the train, descendants of the mobs left behind by ruined settlers. But the dray-roads were becoming well worn again, and the train passed many teams bound for the mining towns and the inland stations, or returning loaded down with wool-bales.

It was dry on the Dawson: the grass that had. grown from the few spring storms had begun to bleach in the sun, and the river was low. But May saw the landscape with no less pleasure for that. This was the kind of country she had heard of as a child from her father: the thick scrubs of brigalow, black-stemmed and grey-leaved, where myalls had once hidden from the cattle going through, with spears and throwing-sticks ready; the big grotesque bottle-trees with their sappy trunks, good for cattle-feed in a drought; the big clumps of white crinum lilies, now in flower. The dark soil of these plains was rich and springy underfoot; it held the wheels of the old buckboard and sank under the horses' hoofs.

But how hot it was! The heat seemed to rebound from the soil and strike upwards as well as downwards, biting from both sides like the jaws of a trap. As they crossed the swampy country and the occasional little creeks, mosquitoes sang constantly around them, and the glare gave May a headache. She was glad when at evening they pulled up for the overnight camp at the creek near deserted Rio Station.

They set out again soon after dawn, using the coolest hours of the day. May watched the trees for birds; there were thousands of them, many strange to her. Groups of brolgas, beautifully plumaged, grey and red-wattled, stood quietly to watch the buckboard pass; great flocks of ibis rose, making a darkness with their wings; parrots burst out of the trees in noisy flocks, butcher-birds and friar-birds whistled and gabbled. But the sun, climbing higher, gradually silenced everything; the weight of heat increased hour by hour and the horses began to tire, travelling more and more heavily. Their polished hides were dull with caked sweat and dust; dust lay thickly everywhere and the iron arm-rests of the buckboard burned the flesh that touched them.

Nulalbin now was crowded for the shearing. When May first caught sight of it, it looked like a little settlement, so many tents had sprung up along the creek. A dozen or more shearers were dossing meanwhile in the sheds and on the verandah of the quarters; the nomad tribe whose country Nulalbin had once been had come back from their yearly walkabout and were camped down the creek; even the new house itself, to Albert's annoyance, was occupied, for a couple of travellers on their way west had knocked up their horses in the hot weather, and had persuaded Mrs Turner to let them sleep at the house.

May, sunburned and weary from the trip, could not help feeling strange and a little homesick. Albert was at once caught away from her into the urgent work of the station, and Mrs Turner, cooking and baking for so many men, withered in the hot dark kitchen and had few words to spare for the girl who was taking away her authority. May was faced immediately with household problems, for supplies were very short, the drays had not yet come in, though they were long overdue, and there was no news of them, and rations had sunk alarmingly with the number of people on the station.

There was no knowing when the teams would come: they might have been bribed away to some other station; perhaps a party of miners had bought them out, or perhaps they were caught in the flypaper of some wayside grog-shanty. At this rate, there would not be enough in the store to see the run over shearing, and Mrs Turner complained sourly of thieving as well; she could not set the bread to rise without watching it all the time, for the blacks would send the older children to hide near the kitchen and take whatever offered. The hot dry season had lowered their own food-supply to dangerous levels.

For the first time, May found herself with the responsibility of giving orders and of seeing them carried out. The whole bewildering machinery of the station was suddenly presented to her and must be mastered alone; she had to find her own way among unknown precedents, jealousies and confusions, for Albert had scarcely any time to spare, with the shearing now begun. But she took charge of her problems courageously, and soon began to enjoy her work, for this was the kind of life she was best fitted to understand, and her capacity for winning and using people was now exercised to the full.

It was not long before Mrs Turner was coming to her with questions and appeals, and the men with their ailments. Though Tom Turner and the stockmen were caught up in the whirl of the shearing's business and she had scarcely seen them as yet, it did not take her long to piece together, from Mrs Turner's conversation and from odd bits of talk picked up, the things that it would be necessary for her to know about them, and they soon began to place their confidence in her. The black children walked invisible, now, when the new missis heard of any thieving; even Crooked-toed Jimmy, notorious double-talker and cheeky-boy, an old police tracker who was now one of the elders of the tribe, ran out of range when she lost patience and went for the rifle that always hung near the dining-room door.

It was lucky, she thought, that George Wyndham had taught her to shoot, and that her aim was straight and her hand steady. It did not occur to her that taking aim at untrustworthy old men was anything unusual to be found among the duties of a housewife not yet eighteen; she had heard so many of Margaret's stories that she took her role as a matter of course.

Shearing was almost half-way through now, but still the drays had not come, and the stores were shrinking dangerously. The creek, too, was running lower and lower, and scum was gathering thick on the waterholes. There had never been time to dig a tank for the house water-supply, and all water was carried from the creek in a barrel. Though it was boiled at once, and never drunk except as tea, the taste was not pleasant, and when May went down with the 'Dawson sickness' she was inclined to blame it.

Albert, anxious for her, and for the food-supply, decided to pay off the shearers, and leave the rest of the sheep to be shorn when the drays had come and the stores were full again.

The men moved off to other stations, and the run went back to its normal work. It was a relief from some of her responsibilities, but nevertheless May's sickness grew no better. The weather was rainless and unpleasant, and she could eat little. The 'Dawson spue', a continual and exhausting retching, made her miserably weak.

It was early in December when the storms broke at last. The creek came down in a clearing flood, and after each storm, for a little while, the air was clear and brilliant, before the blanket of moist heat fell again. At such times she felt better, and even went out along the creek with Albert, shooting pigeons and bustard for the failing food-supply.

Though there was plenty of game, there was not enough flour and sugar left to be husbanded more than a few weeks; the tea was almost gone, and the little that was left was kept for the ration cart that took out weekly supplies to the shepherds and the fencing camp. Christmas dinner, if the drays did not arrive before then, would be a problem; the hot weather had stunted the vegetables in the little garden, and it looked as though there would be scarcely anything to eat.

Christmas drew near, and the heat became fiercer daily. News came at last that the drays were on their way, and would be at Nulalbin by Christmas, but now the storms began again, the Dawson came down in flood, and the drays were stranded on the farther side. There would be no Christmas mail, and it looked as though the wet season had begun in earnest. The drays might be months yet on the way, and the household was reduced to half-rations. Meat tainted in the steamy heat almost as soon as it was killed; only stiffly salted meat would keep over a day.

The sandfly season, too, was beginning, and May now was ill again. She could not even make a pretence of eating the bustard which Albert shot and Mrs Turner cooked for their Christmas dinner. She had lost her firm and glowing look, and had grown wasted and sharp-boned. Tormented by the sandflies, she sometimes lay awake all night.

Albert grew really alarmed. He sent his most trustworthy black-boy on an eighty-mile journey to Bauhinia Downs, where the white missis was reputed a good bush doctor. Mrs Dutton sent over whisky, arrowroot and a letter of instructions, and Albert turned nurse, and cursed the weather, the drays and the sandflies.

While May lay ill, the household, it seemed, kept augmenting. First came a couple of men from stations farther up the river; all the stations now were out of supplies, and they had come down with packhorses to beg flour and sugar, if any were to spare, or to try to cross the flood and bring food from the stranded drays. But the water was too high; they returned to Nulalbin to wait, and had to be fed and given beds until the river should fall. Mrs Turner, at her wits' end, grumbled day and night; the rations now were almost gone, and even ammunition threatened to give out, so that the hunting-parties after game had to husband every shot.

Then one night old Stapledon, the shepherd from the Mimosa, a hatter who had not come to the homestead for years, stumbled in almost exhausted. His legs were swollen as if with dropsy; when he was lifted into a bed he crawled out again and tried to go on with his painful journey, raving and blank-eyed. Albert diagnosed a bad case of scurvy. May, who was now beginning to recover, took over the nursing. But the old man was almost impossible to deal with, for he refused to be washed, and could not be induced to eat anything except his usual monotonous diet of salt beef and black tea.

He would wander at night round the slab room in which they had locked him, trying the door and window continually in an effort to escape and go on his desperate journey; sometimes he would suddenly begin to shout, repeating endless verses of poetry in a language which Albert managed to identify as Greek. It was a nightmare to May that he might escape and die in the bush; she listened for the breaking of the door or the fastenings of the timber window-flap, as though a wild beast were in the house.

It was not until late January that the drays at last managed to cross the river. By that time, everyone was weary to death of the monotonous salt meat and game which must be choked down at every meal, with weak sugarless tea and without bread. When the drays unloaded. rain had soaked through the tarpaulins, turned the coarse brown sugar into rock and caked the flour to the bags, but it was nevertheless a day of rejoicing.

Furniture, cases and barrels of household stuff which had been bought in Sydney on the honeymoon were at last unloaded, and the house took on a new air. Old Stapledon, too, now sewn securely into his blanket with a packing-needle, was dispatched on the drays to hospital in Rockhampton, and May and Albert had the house to themselves at last.

May had recovered quickly; she was beginning, too, to get a little immunity to the bites of the sandflies. She was certain, now, that in spite of her weeks of illness there would be a baby. She began to be busy again, arranging the new furniture, changing the rooms to her own liking, painting the battered old tables and bedsteads, and preparing for her lying-in.

Shearing had begun again, but the few remaining unshorn sheep were soon finished. When the sandflies began to lessen a little and it was time to gather the cattle and draft out the fats for market, she began to ride out with Albert now and then, or to drive over the run with the quiet old horse, Bolliver, in the sulky. She was interested in the working of the run, and now that she felt well and energetic, she began to question Albert eagerly.

She had always loved riding, and especially cattle-work. At Dalwood her uncle, young Regi Wyndham, had often taken her riding among the stud beasts he bred, which were famous then in the valley. Amused by her interest, he had taught her something of their points and breeding. Now she found her opinion asked and her knowledge respected, and because Albert thought highly of her capacities, she began to develop them for the pleasure of hearing his praise.

He had already begun to improve the herd, culling the scrubbers and the bad doers, selecting and breeding; now she began to persuade him to buy a few of the Wyndham bulls and breed to a better strain. The rough mongrel cross cattle, wild and long-legged, which made up most part of the Dawson herds, were restless and bad fatteners; the pure-bred red and white cattle among which she had ridden so often in her childhood, quieter and more easily worked, would do better, she was sure. Albert listened, and soon began to believe her ideas his own; soon he was committed to an expensive policy of herd improvement which his neighbours at first thought a crazy waste of money.

It was the beginning of many consultations between May and himself. Always humble, he regarded hers as the better mind of the two, and indeed her intuition and quick decisions made her a useful partner for his slower and more thorough nature. Her nimble grasp and masculine love of problems soon taught her as much as he himself knew of the possibilities for improvement of the country, which was still wild and heavily timbered, watered only by creeks. She followed for him, too, the trends of the markets, and the changes in the now quickly-moving times.

These were the last years of the age of wood on those far-out properties. In the south, here and there, a property might be found entirely fenced with the new cheap wire of which there was so much talk, but as yet the big properties of the cattle country were innocent of any kind of fence, except perhaps for a holding-paddock or two enclosed by wooden dog-leg or by a more solid line of chock-and-log. Sheds, huts and houses alike were made wholly from the station timber, as was most of the furniture; roofs were of bark and ceilings of bagging.

But now in a rush the age of iron was coming in; sheets of galvanized iron would soon be cheaper, on a long view, than the old stringybark which must be replaced every few years, for time and labour, which had once been so plentiful, were becoming valuable again.

The first breath of a new era was blowing. The first settlers, the devil-may-care boys, the young Englishmen out to spend their money and get experience, the adventurous young men who had taken up this northern country, had long gone under and were forgotten, and now that prosperity was on the way again, the second generation was bent on finally taming the wild country that had defeated their forerunners. Albert, whose life had been spent among the crude and makeshift devices of the bush, could feel the upwelling of change, and could not help a little resenting it. Yet, had he not spent his youth in bitter hardship for the lack of money and security?

G

He too now caught the infection of the age, though as yet he was barely conscious of its direction and aim.

But May, brought up in the comfort and civilization of longer-established settlement, welcomed every innovation. She scarcely noticed what was passing away as the new excitement began. It was all the thing, now, to fence your run and do away with the worry and expense of housing and feeding shepherds. There was clearly money to be made out of importing good cattle and breeding more suitable types. Now that the overland telegraph was in use, and the papers carried English news only a few days old, it was exciting to read the weekly mail and to guess what effect this or that piece of news might have on the tallow trade or on meat-preserving, and so upon the economics of the run.

Her mind was direct and practical, and Albert began to depend upon her to know the things he had no time to find out. It was cattle and horses that he knew about; money matters and the transactions of buying and selling were to him the more unpleasant part of his life, worrying him and making him doubt his own judgement.

He gladly shared such decisions with her, and in this way their partnership began gradually to solidify. He accepted her suggestions as readily as she deferred to his knowledge; he would begin to fence the run as soon as wire could be got; he would buy those eighteen bulls of the Pearl Diver blood as soon as a reliable drover could be found to bring them north; he would begin to sink wells in the drier parts of the run, and to clear the timber from the flats.

Though he was among the first to turn to the new ways of working, the settlers in the Dawson country were all beginning to feel the inflow of change. As yet there was only a difference in emphasis, a slight shift in the subjects of talk when neighbours met, a raising of new problems. The bad times still lingered; the common dress of the land-owner and the stockman and drover was still the same, the old ration-issue blue Crimean shirt and coarse moleskins with rusted iron buttons. Few men had town suits; only the young swells wore them. There was no money to spare for luxuries, and food was monotonous and often scanty. Work was hard and exacting, leaving even in the slackest season no time for the leisure occupations of reading or of learning.

For a few years after he had been forced to leave school, Albert had carried his French grammar, an algebra book, and a copy of Homer with him; he had vowed to spend his spare time studying, for he felt keenly over the loss of his school-days and the books he had loved. But there had never been time to do any of the things he had vowed; gradually he had forgotten the little he had learned, until now the books, when he came across them in his trunk, looked unfamiliar and incomprehensible. Now, with the years, hard work had a little dulled and rusted the edge of his intelligence, so that he scarcely read more than the newspaper. Weariness and the flickering of the smoky slush-lamps or candles usually drove him to bed soon after dark.

His work grew no easier; indeed, nowadays the times demanded more and more work, and an ever-widening span of attention. The pace grew faster as the world outside came closer; it was no longer enough to be a good cattleman, a good bushman, and a good rider, for now one must be a judge of markets, a bargainer, a clever buyer, a man with wide experience and a knowledge of the times. It was here that May helped him most, and here that he came more and more to rely on her help.

Gradually the once-deserted country was filling again. Mobs of cattle passed more and more frequently along the stock-route that crossed Nulalbin, and travellers went through in increasing numbers, many bound for the western country that was the new Eldorado of the pastoralists. Albert had built a hut on the route, which served for hospitality to such travellers. He kept it supplied with rations, and often enough the man on the ration-round would find men camped there, ill with sunstroke, fever or exhaustion. It was May's responsibility to doctor them, and the work kept her busy.

Mobs of horses, too, often passed through. Horse-dealing was a thriving trade, for the new stations were hungry for any kind of nags, and the dealers who bought mobs of weeds and outlaws in the south found a ready market. There were more drays on the road, too, and competition among the teamsters was growing. It was not likely that the Dawson stations would be stranded short of rations again. Hawkers came with their covered carts, and itinerant saddlers, watchmakers and other tradesmen began to arrive, travelling along roads which had long been grass-grown and blocked with fallen timber.

In late autumn, the weather grew cooler and the intermittent rain blew off, leaving a clear pale sky and bright weather. May drove old Bolliver out every day, through country that was fast becoming familiar to her. There were none of the bright and various greens of the cultivated valley she had left: the blue-grey leaves and dark-sheathed stems of ironbark and brigalow gave the landscape its prevailing colour, and the olive plumes of casuarina and the wilgas with their delicately drooping boughs diversified it. She was used to the sight of the big swollen bottle-trees now, and they no longer looked comic and clownish. She watched for birds—there were great flocks of them, now that the grass-seed was ripening—and shot them sometimes from the buckboard, not only for food, but to keep up her reputation as a markswoman, if she suspected that the blacks were watching from the brigalow scrubs.

It was often hard to be sure if they were there or not, their bodies melted so strangely into the darkness of the stems. Sometimes in the long grass Bolliver would almost step on the body of a child crouching, still and invisible. It would dart out from under him and disappear again in a moment, to go on with the game of watching without being seen. This sense of continual surveillance made May a little uncomfortable.

It was somehow unpleasant, she thought, to live among these people who were not people at all, whose minds she could not reach, whose games and dreams were incomprehensible to her. The gins who worked at odd jobs round the house were easy enough to teach; they quickly picked up their scrap of English and used it cleverly, and for a while they would enjoy the work they were given. But soon they were bored with it, and then anything at all—a trail of ants running over the clay floor of the laundry-shed, a packet of matches left behind, a button come loose from the shirt they were washing— made material for some endless and absorbing game, until May or Mrs Turner heard the laughter and came like stern schoolmistresses to order them back to work.

The wild-haired, attractive children—she had often tried, when she was lonely, to make friends with them, to teach them something useful, since to her mind, children should learn and enjoy learning. They laughed, they imitated what she did, but she could never get them to stay long or to forget their animal shyness. If she turned away from them for a moment they were gone, leaving her feeling a little ridiculous.

Driving alone now, she remembered the old hands' warnings—'make friends with them and sooner or later you're speared or knocked on the head'—and thought, as all the settlers so often did, of the massacre at Hornet Bank, not so far away or long ago. She had begun to agree with the old hands—there was only one way to treat these people: to be firm and to keep them at a distance, not as an inferior race, but as some superior animal. Their ways were not hers, and nothing would teach them human ambition or drag them out of their curious dreams.

When the water-lilies ceased blooming in the big pools of the creeks—the pink lotus lily and the blue whose long white stems formed part of the blacks' food-supply—the camp was shifted. May sat sewing on the verandah, whipping lace on the baby's long linen dresses, or gathering frills on the white lawn caps, and watched them pass along the creek, moving no one cared where, to some crop of wild fruits or nuts their tribe had known of and had rights in for many centuries. First came the proud young men, the warriors of the tribes, greased and shining all over with goanna-fat and wearing only their weapons; after them straggled the younger women, carrying babies on their backs, and the older children, with the camp possessions of possum rugs and bark coolamons filled with odds and ends. The sick and the old trailed after, the small children kept up as best they could, and the whole procession was fringed with camp dogs, incredibly thin and cowardly. The continual high shrieking treble which the blacks used for distant conversations sounded, from a distance, like the chatter and screaming of a flying-fox camp.

Among the men, she knew, went most of Albert's black-boys. She could see Wackemall, Captain and Charlie there, and thought how awkward and annoying it was that the tribe could never be persuaded to stay over the traditional time of walkabout, but went as inevitably as the season came, taking the boys just as they would have been most useful. Albert was out now, camping on

Tearaway and getting the last of the fats. Captain was the most intelligent stockman and the best tracker among all the boys, and Albert might be away for a week or more because of his desertion. It was a great nuisance, with so much to be done, and Albert hurrying to get the place to rights before he must take her to Rockhampton for the baby.

But it was no use explaining that to the boys, and no use offering them extra shillings or more tobacco. Migrating like birds, they were driven, she felt sure, by the same instincts, and she felt for a moment the deep emotional repulsion that was half attraction, for a way of life so unconscious and unquestioning. It was the repulsion of will and intellect from their own opposites—the kind of fear that had prompted the white men to kill and kill, not because of the little damage the blacks could do them materially, but because of a threatened deeper damage, the undermining of a precarious way of life that existed by denying what the aboriginals took for granted. It spoke in her darkly like the unborn child: 'My children would be like them, if they were left among them.'

She put down the spotless elaborate baby-linen and watched the naked dark infants that clung in bark slings to the mothers' backs. There was Clara, Wacky's gin, who had been polishing the knives yesterday, for once obedient and cheerful, calling out 'Yas, missis' to every new order. Now she gave May hardly a glance, trudging past bowed under the weight of her two babies and carrying on her head the dented old saucepan she had begged from Mrs Turner. She had withdrawn into the shelter of the tribe, losing all identity. They ate with the dogs, they had no pride, May thought; yet there was pride in the way they spoke and acted.

Could they have souls? Albert thought so; he treated them sometimes almost as equals, speaking many dialects of their language, which she had never tried to learn. She remembered what he had once told her—how, riding over a bare plain in a drought, without long grass or cover anywhere, he had seen to his surprise a warrior standing alone by the one dead tree on the plain. He had called out and ridden across, for he did not know of any tribe near, but when he came close there was no one there, and never could have been. If they had ghosts, they must have souls; yet it did not seem possible to her.

She picked up her sewing and moved inside, for the last of the procession was passing, and the sun was growing too hot.

8 THE FIRST SON

MAY HAD BEEN more than two years at Nulalbin, and little Weeta was not yet eighteen months old, when Albert took them to the valley for the first holiday since his marriage. He had hoped that the rest would soon make a difference to May; her second baby was due in June, and fever in the summer had made her thin and weak. But the journey down by sea had been terrible—he shuddered to remember it—and everyone at Dalwood had exclaimed at the change in her, so that he had felt wretchedly guilty and anxious.

At her mother's request, he had agreed at once that she must stay in the valley until the baby was born. Indeed, he had refused to listen to May's own protests that she was perfectly well. She had finally given way, partly perhaps to please her mother, for now that her father was dead the household at Wouillah was a lonely one, and it would give Weeta Mackenzie a new interest in life to look after her and the elder baby for a time.

But now that he was returning to Nulalbin alone, Albert began to feel dismally lonely and anxious. If May were really as changed and ill as everyone seemed to think her, how could he ask her to live much longer at Nulalbin? He sat on the crowded deck of the steamer, watching the green and white shore of Curtis Island flow steadily past, and worried over her.

Perhaps he should try to sell out, to find another station away from the heats and ague-weather, the droughts and rainy seasons? But how it was to be done he did not see, for the mortgage on Nulalbin was far from being paid off yet.

In any case, stations were still very difficult to sell. Avon Downs, whose mortgage he and Fred now held in partnership, and where Fred was still in charge, had been up for sale for a year or more, and there had been scarcely a nibble as yet. With new country being thrown open every year, the few buyers preferred to wait and see; there were still not enough settlers to occupy the available good country, and Avon Downs in particular had a bad reputation for fever and spear-throwing blacks. It seemed that Fred and he might have made a bad bargain in taking on the two runs, good country as they were.

But the hard work of these last years had done a great deal; another two or three good seasons and he might be free of debt. Then he would perhaps be able to sell, for prices seemed likely to keep up now; perhaps they would even rise, when the rush for new country steadied. But could May stand another two or three years? He thought in a circle of anxiety, and scarcely saw the calm blue of sea and sky.

When he reached Nulalbin again the house, after his two months' absence, looked dismal and unfamiliar. His meals, now that Mrs Turner found herself free of supervision, were sloppily cooked, and the tablecloths (which were May's innovation, Mrs Turner preferring the bare boards as being less fanciful and easier to keep clean) were dingy and mould-spotted.

In a fit of miserable impatience with the house, he decided to go out on a week's camp to look at the new fences, and to see how they were standing up to the emus and kangaroos. Wires were often broken and posts torn out by them, for the fences crossed their familiar paths to water and feeding-grounds, and cut them off from their companions, and they could not learn that the frail webs of wire were stronger than they looked. Often he found animals and birds entangled among the wires and dying there.

Also, the kangaroos and wallabies were increasing in numbers alarmingly since the fences had gone up. As he rode across his newly fenced paddocks, he disturbed mobs of them grazing on his cleared pastures; they scarcely troubled to move out of his way. The dingoes, which had kept them down before, were as yet puzzled and mistrustful of the fences, which they avoided as possible traps, so that in the shelter of the paddocks marsupials flourished and bred more than ever before. He had put the blacks on hunting them, and ears and tails were paid for at the ration-store with issues of sugar or tobacco, so that the tribe was doubly feasted, and the boys were growing fat and disinclined to work.

Everything that was done to tame this country, he reflected in exasperation, seemed only to give it another weapon against you.

Still, he looked with pride at the grass in the clearings and among the newly ringbarked trees; it had grown thick and deep, and cattle stood in the open plain fat and contented.

It was good breeding country. The heifers he had bought four years ago had done well; their first calves had been marketed now, yet the place was growing over-stocked. He must think about sending a mob to Avon Downs next year to lighten the load on Nulalbin. But the thought of Avon Downs set him worrying again about selling the station, and about May.

His horse splashed through a swamp that needed draining and was treacherous with holes and fallen trees; some day a beast would be caught, coming in after the lily-stems. A drain could be dug across to the gully there, he thought, and as he looked across to take the line he saw a big gum-tree on the edge of the cut-road along the fence line. It was too tall, and would be dangerous to the fence; the men should not have missed it. He rode across, with old Sally the packhorse trotting behind, and dismounted, taking the axe from the top of the pack; he had better get it felled now. The hard work drove away his melancholy for the time being.

But he had been out only a couple of days when the weather changed, and a big rain began to blow up from the north-east—the quarter for floods. He had to abandon the rest of the trip and make back to the homestead. Clouds hurried in from the coast, ragged and dirty-skirted, and the close hard rain of flood-weather began to press against the house, driven by the wind into every crack and deep into the timber of the slabs.

He began to shiver with ague again in the saturated air, as he sat at the endless accounts that filled in the time in wet weather. It was a blessing May was not here, she would have been down with fever again to a certainty. Yet he was lonely enough without her, in the sorrowful darkness of the air, that reminded him of all his fears again.

The roof of the kitchen, the shingles on the men's quarters and the bark over the ration-store all began to leak. And Mrs Turner's complaints, as he wrote to May, in a temper, were as bad as her cooking. But the letter could not go, perhaps for weeks; the Dawson was sure to be up by now, and the heavy mud would bog the mail-man.

Suddenly it occurred to him that May might be ill, seriously ill; there might be a telegram for him at the post-office, asking him to come quickly, and the weather might not let up for weeks yet. Lord, what a country!—and he sprang to his feet, leaving the papers on the table, and tried to think of something to do that would keep away the wet-weather devils. He would clear the cockroaches out of May's piano; when he looked inside the lid, they scuttled and hid everywhere. They had eaten the felt mufflers almost away and the notes sounded strange when he struck them, for wet weather had warped the keys a little.

When the rain slackened at last, the creek was higher than he could remember it, racing past with a noise like a continual wave breaking, and full of debris of logs and bones. A hot sun came out, drying a crust over the deep mud, and cattle and horses began to bog. He and the men rode out with ropes, and spent a strenuous week dragging beasts to dry ground.

The sandflies had begun their yearly torture. Everything seemed to steam and sweat, and the leaves of trees hung limply, stirred by no movement of air. At last the mailman and his packhorses managed to struggle through from Banana; Albert had ridden across to the route himself and was waiting in angry impatience. It was a relief beyond words to find May's letters. She was well; there was no news.

He turned with pleasure to the cattle-work, after his enforced imprisonment. The yearly draft of fats was now to be got ready for the trip to Rockhampton, but rain blew up again persistently, and the mud would scarcely dry a little before another storm undid the good of the sunny weather. Horses, exhausted by the sandflies, struggled through the deep soft soil, and often knocked up before the day's work was half finished. It was well on into April before the work was finally done and the mob sent off down the river.

Albert did not go with them this time, for he had decided to go to Avon Downs to lend Fred a hand. A big mob of cattle was to be got there, for a buyer who had taken up new country on the Thompson; it was an important deal, and the station was short-handed. He rode with two changes of horses, as well as packhorses, for the mud was still deep and treacherous and the weather threatening. On the way he found all the creeks high, and had to swim his horses;

low ground was swampy and treacherous, and the Mackenzie River was in high flood, holding him up for two days before he managed to cross in a crazy boat, the horses swimming behind it.

He had been wet through for days now, since the persistent showers would not let his clothes dry out; he was shaking with ague, and when, two days from Avon Downs, he met travellers with bad news of fever on the station, his heart sank with painful apprehension. All hands were said to be ill, and the memory of 1869 came back to him with dreadful vividness. If he were to go through that again (and he remembered the desperate nightmares of that month lost out of his life) what would happen to all the irons he had in the fire?

He halted overnight in Clermont, and bought all the medicines he could; quinine was scarce as always at this season, and very expensive. The old hands dosed themselves with red pepper, brandy, and even vitriol when quinine was unobtainable, and of all these he laid in a plentiful supply. When he set out again, the showers had turned to heavy rain and wind, and he finished the journey riding half-blind against a wall of streaming air.

But his alarms had not been necessary after all. The fever had not been serious, and was already on the mend. The change of weather that came after this last lash of the rainy season brought it to an end soon after he arrived, and he had little nursing to do. Autumn sun and wind cleaned the air of the dirty and dismal quarters, and took the fever-sweat and mould out of clothes and blankets. It was not long before work began again, and the air was like a draught of sweet water after the hot and clinging steaminess of the wet season.

The soft earth hardened to springiness under the horses' hooves, and magpies sang round the camps in the early mornings, clear and joyous. Even the cattle seemed to move more willingly; they obeyed the whips and dogs, running together in long bellowing processions into the clearings; it was an easy muster and the number was got early.

It was a fortnight that felt like a holiday. The ten white men, relaxed by the passing of the fever and the bright convalescent vision of these autumn days, seemed subdued by work and weariness into an intimacy that went deep. They yarned together round the fires in the dark, cracked companionable jokes with the black-boys, and felt for each other a deeper than customary brotherhood.

Albert drank in the bright weather and the comradeship, and his own ingrowing tension gave way for the time being. He himself scarcely knew how much, nowadays, that tension had taken possession of him; only in this temporary freedom from it did he recognize the change, and puzzle over it. In fact since the loneliness of the first travellers and settlers had passed, a new spirit had begun to thrust into the lives of the white men. Once, isolated in these little-explored districts, they had felt the solidarity of comrades united against the hostile unknown—against the bush whose distances and hardships they felt equally, against the blacks who far outnumbered them and of whose intentions they were never certain. Now the tide was setting in a new direction. The country was hostile still, but its dangers were measured and known; the blacks might still, had they known how, have swept the settlers from the land by a concerted attack, but by now their invaders knew that they were too bewildered, too divided, too easily appeased ever to do so. That gathering of the tribes in open warfare which had once been the secret fear of every white man could now be discounted. But it was now white against white—the competition of seller and buyer, the division of employer and employee, the struggle not for physical but economic survival. Men were not comrades now, but rivals; they set themselves hard to withstand the pressure, and to hold and increase their own possessions, which meant safety. For May, the baby and the baby to come he had hardened himself in continual work and struggle, for in them lay his happiness.

But happiness, he found, was here too, and a little point pricked his conscience because of his secret relief and joy in a company from which May was absent. He had ceased for a little while to spur his own sides, and for a time he tasted a companionship he had almost forgotten.

But when the great mob had been collected and handed over to their drovers, and he was on his way back to Clermont, the thought of May filled his mind again. His pockets were stuffed with letters for her, and he called at the little post-office to send them off, and to see if any were there for him. When he saw the telegram, his heart leapt with terror; he tore it open. 'Boy born today, seven weeks early,' he read; 'both very well.'

He waited at Nulalbin only long enough to set things in order. His mind was occupied again with feverish plans for the future as he rode to Rockhampton to catch the steamer. Waiting there for a day, he found talk optimistic for the country's prospects. Capital was coming through freely from the south, a mild boom in cattle and stations was expected, and things looked rosy. As usual, the relief of his own good news had changed his outlook; he began to forget his fears and problems. They would make their fortunes on Nulalbin yet.

The sparkling weather of early winter was on the Hunter Valley country as he watched it through the train window. The first frosts had browned the grass, and instead of the green-squared pattern of crops he had travelled through so dismally in January, pale golden stubble-fields and parchment-coloured blocks of standing maize alternated with the warm earth colours of ploughed paddocks. Over the stubble dairy cattle grazed, and the pastures, he saw, were taking over more and more of the old arable land.

He remembered how, travelling to school, he had seen from the coach windows an almost unbroken plain of wheat on these flats; the stone mills, like prison-towers, still stood there, derelict now or turned into dairies and housing the big milk-cans that the train gathered in at every siding and station.

The wheatfields had then belonged to the big houses, the valley's old landmarks. The railway, which had been built to bring those houses more prosperity, had gradually brought about their humiliation, for the price of land had gone up, the little farmers had come in and bought, and worst of all, rust had ruined the wheat crops and brought disaster on the obstinate conservatives who had stuck to old ways in the face of the new times. Now the big houses looked sad and unkempt, out of place among the wash of little farms and dairies that swirled up to their very gardens.

These were the houses that remembered the last days of the forest, the chain-gangs, the official barge that had travelled up the river with triangles set up in the bows, ready for summary punishment to any assigned servant whose master had a complaint to make of him. Their day was over now; indeed, their greatest prosperity had begun to decline when the gold-rushes came. Some of them still looked prosperous and well cared-for, but these, for the most part, were supported by stations up the country or in the new western sheep-lands. Like Dalwood, they lived on the profits of rough and lonely lives spent in outpost bush, among hardships they themselves had long lost sight of.

Now the dark river soils, their forest richness beginning to fail, no longer grew the heavy crops that older men remembered. But this was still the day of the small farmer, the grower of potatoes, maize and vegetables. Little roads ran everywhere, fences jealously marking the limits of their encroachment on the cultivations on either side; farmhouses and little gatherings of townships had sprung up more and more thickly along the railway line. Albert looked out at the peaceful business of this countryside without much interest; he had the cattleman's slight contempt for the farmer.

And after the years in which his eyes had become accustomed to the bluish-greens and greys of the Dawson landscape—that hard and subtle country with which he had so long wrestled—these coastal valleys always seemed insipid to him. This was soft, easy land, a green velvet cushion beside his hard and feverish plains. Something stirred in him at the thought of those plains, the exhilarating response of their springy soil under a galloping horse's hooves, the level sea-like distance of their horizons.

In the years he had spent in that heart-breaking stubborn toil, the country had begun to set its mark in his bones. He would never love it, for he was of the lost first generation, brought up on stories of a country they had never seen; yet in the fight to master the land, it had in fact begun to master him. The long occupation of his whole mind and life with the problems it set had made him more its own than he realized; the ways of thought it imposed on him had become the yardstick by which he measured what was strange or foreign to him. His struggle with it was forcing him into an ever narrower intensity of focus.

The marks of this same struggle between land and man, had he been able to interpret them, were just beginning to show in the winter landscape of the valley that ran past the train window. Storms on ploughed ground had left there little disregarded gullies, washing away the fertile topsoil so that the crops grew less and less profitable, and the fields were left at last to go back to pasture again. It was on the slopes of the cultivated foothills that these little claw-scratches had first appeared, but under the repeated crops of heavy maize even the richer river-soils were beginning to stagger a little.

The small farmers, who had bought their land at the high prices of the first railway boom, were getting their money back quickly, for capital was plentiful just now. Few of them were farmers by choice; they were generally anxious to buy stations, to return to England, or to find some profitable business in the towns. The gold-rushes had taught them to look for easy profit, and the rich soil lay waiting to be minted. They put in the same money-making crops again and again, and the soil wilted under them.

Dalwood, in spite of the deep divisions that were undermining it, still seemed prosperous enough. Its wines kept their reputation; good cattle and horses were still bred there, and as he drove up the house still wore its old air of serenity. But he knew that already the money-troubles were growing serious; too many people depended on the old estate and what it still yielded, and there was bitterness in the house. He was doubly glad to go on to Wouillah where May was waiting.

She had made a quick recovery after the birth; she ran out radiant and smiling. The rest had certainly done her good; she had colour and roundness again, the hollows between her bones had filled a little. He renewed his pride and confidence, seeing her so gay, and for a time he had eyes for no one else. How much he had missed her!

But the baby—little Albert, who was to be called Bertie—lay so quiet and small in his crib, that Albert's pride in his son was darkened by an anxiety that he could not help feeling. Everyone said he was well, a healthy baby now, though being premature he had given a lot of trouble. . . . He would have to be looked after. But it was May who occupied Albert's thoughts; the children were not yet quite real to him, but May filled his world.

They were to return to Nulalbin almost immediately. May was anxious to go home and confident that the climate would not trouble her again—she was so well now. She would not hear of his putting the place up for sale when he suggested it, and secretly he was relieved of a painful burden by her refusal.

They were back at Nulalbin before June ended. The shining winter weather, the clear air and the sun's brightness reassured and exhilarated him, and little Bertie had stood the trip well and seemed to gain weight and colour in this northern warmth. After the heavy rainy season, the grass and the garden had grown wonderfully; winter feed was assured, and the country looked rich and pleasant.

May's piano came into use again. In the evenings in the little parlour, the children safely asleep, she would light the candles in the brackets and sit down to play. This was the slack season, and he was not too weary after the day's work to listen with pleasure. Sometimes they sang duets, while he stood beside her and turned the pages—Tom Moore's songs, the sentimental drawing-room songs of their generation, or old tunes like 'Ben Bolt' that never failed to move him. The children lay in their cots; the night receded from the circles of candlelight that bloomed over the delicate colour and curve of May's face as she played. From the men's quarters came the sound of concertinas and jews' harps, and a chorus subdued by distance. Everything was well.

9 THE NORTHERN VENTURE

IT WAS THE fifth year of his marriage; a dry and frosty winter had crisped the grass, and westerlies were blowing. There should have been plenty of dry feed still; but the last season or two had been good, and the herd had increased to a point where the run was over-stocked. Albert rode out through the fenced paddocks to see how the cattle did, and noticed that the feed near the creeks and waterholes was already beginning to give out, and that the cattle had to walk farther for their grass now than was usual at this time of year.

Then, too, there were the great mobs of marsupials, still increasing in the shelter of his fences, since the clearing of the scrub had resulted over these last seasons in so great a growth of the native grasses. Kangaroos and wallabies grazed everywhere, and hardly moved out of the way as Albert rode among them. The dogs could no longer be troubled to chase them. He had put the blacks to work spearing and shooting, and this winter he had already paid for more than a thousand tails. But even this seemed to make little difference to the numbers of kangaroos; and the tribe now was becoming so well-fed and well-paid that they were tiring of work, and preferred to stay round the camp all day and make corroboree all night. May could scarcely get the gins to help in the house, and even Captain and

Charlie, old and wise in stock-work as they were, had refused duty at times. Albert flicked his whip irritably at the kangaroos; they were eating the grass and drinking the water that he felt belonged by right to his sheep and cattle, and in the dry season this made him impatient and uneasy.

Perhaps he should begin to get together a big store mob for sale, as well as the fat cattle. There were plenty to spare, and if spring and summer should happen to be dry, his grass would not last much longer. He had begun to watch the waterholes, as always at this season, for as the water-level sank their muddy edges grew treacherous. The morning had been spent in clearing them of branches and snags brought down in the February floods, and now beginning to show above the surface. Now he was riding across to the stock-route, which crossed Nulalbin.

Eight years ago, when he had first come here, the stock-route saw few mobs pass, except those from the mortgaged stations travelling out for sale at any price. Now the mobs travelled the other way, for the most part, inland to the new country that was being taken up out westward. Mobs of thousands had gone through this year, and he and the men had spent much time in clearing the Nulalbin cattle out of their way as they passed through the station, for the route was still unfenced. He would go out and see whether the last travelling mobs had left the Mimosa waterholes sunken and boggy for his own cattle.

Today the westerly wind was colder than ever, frustrating the coming of spring. No rain could be hoped for in such weather; and fires, if they should start, would be hard to check. He kept a close watch on the horizon for signs of smoke. He was restless this spring; the continual drag of the wind seemed to vex his mind, like the drag of his increasing responsibilities and unceasing work, and to put into his thoughts, unacknowledged, the desire to leave this difficult country and the burden of his commitments to it, and begin again.

Yet, he reflected, the last two years had been good years. Not only had the seasons been fair, giving him plenty of grass and water, but he and Fred had managed to sell Avon Downs—a lucky sale, which had almost cleared him of debt when the partnership was wound up, and left him free to devote all his time to Nulalbin. He had fenced more country, bought more well-bred beasts to improve his herd; he felt more secure than he had ever done.

But his increasing family—there was a third baby now, another boy, born this time in Rockhampton—was constantly on his mind. May had had bad attacks of fever and ague in the humid wet-season weather, and so had the baby, and little Bertie—Bangs, they called him—was too often ill. Albert was still planning a long holiday for May and the children in the south, but there was not enough money for that, since the fencing and the cattle were still to be paid for, and May refused to go unless he was able to come with them, which could not yet be thought of.

He was always secretly relieved when May brushed aside his arguments and stayed on at Nulalbin, in spite of his worry over her health. Without her, he was lonely and unsure of himself; with her, her wishes and ambitions and her view of life became his own. Now, riding through the fretful gusty wind and noticing afresh how his pastures were thinning and his cattle increasing, he translated his restlessness into terms of those ambitions, and began to think of the new country.

Since Avon Downs had been sold, he had lost his outlet for surplus cattle. Before that, if seasons were dry, he could always send a mob of weaners to the other run to lighten the burden on Nulalbin; but now he must either sell cattle to some man taking up country, or find more land. Prices for cattle were good, and he would easily find a buyer for a store mob, since there were rumours of more new country soon to be opened up, and speculation in cattle was running high. But why should he not take up new country himself?

The idea was not novel to him; he had listened often to the talk of men passing through with cattle, and had envied their freedom and half-wished to join them. And wherever one went nowadays the story was the same. Everyone seemed to have some stake in the new country, or to know something of it. Good reports of the Gulf country, of the far north, of the far west flew round from run to run. But Albert had dismissed the thought of such speculation for himself; Nulalbin was enough for him to handle, and he could not leave May and the children.

Yet this morning, it seemed, the windy spring weather had fired him. If he were to find some younger man—a man without ties, who would take charge of his surplus cattle and take them through to the new country, in partnership with him—he might take up a good-sized run and stock it straightaway, in fulfilment of the conditions. He would have to borrow again, of course, but the new land was cheap enough, and if he were lucky, in a few years the debt would be wiped out by the rise in value of the land. Fred might come into the partnership, lightening the debt; their younger brother Harold, still at Bickham, was talking of coming north to join them and might be interested in the venture too.

It should be easy enough to find a partner for such a scheme, in any case, for Queensland was once again a magnet for young men, after the depression years, and most of them were eager to join the rush to the northern and western country, though few had the means of stocking it. Rumours ran through coastal towns and inland stations alike. There were tales of thousands of miles of treeless downs with grass as high as a horse, of fever-swamps and myalls with poisoned spears; of men who had taken up country, stocked it and sold at incredible prices, and who would sail for Home next week; of so-and-so who had been flooded out on his way through the Gulf country; all his cattle were washing about in the Gulf and he was drinking the last of his bank loan in Potter's Pub on the Cloncurry road. It was the recurrent infection of the gold-rushes over again, working in everyone's blood with visions of quick wealth.

Though Albert meditated plans as he rode, his eyes were still busy with the recording of details—the state of grass and fences, the way the cattle were grazing—and watching for signs of trouble in the cows near calving, or possible symptoms of pleuro-pneumonia. He saw through the scrub the movement of a roan side, and was alert at once. His herd now were almost all Herefords, red and white cattle; he was proud of their uniformity, and the colour of this beast was unfamiliar. He remembered an old scrubber bull he had seen in the range country, a dangerous old animal and a breaker of fences, with a hide of that colour. He had spoiled many musters and enticed away cows to his own wild herd, and Albert was anxious to get rid of him. Probably the dry spring had tempted him down from his timbered country and he had broken the fence to get into the clearings where the grass grew higher.

Albert worked round against the wind and identified the old bull. He dismounted and unstrapped the revolver he always carried, and crept through the scrub. The wind muffled the noise of his movements and kept the old bull from scenting him, and he shot it cleanly, and skinned it at once for greenhide, to be used for ropes and repairing harness and saddles. He rode on about his business feeling that this might be a good omen; the old bull had been a legend in the range since Albert had first seen Nulalbin, and had long been an enemy of his.

That night he discussed the new project with May, and soon it was decided on. Letters were written to Fred and Harold, and Albert went to Rockhampton to enquire into the chances of another bank loan, and to see if he could hear of a possible partner and of country that would be suitable.

Soon he was in touch with a young man named Haydon, who was ready to start for the Gulf to look for likely country. Haydon rode to Nulalbin, and an agreement was quickly reached. He would start for the Gulf immediately, Albert supplying the horses for the trip, and look round for a suitable run. When it was found, he would take it up straightaway and ride back to Nulalbin for the cattle. Albert, meanwhile, was to draft off a suitable mob for the journey and have them ready for Haydon's arrival.

Haydon left for the Gulf in the middle of August. Albert was eager now to have the cattle on their way, but it would be foolhardy to start them too soon. The cold dry winter had weakened them, and no rain had yet fallen; the stock-routes northward were dangerously dry and good grass was scarce.

Albert fretted, as Haydon rode off, at staying behind; he fretted, too, at the weather, which might delay his plans. Scanning the newspapers, he read glowing reports of this and that new district, and feared that the Gulf country might not be the best speculation after all. The Atherton Tableland, inland from Cairns, was now the most highly praised of the new districts. Perhaps he had chosen wrongly?

The continual cold winds changed gradually to hot winds with the advance of spring, but the sky remained cloudless and the air grew dustier and drier. The grass on his cleared flats, grown wispy and thin, began to loosen and blow away as the cattle trampled it down in their ever-lengthening search for water. Fires began to break out, and were beaten back with difficulty from the precious feed, and reports of the stock-routes and waterholes on the roads to north and westward grew more and more discouraging.

Albert waited impatiently for news from Haydon. None had yet come, and he was in a fever of impatience, when one day he got news of almost two hundred miles of country available near the Walsh River, in the far north of the Atherton Tableland. Its owner wrote that he had heard that Albert was looking for country, that this was going for a song, and would certainly suit him. The owner, a man named Uhr, had taken it up purely on speculation, since he had not the capital or the stock to comply with the conditions of the lease, and he wrote that he would let it go for only two hundred pounds and the partnership, and in addition was willing to come south and get the cattle, and take them north himself for only a drover's wage.

Albert calculated desperately. It was possible that Haydon might never get in touch with him at all; plenty of men travelling on such errands as Haydon's through wild and unknown country had not returned; and even if all went well, Albert could still manage to find a second mob for the Atherton station. And Fred, who had now bought a nearby run, Banana Station, might be able to supply more cattle. If he took up the Atherton country, he might still honour his agreement with Haydon, though it would mean more borrowing and extra risk.

He rode across to see Fred, and infected him with some of his own enthusiasm. It was agreed that Albert and Haydon should remain partners in any country taken up on the Gulf, and that Fred and Albert should join with Uhr in the Atherton country, Fred providing half the cattle. Albert sent a telegram to Uhr at once and closed with his offer.

He was now only impatient to hear from Haydon and to begin gathering the cattle. But it would be useless to start the work until rain fell. Time drew on to the end of October, and the usual spring storms had shown no signs of gathering. He had enough work on his hands to keep the Nulalbin stock in grass and water, and with a heavy calving, the run was seriously overloaded.

Now, as he had feared, the fires began to grow serious. One big fire broke out on the unfenced part of the run, in the Tearaway country, and pushed aside his other preoccupations for a week. By the time it had been got under, with fighting and firebreaks, it had burned a good part of the grass that was left for the Benleith and Tearaway cattle, and by early November, weak and old cattle were dying.

Albert was continually out, camping on the run for a week at a time, pulling weak beasts from the bog-holes in the creeks and cutting saplings to lay new corduroy approaches to the waterholes. He had already begun to feel the first edge of his enthusiasm for the northern venture blunted, and by the time rain at last began to fall in mid-November, he was too wearied to feel much pleasure in the prospect of getting the cattle away, at last.

He had now heard from Haydon, of whom he had begun to despair. Haydon wrote with news of a big and well-watered block in the Gulf country, not far from Normanton. He had already taken it up, and was now travelling south to get the cattle according to their agreement. Uhr, too, was coming to Rockhampton for the cattle for the Atherton runs, and Albert decided to ride to Rockhampton himself and meet them there.

He must call at the bank to sign the documents for the overdrafts arranged with them, and also the terms of partnership must be drawn up between himself and Haydon, and with Uhr for the Atherton runs. He felt himself reluctant at the thought of the errand; he had so recently rid himself of debt that the idea of taking up again such a crippling burden was unpleasant. But May cheered him with her confidence and the pleasure she obviously felt in the venture; and indeed it seemed likely, if luck were with the cattle on the droving trip north, to turn out well.

Money was easily to be got now for the development of the new stations, provided that the cattle were available for security. The sudden expansion meant that cattle were selling at fantastic prices in the north and west, since to comply with the conditions of the land leases they must be brought in to occupy the new country at once. Many of the squatters and speculators held a great deal more land than they could stock, and could not comply with the conditions of the leases. Cattle were pouring in from the south, certainly, over-landed from New South Wales and even from Victoria; but mean-while Albert's cattle were the most valuable of guarantees against loss.

Uhr and Haydon met him in Rockhampton, and, when the agree-ments were drawn up and financial matters arranged, they all rode back to Nulalbin. It was a formidably large party, for both Uhr and Haydon had drovers and drovers' plants; and when the camps were made by the Nulalbin creek the place seemed more populous than it had ever been except at shearing.

Now began the station's biggest muster. For weeks past Albert had been collecting cattle, drafting them and placing those fit for the journey in his two fenced paddocks, but many more remained to be got. For a fortnight the scrubs and the range country were combed. Mob by mob, the cattle poured into the inner paddocks. Still poor from the long dry spell, they had begun to pick up a little condition, for the creeks were running again, and the herbage that had sprung up after the rain was growing green on the flats and clearings. All told, there were thirty men on the mustering and drafting, and at last the work was done, and the cattle for the trip were gathered into the Brigalow Hole paddock.

Horses, too, were brought in; with the extra hands on the work, they succeeded in yarding a number of the brumbies from the range mob, after a few days' chase, as well as a few unbroken two-year-olds of Albert's own, and some other horses that would be fit to act as packhorses on the trip. The brumby youngsters were branded and broken with the rest, the old mares and the other brumbies that would be useless were shot. The run was like an antheap for activity.

Twelve hundred cattle were started from Nulalbin to Rio Station, where they were to join up with Fred's cattle for the Atherton runs, and a few others bought to make up the numbers. They set out the day before Christmas, after three weeks' hard work during which the men had been almost always in the saddle.

First went the drovers' carts with the camping gear, which travelled ahead of the cattle to warn the runs on the route to clear their own cattle out of the way, and to make camp at the waterholes that marked the end of each day's stage. Then, gradually, the great mob was pulled together and headed after them, silent dogs at the heels of the tailers, and the men riding each in his station to guide the nervous rushes of the cattle on the wings of the mob. After a few miles of travelling, they would settle down a little and become accustomed to the sight of men and horses, and weary of useless struggles to break away into the familiar scrubs where they had lived, almost unmolested, from season to season.

All the cattle were to travel together until their routes diverged. Then Haydon would take his number and swing away north-westwards for Normanton, while the rest continued towards the Atherton Plateau. There was no saying how long the trip would take, or how long it would be before Albert heard of the safe establishment of the runs, for it was late in the season for travelling, and the wet was almost certain to begin before the cattle could reach their destinations.

They should have gone long before, Albert knew; now they would be travelling through January, perhaps through February as well—the worst months of the whole year for their northern trip. Floods might set in and cut them off for weeks from further travelling, so that scarcity of feed on the stock-route would perhaps force the men in charge to find agistment on some already established run, which of course would have to be paid for. Well, he would not care about that, if the cattle did well and there were no great losses.

He rode with them to the boundary of the run, to see them away and all well. Passing through the country they knew, the cattle were restless and fractious, trying to break away into the scrubs or back to their old haunts. It took some time to get them safely to Nulalbin's boundary, and it was already mid-afternoon when he turned his horse homeward.

Two bullock-waggons followed the mob, carrying supplies and tucker for the new stations. They travelled slowly, and Albert met them on his way home. The waggon for Haydon's Gulf station was under the charge of Johnny Power, who had worked on Nulalbin for years, and the bullocks that drew it were a team that Albert himself had driven often. He lingered with Johnny almost wistfully, re-testing yokes already gone over, making sure of the list of stores the waggons carried, checking his notebook list of bullocks against those that had been yoked. He knew the bullocks as well as Johnny did, the whole nine yoke, from Yellowman and Dragon back to Bonner and Boxer. Johnny understood this unaccustomed fussiness. When Albert finally shook hands and mounted, it was clear to Johnny which way he would have liked to be riding.

But, wistful as he had felt at the sight of the mob's dust growing smaller to northward, he knew he could not spare time from the work on Nulalbin for such a journey. He would be short-handed now, for Johnny and two other men had gone with the mob. Besides, he was needed at home. Bangs was ill again; it was sandy blight this time, May was afraid, and the other children were almost sure to get it. Poor Bangs cried and twisted with pain, in bed in the darkened room, his eyes closed and his eyelids red and swollen. The fever season, too, would soon be here.

May had the fever in her bones, now, as the old hands said. Every year she went down with it, and each year was worse than before. With the fourth baby due in five months, he could not think of leaving. Yet he sighed as he rode back, going over in his mind each day's stage with the mob, as far as he knew the route, and speculating on what he had been told of the northern part of it; thinking what water they might expect, what the feed would probably be like, wondering whether the blacks in the north were likely to be hostile, and how soon the floods might be expected this year.

It was a good season, but work around the station seemed flat, and the branding was small now that so many cattle had gone. The grass grew high and thick; at the Island, when he went to muster there, he could tie it over Star's neck. But he wondered whether so good a season here might not mean bad floods farther north, and the suspense of waiting for news was made more anxious by the children's illnesses. All three had sandy blight now, and fever and ague were beginning.

May nursed the children day and night, growing pale and sharp-boned again. Between their needs and the fever-pains that kept her awake, she got little sleep. At last, when he came home after a week on camp around the fences, he found her, too, down with sandy blight, almost blind and in great pain.

It was a stubborn and recurring complaint, and it made her almost helpless. Albert had to alternate the station-work with the duties of a nurse. The sultry heat of the rainy season, the myriads of sand-flies and mosquitoes, wearied them all, and continued far into autumn, and the house was full of sickness. There was no news of the cattle.

Albert was thankful when at last it was time, in any case, to take May to Rockhampton for her lying-in. The three children had to be taken, too, for there was no one to look after them at Nulalbin. The Turners were leaving, infected by the talk of the new country, to try their luck farther inland, and unless a new housekeeper could be found in Rockhampton May would return with the new baby to all the household work and the work of the store as well, and he himself would be faced with the winter work of the run, more short-handed than ever.

He found himself almost as busy in Rockhampton as he had been at Nulalbin, after a nightmare journey with May and the children in the waggonette, with all the creeks high. May's sandy blight still kept her almost helpless, in spite of the doctor's treatments, and a spell of fiercely sultry heat, the last of the season, brought back Bangs's fever and ague. He scoured Rockhampton in search of a nursemaid, but there were none available.

By good luck, however, an immigrant ship was due in Rockhampton. He met it, and managed to hire an Irish girl, Ann Carlon. She was six feet tall, bare-footed, and new from Ireland. Her brogue was hard to understand, but she was kind and easy, and the children liked her. Under May's anxious supervision she looked after Bangs, but May was exhausted by her sleepless nights, and still half-blind and feverish, when, a few days later, their third boy was born.

Meanwhile, Albert's younger brother Harold had passed through Rockhampton, on his way north to join the cattle travelling to the Atherton run. Neither Fred nor Albert could make the trip north to see for themselves how things were going, and though Harold had no experience of conditions in the north, Albert felt that he would at least keep him in touch with what was happening there. By now he must have joined the mob travelling to Atherton and taken over some of Uhr's responsibility.

Albert knew that the wet season had set in, near Cairns, and he was fretting for news, but it was not until he had brought May and the children back to Nulalbin, with Ann Carlon now the only other member of the Nulalbin household, that news began to come through.

The mob for the Gulf station, it seemed, was doing well enough, and had almost reached its destination, but the Atherton mob was camped near the Barron River, which was uncrossable as yet. Harold wrote that the new country had been taken up as two runs, Wangarinda and Corunna, and that the cattle were to be divided between the two. His letters were full of the beauty of this rich country, its forests and mountains and waterfalls. Albert read them wistfully; but he would have liked, too, more news of how the cattle did there.

He wished Harold had had more experience of the north, of the wet season and of the troubles to which cattle were subject in its constant rain and heat, and more experience, too, of handling men and averting possible trouble with the tribes, of which bad reports were beginning to come through.

Sure enough, it was not long before Harold's letters began to lessen in enthusiasm and to take on an anxious note. The cattle were over the Barron now, and established on their permanent country, but they were not doing as they should. Some were showing strange symptoms; a few had died unexpectedly. Evidently there were poison-plants about, but he could not find out what they were. The cattle not affected by the poison were losing condition badly, and the country was rough, with many deep ravines and gorges, so that it was hard to keep track of them.

Further, the blacks were showing signs of resentment. They were an isolated, untouched tribe; their solitary hunting-grounds, in this wild difficult country, had never before been invaded. At first, they had kept prudently to the shelter of the scrubs, but now they knew how few men the white camp held, and they had begun openly spearing cattle, and threatening the stockmen from a decreasing distance.

Harold, to whom blacks as he had known them in the quiet long-settled Hunter districts were merely a useless and harmless form of existence, was puzzled and alarmed by the situation. His attempts to teach the tribe a lesson had bad effects. His letters grew more and more disillusioned. The country, however beautiful, was certainly bad for cattle; losses were increasing; and now the tribe was collecting on the northern run and apparently planning some kind of attack against the invaders. What should he do now?

Albert read these letters in an increasing fury of anxiety. If the runs were really untenable for cattle, they must be given up and the cattle must be got out and sold as soon as possible. Already the rush to the northern country had slackened, and prices for cattle were dropping sharply. If he could only make the trip north himself, he could find out for certain what the country was like, and take action before the cattle began to die wholesale. Moreover, he could pacify the tribe and come to some settlement with them, as Harold seemed unable to do.

But how could he leave Nulalbin now? May was still weak, the baby fretful and troublesome, and the children were seldom really well, especially Bertie, whose last attack of fever had been alarming. Ann Carlon, though strong and cheerful enough, was far too inexperienced and ignorant of the country to be of much use as yet. It was hard to find labour of any kind, with the new settlement taking all available men; so that Nulalbin was very short-handed for stockmen, and the outside work was already behindhand.

Albert rode over to Rio Station to consult Fred. It was clear that someone must go to Harold's help, if the northern runs were not to become a dead loss. Fred was busy enough, but he agreed to sail to Cairns by the first steamer from Rockhampton, inspect the runs and give a final report on them.

Meanwhile, Albert watched the market-news in the papers that came by the weekly packhorse-mail that passed twenty miles from Nulalbin. He added endless columns of figures, and was depressed by the results. Whatever happened, the northern venture must be a loss, even if Fred should report better of the runs than Albert now expected. If the cattle had to be sold now, the price would barely pay for the cost of droving and supplies, and with every week the northern market fell more steeply.

Fred's first letters came, with as bad news as could be. Both the runs, he reported, were useless for cattle: beasts were dying daily from poison-plants; many were lost, too, in the steep rocky gullies that made mustering difficult. He had not been able to get in touch with the blacks: they had been badly handled and were incurably hostile.

There was not a good word to be said for the country, in his view, and he suggested abandoning it immediately, gathering the cattle, and starting them either for the Gulf station to join with Haydon's mob, or for sale in the more settled part of the Atherton Tableland, as soon as they could travel.

But their condition was now so bad that to start them at once would certainly mean many losses on the road, for they must not only recross the rough mountainous country that had already weakened them, but must be swum over the Barron River, a difficult crossing at the best of times. There was little good pasture now, but with spring near, the grass should improve and the cattle pick up some condition.

Albert answered at once, agreeing to abandon the runs. If the cattle could be sold immediately, so much the better; he had no mind to wait for a possible improvement in prices, since he had begun to fear that all the northern country might now be found unsuitable for cattle. And by this time his mind winced away from the thought of this whole northern venture. To travel the cattle across to the Gulf country would mean for him more risk and more sleepless nights of anxiety. Spring in the north was a dry season, and water on the westward route, he knew, was scarce and uncertain. If drought struck the mob on its way westward, he might lose all the cattle, and though Haydon had now settled his own mob on the Gulf station, Vena Park, and seemed optimistic, Albert could not take the risk of overloading its as yet unproved pastures. No, the cattle must be sold in the north, and sold quickly, no matter what the loss might be.

Reckoning up his accounts, he stared aghast at the total of bills due, cattle dead and lost, interest due on his loans, and fallen prices. This unlucky venture had taken all the credit he had gained from the years of planning and work on Nulalbin, and left him once more deep in debt. And it was clear that, though the Gulf station was showing no losses as yet, much money would have to be spent there before it could become a profitable investment. Certainly, it was not likely to help his finances for years to come.

Now that his hopes were centred on selling the Atherton cattle, he waited anxiously for news of Harold's moving out with them. But the few letters that reached him told of delay after delay. The blacks had driven off a mob, and had had to be dealt with; the men fell ill with fever; the numbers could not be got and the country had had to be mustered over again.

It was December when at last the mob was ready to move, and now Harold met with another disaster, for the wet season set in early this year, and when he reached the Barron River crossing he found his way blocked by high floods. He was now cut off by floods both from Cairns and from the other new settlers on the Tableland, and had to make camp and wait for the river to fall. He had managed to get the letter over the crossing by swimming his horse over, but it was far too dangerous to risk the mob in the current.

Albert had no more news for a month. When at last he heard from Harold again, the letter did nothing to cheer him. Harold wrote that continual wet weather had kept him in camp beside the crossing for a month, and then he had only just managed to bring the mob over the river before fresh floods came down. Six feet of rain had fallen in a week, and it was now impossible to travel the cattle farther. In any case, they were in desperately poor condition after the long spell of wet-weather travelling on rough country with little pasture, and must be rested if they were to recover.

Accordingly Harold had sheltered at an Atherton out-station, and had got agistment for the cattle there for the time being. He would wait there until the wet season was over. Moreover there seemed no chance of selling the mob at present, whatever the price. Too many cattle had been poured into this unsuitable country, and were now flooding the market.

Albert knew that there was nothing to be done, though he longed to go north himself and try to find some way out of his difficulties. Fretting was of no use, but as usual, he could not prevent himself from fretting—the more so as the wet season had set in again at Nulalbin, too, and the household was again full of fever and sicknesses.

Himself, he seemed to have developed an immunity to fevers now. Perhaps it was the terrible month at Avon Downs, years ago, that had ended that trouble for him. But May had never been able to get through the wet season without sickness, and the children, even down to the baby, fell ill with sharp attacks that recurred regularly. Ann, too, was ill; she had not been much use as a nurse, but she had at least been able to keep the children quiet and amused with her Irish stories and songs. Now the whole burden of the household and the nursing fell on May; her own aches and agues had to take second place, but her sleepless nights and ceaseless work had exhausted her, and for once she, too, seemed to have lost heart.

He repented now that he had not sent them all south to Dalwood for these months of burdensome heat and rain. There could be no question of it now, with losses piling up daily and the Atherton cattle still unsold. He decided to try, at least, to make a little extra money to give them a holiday later. He would take advantage of the sandfly season to try to get the wild mob of horses that ran in the Dawson Range. They had been sighted several times, during the big mustering before the cattle had left for the north, but they had not let the stockmen get within range. There might be thirty or forty youngsters among them that could be broken and sold to the new stations, bringing in perhaps two or three hundred pounds.

This Dawson mob, too, was an increasing nuisance to the station. At mustering time, they would come round the camps at night and try to entice the stock horses to break away and join them. They broke fences, spoiled musters, and occasionally came down into Albert's cleared country and made inroads, as the kangaroos did, on the sweet rich pastures over which Albert felt so possessive. There were certainly a number of good station horses among them now: some were wanderers from Nulalbin, some lost from passing drovers' outfits, some the progeny of the horses left behind on runs deserted during the slump.

Albert laid careful plans, built a strong yard on the creek at Tearaway, concealed in the scrub, ran long wing-fences out on either side of the entrance at a point where the horses might be expected to make for a gap in the range, and equipped five of the black-boys with new gear and good station horses. He ran in a mob of forty quiet

I

horses, to be used as coachers, in the hope that they would lead the wild mob into the yard, and he and the stockmen set out for the range with a week's supply of flour and corned beef, driving the coachers ahead.

But Albert was to have no luck this year, it was evident. After a two days' search, the mob was sighted in the thickly-timbered foothills of the range, where they could not be manoeuvred out into clearer country, and after another four days' chase, finding, losing and tracking them again and again, only a few light and weedy animals and a mare or two with foals had been got. By now the station horses were knocking up; one had been badly staked by fallen timber, and one of the coaching mob had broken a leg in a swamp-hole and had had to be destroyed.

At last the mob eluded the hunters altogether and crossed the range through rocky country where their tracks were difficult to pick up. By now, after a week's hard riding, Albert and the stockmen were thoroughly tired of the venture, and they had fifty miles to ride home with the coachers. A fortnight's work had been wasted, and there would be no holiday for May and the children.

The rainy season hung on week after week, far into the months that should have brought a spell of cooler autumn weather. It was interfering with the autumn work of the run, the routine of mustering, branding and drafting; and no sooner was one of the children safely over an attack of fever than another fell ill. All of them were now pathetically thin and pale, and it wrung Albert's heart to know that May lay sleepless listening for their crying.

If only the northern venture had turned out well—if, even now, the cattle could find a sale at a fair price—he might have been able to break away from Nulalbin and buy another run, in a fever-free district, as he and May had often talked of doing. He reproached himself bitterly for his bad judgement. Yet others had taken the risk and had prospered; the luck had gone against him. Well, he would work harder than ever; for next summer, he was determined, he would send May and the children away for their holiday—the first since Bertie's birth—whatever it might cost him. They would not go through another year like the last two.

May, after her six years of hard work and child-bearing, was still cheerful enough in spite of her fevers and pallor. She had never complained, but he knew well enough how, after a year or two, the unbroken monotony of the inland life, with its loneliness and its poor unvarying diet, turned into a deadly weariness. The cool bright days of late winter and spring, the best time of the year here, lasted too brief a time, and then came the fierce heat of summer, followed by the steaming fever-season of the rains, which for the last years had been so prolonged and heavy. The vegetable garden which provided the only variety in their meals withered and died before Christmas and could not be replanted until late autumn, and meanwhile the eternal corned beef, stiffly salted but always tainted by the heat, the flour that mildewed almost before the drays brought it from Rockhampton on their three-monthly trips, the sugar that had to be hewed out of its wrappings with an axe, the few eggs laid by such hens as May could rescue from the blacks, and an occasional plains-turkey or duck shot on the lagoons formed the children's diet.

May did not trust the marshy-smelling creek-water that was the household's only supply. She boiled all the drinking-water herself, in the big iron kettle that always hung over the kitchen fire, but for all her care, boils and sores kept the children miserable, and the 'Dawson spue', that sickness of malnutrition, broke out again and again in the household.

Then, too, there were the other hazards of the hot weather; scorpions that nested under the wood-heap that supplied the kitchen fire, centipedes lurking in dark corners, snakes—May had often killed them—lying on the earth-floored back verandah or looking for coolness in the house itself. And in the heat of summer May would scarcely allow the children outside the house, for fear of sunstroke.

Yes, this year they must go to Dalwood for a time—in December, at the latest—and get rid of their sicknesses and gain strength. He began on his solitary rides to add up the money that would be needed. There would be clothes for the children, who grew so fast that May's sewing was always behindhand, a new dress for May herself, whose old clothes hung on her thinness pathetically, fares, expenses. . . . And he would begin—he must begin—to look for cheap stations, away from this fever-country. It would mean more debt, when already he did not like to think of the mortgages on his future, but somehow it must be managed. . . .

When at last news came of the sale of the Atherton cattle, at a price lower than even his worst fears had imagined, he scarcely glanced at the telegram. At any rate that venture was done with. He would dismiss it from his mind; he would not think of it again. There remained the Gulf station, where Haydon seemed hopeful of the future. Something might be saved in the end out of all this loss; but he would not allow himself the luxury of optimism.

He turned back to the work of Nulalbin and to his resolution of selling and finding better country; he worked on, stubbornly and without respite.

10   *DEPARTURE FROM NULALBIN*

YET, ALBERT THOUGHT, as he sat over the endless accounts at his crowded little table, more than four years had passed since he had taken that firm resolution to leave Nulalbin, and nothing had come of it. If he had acted then, had cut his losses and walked off the place, how much they would all have escaped, how much of bitterness and loss he would have been spared! He sighed to think of those years.

It was the drought that had betrayed him, month by month, into staying a little longer, hoping for rain, for grass, for a little luck to mend his finances, for some good news from the Gulf station where drought held Haydon also. A year of drought had passed; surely the next would make amends with a good season, and he had stayed on; but that year too had passed, and the next, and this season now seemed likely to be the worst of all. He had forgotten, almost, what it was like to see the creeks in flood, to see the grass high on the river flats, the cattle grazing easily on good pasture.

Outside the unglassed window-opening the landscape was bleached and dry; a few heaps of white bones showed on the plain. It was January, and again the wet season was late in coming, and perhaps would not come at all. Twice it had failed, except for a few late storms; a third time would be certain ruin, for the cattle, though they stayed alive so stubbornly, had little strength left to face a dry autumn and winter. The few scattered rains that had fallen in November, starting the grass into growth for a few weeks, had not set the creeks running. Now a month of burning winds had dried the grass and withered it almost to the roots, and the waterholes shrank daily. This had been the way of it for years now; just enough rain had fallen to keep his hopes alive, saving him from actual bankruptcy, but condemning him to ceaseless and killing work that had narrowed his horizon more and more, into a burning circle of hardship and anxiety. He was running in a treadmill, gaining nothing.

One relief at least the drought years had brought—the fevers that had so oppressed the household had vanished. There had been no wet seasons, so that the mosquitoes and sandflies had found nowhere to breed. The children now were clear of the disease, and though May still sometimes fell ill, burning and shaking, with a recurrence of the old infection, the new baby, Elsie, had never had it, though now she was two years old.

But though they had abated the fever, these drought years had struck a yet crueller blow. Thinking of it now, Albert moved restlessly in his chair as though a thorn pressed into him. He could never recall Bertie's illness without that recurring pang of self-reproach and fear, nor see Bertie himself—so pale and quiet now, with the great swelling that pulled his head sideways on his neck—without remembering the doctor's words that had marked him like a hot iron.

It was a cold and arid midwinter, two years ago, when Bertie's illness had begun. He had always been the first of the family to sicken and the last to recover, in any bouts of illness; Albert and May had gradually grown used to this, accepting him as a 'delicate child', and no longer worrying overmuch about him. But this time his illness had grown worse and worse; his throat had begun to blister and swell, until at last he could not swallow and May had had to find ways of feeding him, somehow managing to slip down his throat spoonfuls of the precious milk that the few half-starving house-cows still produced. It did not seem possible to take him on the rough two-day journey to the hospital at Rockhampton; and though Albert had sent urgent messages to the only doctor there, it would be at least five days before he could appear, even if there were no other more important calls on his time.

Meanwhile, May went desperately through the volumes of the old medical book, trying to identify the disease, which was mysterious to her. She was a resourceful and reassuring nurse, and after a few sleepless nights with the child it seemed that his fever had begun to lessen a little. By the time the doctor's horses were seen across the plain, it was clear that the worst of the attack was over, though she was still secretly terrified by Bertie's weakness and pain.

The doctor avoided giving the illness a name, probably because he too was puzzled by it; he gave May medicines and directions, and agreed that the boy seemed on the mend. But when Albert pressed him for a possible cause, he was explicit enough.

'These children are drinking bad water. You boil it, do you? Well, it would take a lot of boiling to make water wholesome, in the condition this stuff is in. I don't say that *is* the cause of the boy's illness—but even if it isn't, it will be the death of all of them sooner or later, if something isn't done.'

Albert was stricken to the heart. It was years since he had first intended to get a tank dug for the drinking supply. Each time he had thought of it, it had been put off—by the urgency of the outside work, by the lack of labour, by the expense. . . . He had known, of course, that the long drought had made the house waterhole stagnant and impure; no flood had gone through it for years, and sometimes the carcases of bogged cattle might lie in the water upstream for weeks before they were found and dragged clear.

The blacks were supposed to camp on the lower waterholes, but they too were short of food and had moved nearer the house so that they could get their daily ration of meat and flour, and often, he knew, the gins and piccaninnies used the house waterhole for washing and swimming. May had reminded him about the tank, and he had promised; but the increasing pressure of work and worry had so filled his attention that he had forgotten it again and again.

He took the two stockmen from their work immediately and set to, with them, to dig the tank. The cattle might die where they stood, the brumby mobs move in on his precious waterholes and the work of the run go hang, but the tank must be ready to catch water from the first spring storms. But he was bitterly conscious that the work was done too late to help his eldest son.

Bertie had recovered; he was walking and even running now, though he did not laugh and play as the others did. But on his neck remained the extraordinary swelling. It did not go away, as the doctor had at first prophesied; and all the treatments he had given had done no good. There was nothing for it, the doctor said, but to take the boy to Sydney and consult specialists.

The thought of the expense made Albert flinch for a moment, but he was immediately ashamed, since for Bertie nothing now could be too much sacrifice. And he was still afraid for the other children, with the fear of his own guilty conscience. He decided that they must all have a holiday. It was years since he or May had left Nulalbin, except on the trip to Rockhampton for Elsie's birth. He would manage to pay for a holiday somehow, no matter what the bank manager said.

He sent May with the other children to the Hunter, and himself took Bertie to Sydney. It was a weary and heartbreaking round that the two of them followed, from one doctor to another. Each doctor, it seemed, had a different opinion on the cause of Bertie's trouble, but they all agreed that nothing could be done. As for the future—they shook their heads. It was impossible to tell. The boy might shake it off, grow out of it completely—but on the other hand . . .

Albert's heart, as he walked with the silent little boy from building to building, from one false hope to another, ached with misery and love. He could not bear the thought of his own possible responsibility, and during this time of their constant company he had come to feel more and more deeply for the child, as he helped him through his occasional attacks of illness and watched his pale submission to the doctors. Whatever happened, Bertie must be saved.

At last, in despair, he had taken him to a foreign doctor, who specialized in some new treatment called galvanism. He was said to be a quack, but by now Albert was indifferent to opinion. If no one else could help the boy . . . And Friedland, after a quick examination, had been quite confident. Perhaps his treatment had really done some good; Albert could not be sure. . . .

He wished, though, as he gathered together the threads of his neglected work on their return to Nulalbin, that it had been possible to afford to keep Bertie—indeed, all the children—longer in the coolness of the south. This was the worst time of year; these January days, always hot and angry, were aggravated by the violent winds that raised dust from the bare ground and swirled dry leaves from the thin trees. Sitting at his desk now, his mind reverted to May's worry over food for the children; the little vegetable garden, neglected in their two months' absence, was burned dry; the blacks themselves could scarcely find game enough to survive, though May had shot a pigeon or two and a few bustards too tough and thin with drought to make more than a pot of soup.

The few house-cows, which gave little milk at the best of times, were miserably poor; there was scarcely a drain of milk to be got from them, and that little went to Bertie and Elsie. The rest of the household were back on the monotonous diet of salt beef and bread, and Albert knew that the old malnutrition sicknesses, Barcoo rot and spue, were not far off. Would he never have the luck to sell out and get away—to find that station in the easy country? Next year, perhaps, if rain fell to rid him of his more pressing debts—but it was always *next* year.

At present, it seemed he would be lucky indeed to get enough salable cattle from the run, for the autumn draft, to pay his rent and the interest on his loans for the year. The station was short-handed as always, the work had been neglected in his absence, branding was in arrears and the heat and drought had weakened both cattle and horses, so that little work could be done now until rain fell. And he did not like to think how much had been added to his debts by those two months away in the south.

The thought recalled him to his account-books and he sighed again and bent to the work. He must make up the accounts for the partnership in the Gulf station, in the hope that this year, in spite of the drought, Haydon and he might begin to make a little profit. Until now, the necessity of improvements to the land and the ill-luck of continued drought had left little more than enough to make it worth while keeping Vena Park in work.

Haydon was always optimistic of better times; but Albert no longer expected much. He did not feel satisfied that Haydon's management was good; the station always seemed too expensive to run. But he had never been able to spare time or money to make the trip to the Gulf and see for himself; though once, he remembered, he had looked forward to it with the excitement and impatience for adventure that he had felt when first the steamer brought him to Queensland.

This morning he had determined to make up the Vena Park accounts for the whole four years of his partnership with Haydon. When he had reached the totals, he sat staring at them without hope. Apart from the interest on his bank loans, there were now liabilities of more than seven hundred pounds to reckon with, and if the drought continued much longer, there might not even be enough cattle left on the station to cover them. Oh, if only he had never entered on those unlucky northern ventures! Surely he had had enough millstones round his neck, without adding others.

He remembered that only a year before, he had again been half-tempted to try to recoup himself by entering another such partnership. His sister Mary's husband had written and offered to let him join in a station which he was taking up in the far west of New South Wales. This was the famous new sheep country, the saltbush country on which fortunes were being made. Wool prices had risen, and millions of sheep had been taken out to this dry plainland, which before had been reckoned almost useless. The run was newly taken up, near Bourke; Jack Suckling wrote that he was taking out thirty thousand sheep, and that the country was a gold-mine.

A gold-mine: perhaps it was that word that had decided Albert against entering this further venture. He had heard it too often; it was the word of temptation for his generation, ever since his own youth. Easy money—treasure to be got for the taking, from this hard land that yielded so little! He had seen plenty of men who had answered that call once too often; he had answered it himself, for that was the word Uhr had used for that unlucky Atherton country. He would not answer it again; work, hard work and forethought and a modicum of luck, those were the only roads to mastering this country. He would join the rush for no more gold-mines.

He thanked his stars for that decision now, thinking of Mary's last letter, for her news was doleful. The drought had struck at the western country, too; the new run, over-stocked in Suckling's enthusiasm, was now an expanse of dust and moving sheep searching for a mouthful of feed here and there.

It was the old story, Albert thought. This country raised all kinds of hopes, only to frustrate them; prospectors, pastoralists, speculators, all followed a will-o'-the-wisp, and when it vanished only the land remained—obstinate and wild as ever, but now strewn with the bones of sheep, cattle and men. He had been a fool once, but now he would be wiser, for he had a better estimate of the strength that opposed him. If he ever had the luck to buy that new station, he would make sure it was land with a good rainfall and reliable seasons. If you were sure of water, the rest could go hang. He had seen too many cattle and men dying of thirst; he was tired to his bones of the long drought.

January drew to a close, and the dry heat and flaring winds continued. If the wet season should fail again, he was in for a worse year than ever before. At the fag-end of winter, all grass and water would be gone; nothing could save the cattle then. Yet they hung on, now, with obstinate patience, even contriving to fatten a little on the dried grass left from the spring rains. He had been amazed, time and again, these last years, at what cattle could endure and live.

Endure—he had learned to do that too. And today was a day for endurance. The fierce hot wind from the south-western deserts had blown for weeks, and this morning was a lid pressed down on the country, of strangely brassy light; he could hear the dry protest of the thinned trees outside, from the little office where he sat. He had begun to notice, too, a strange grittiness in the air, like a fine metallic dust rasping between the teeth and eyelids; the light seemed curiously darkened and muffled. He rose from the chair, leaving the big account-books and the weighted papers flapping on the desk. Was it a thin cloud over the sky—could rain be coming up?

But it was like no cloud he had ever seen. A high thin veil of greenish or brownish substance, it seemed to hang on the heights of the wind, filtering the sunlight into a diffused and menacing glare. He stared up at it in perplexity; it was something new to him— a mist? A dust? What could it be a sign of? It was certainly ominous

It must be connected with this terrible weather. He watched the sky for a time, half in fear.

Next day it seemed to have passed over, but he could see the last vanishing skirts of it in the east, like a bar of dun-coloured cloud. The sun rose behind, swollen and red, as if it rose through the smoke of a bushfire. The house this morning was thick with dust, the mirrors and glass filmed over, the food gritty. Dust—but where had it come from? He could not yet solve the puzzle.

This had been, though no one knew it yet, the first of the great dust-storms, whipped up by the rasping wind from the bared country of the far west, where the sharp hoofs of millions of sheep had loosened the light soil, tearing up the thin cover of grass and roots that held it. It had been another sign, another wound delivered in the unceasing struggle between man and land—the struggle whose marks Albert himself bore more deeply year by year.

Early in February, a first tentative storm or two broke. It was enough to start the grass again, but as yet it made no standing water. At last, however, he could begin the long overdue branding of last year's crop of calves, and he rode out at once to Skull Creek with the black-boys and the branding-irons.   .

It dismayed him that there seemed to be so few calves. This would be the smallest branding he had ever had, although the cows were not in as bad condition as he had feared. The drought could not have killed so many. Riding through the scrubs he noticed here and there small scattered bones, and a few carcases torn and half-eaten. It was the dingoes, he realized. Made desperate by the long-continued drought and privation of food, packs of them must have been coming down from the range, where ordinarily they hunted, and pulling down young calves perhaps strayed from their mothers, or perhaps with mothers weakened past defending them.

He had never known the native dogs to venture such attacks before, unless with a lost calf or two; but now that the native game was dwindling yearly, with drought and the increasing occupation of the country, and since the great mobs of marsupials that had so troubled him a few years back had been starved out by the lack of grass, it was evident that he had a fresh danger to provide against. He began to make plans; he would put a premium on dingo scalps and set the blacks' camp to work to catch them. They would be eager enough, since the camp was short of food in any case.

As the branding went on, more storms gathered, crossed Nulalbin, but did not break. February was drawing to an end—the month when the wet season should have broken—if it came at all—and as yet there was scarcely water in the creeks. He must begin to think of selling a mob of store bullocks, even at a loss, to lighten the burden on the run. In any case, they could not fatten in time for the autumn muster, even if rain were to fall now.

Ready money he must somehow find, for Bertie was ill again. That it would be of no use to send him to Rockhampton or to Brisbane for treatment, Albert already bitterly knew. Friedland was again the only hope; the boy must be got to him for more treatment. May's younger sister, who was staying at Nulalbin, would return home soon, and Bertie might go with her, for neither he nor May could leave the station now. It would need all the money he could raise to pay for Bertie's visit and the doctor's treatment.

He gathered the cattle, walking them slowly out of the scrubs and from lessening waterhole to waterhole, saving the thin horses and beasts as much as possible. If a beast summoned strength to break away and make a run for it, he let it go; it was not worth knocking up the horses, and besides, beasts strong enough to run might survive better and fatten faster, should rain come.

He managed to find a buyer; a few stations had been lucky with rain in the scattered storms and were able to take a chance on a mob so low-priced.

Early in March, belated signs of wet-season weather came to raise Albert's hopes again. If a flood should come to clear the stagnant waterholes and make good standing water, the year might yet be saved. A storm or two broke, with much thunder and lightning but little rain; but after a few days of close sultry weather the clouds blew off in a westerly wind and the air cooled again.

Albert rode from end to end of the run, calculating his chances. The grass had grown surprisingly well; he had often noticed that, in a drought, even a little rain would bring the grass forward quickly; but without more rain, his water would be gone by spring. Somehow he must increase the water-supply.

He began to study advertisements of the expensive new water-augers, which were said to be tapping water-supplies at unbelievable depths. To buy one of these, he might risk borrowing again, since a good and permanent well would increase the value of the property; and perhaps Fred, whose new station was ill-watered and who was now as deep in drought-troubles as himself, might join him and share the expense.

Meanwhile, he must get a well dug as quickly as possible in the western part of the run, where there were few waterholes likely to last any time. He would be lucky if the cattle could hold out here until the well was finished—if he had the luck to strike water.

Now Bertie was to leave with his aunt for Rockhampton to catch the steamer south. Friedland, in his letters, had reassured May; this relapse was certainly not serious, perhaps had something to do with the child's restricted diet in the drought-weather; with another few weeks of treatment he was sure of curing the complaint. But as for Bertie himself, at the thought of the long trip without either his mother or father, and of the terrifying treatment at the end of it, his stoicism gave way. He wept and clung to May, whose steadiness and cheerfulness had always comforted him, whose gay songs and stories had brightened his long illnesses since he could first remember.

May and Albert were torn by the thought of the parting. Night-long they talked, seeking some way out, but there seemed nothing for it. There was simply not money to afford another trip for the family; the younger children could not be left, and there was no one who might take over May's responsibilities for a time.

Albert went to Rockhampton to see Lilla and Bertie on to the steamer. While he was here, too, he might be able to arrange a loan to get the water-auger. He took them to the wharf, and stood waving as the ship pulled out, very heavy-hearted. Bertie stood beside Lilla on the deck, the books Albert had bought him under his arm, and waved as bravely as Albert could have wished; he had been a little restored by the knowledge that he was an important and adventurous member of the family. But Albert saw with renewed fear how very thin and small he seemed, with the big deforming bulge on his neck that pulled his head awry.

Turning away at last, as the steamer disappeared down-river, he took his way towards the bank, trying to console his heart with remembrance of the doctor's confidence, and to distract himself with renewed plans for countering the drought. But the picture of Bertie—little Bangs who had always been the delicate and shy one— would not go away. Returning to Nulalbin, he had to make a great effort to seem cheerful and confident; May, who was grieved enough already, must not suspect his fears.

He began now to wean the young calves. It was too early, but any that were fairly strong must take their chance, to save the cows. Even the worst of his years here had not offered such a prospect as this did. The wind had risen again, and the short green feed was beginning already to dry into standing hay; there would be no more growth this season, and it was now a question of how cunningly he could distribute the cattle, to make both feed and water last as long as possible.

He was thankful that he had managed to sell another big mob of stores, even though the price was not good and they could not be delivered until midwinter. The load on the station in the critical months of early spring would be a good deal lessened by the sale.

Also, it was becoming clear that he was beginning to reap the profit of those expensive bulls he had bought, and of the other improvements he had been making year by year in the breeding of his herd. The Nulalbin cattle looked better and had more stamina than the usual run of cross-bred and carelessly handled cattle which were run in the district; they fell away from condition more slowly and fattened faster. Pleuro-pneumonia, the disease all cattlemen dreaded, had always been in the herd; in certain seasons, he had learned to expect big losses from it, even though he had begun to use the new inoculation technique as soon as he had heard of it. But as the quality of the cattle improved each year, his losses sank; the drought had not yet struck as deeply into the herd as he had feared it would.

He finished the cattle-work as early as possible; it was better to leave the poor beasts undisturbed in such weather, even at the cost of leaving some of the weaners unbranded and the heifers unspayed. Instead, while the horses were still fit for work, he turned his attention to moonlighting again for the scrubber cattle—those lean inbred beasts, speedy as deer, which hid in the scrubs by day and by night drank at his precious waterholes and broke up the dry hayey grass which would scarcely last his well-bred beasts till spring. Their hides and tallow were worth something, and every penny counted now. He spent a week with the men, coaching over the range, and this time had luck enough to get a good number, though one of the men was badly hurt in a fall and one horse was lost with saddle and bridle.

All through the early winter high winds blew, growing colder and colder. He began riding out each day to the dams and waterholes, pulling out the bogged beasts that still lived, and burning the dead so that they would not pollute the water, clearing the mud away, digging holes deeper as they dried. A well was being put down now, in the driest part of the run; it had struck water and the flow seemed good. Perhaps his luck was turning.

In June, letters came from the doctor in Sydney—it seemed his luck had really turned indeed. The treatment, Friedland said, had done all that he expected; the boy was improved beyond belief. Soon he would go to his grandparents at Bickham, and then the cure might be pronounced complete.

Albert and May stared at each other, scarcely able to believe their joy. Bertie cured—it was a miracle! May wrote a rejoicing letter of thanks, for Albert to carry to the mail, and Albert set off almost lightheartedly; he was taking the mob of store bullocks to be delivered to their buyer, and for once the world seemed rosy. He left the mail-bag on the route and went on with the cattle; he would return in a week's time and pick up the mail for Nulalbin, to take back with him.

The bullocks were slow on the road, for water and feed were scarce and they had to be rested at each camp. He was in a hurry to get home, with so much work waiting to be done, and when he returned to pick up the mail at a wayside station, he would not have glanced at it, if the envelope of a telegram had not caught his eye. Telegrams were rare events; the news they carried was always of urgent importance; and he tore it open at once. 'Deeply regret tell you of Bertie's death,' it read.

The ride back to Nulalbin was the bitterest of his life. His heart hung in anguish on two nails—his own grief, and the thought of May's when he should tell her, May whom he had left so rejoicing.

It was then that for the first time he began to project his own sorrow upon the land, the relentless scene and witness of his defeat.

Many times it had moved him almost to love, in spite of its obstinacy and the tenacity of its apparent opposition to his will. He had often enough made plans to leave it, to find easier country, but he had until now been reluctant to take the final step—always he had been secretly relieved when circumstances seemed to prevent him. But now, the landscape turned for him into a vision of death. The river-oaks hung over vanishing waterholes like funeral plumes, the whining wind was a voice of mourning.

He remembered men he had found on the road through to the west, thirsty, raving, dying, struck down by scurvy, fever, or the sun. He must get away, he must take May and the children away at all costs, before it killed them too. He felt for the dry black earth under his horse's hoofs an aversion that was almost horror; it seemed to breathe up wavering forms of death among the glassy waves of air.

First the drought must be countered; he would at least inflict one defeat on the insidious country that had taken so much of his life and work. From this time he must work harder than ever, riding from earliest dawn to dark, watching for every move the drought might make. He flung himself into the work utterly; he could not help May in her mute grief, or solace himself, but as he worked he had no time for thought.

The windmill was put up at last over the new well in Native Dog; he stood there a moment watching as it began to turn and water flowed out to fill the ditch at which the cattle were to drink. The sight gave him a kind of bitter triumph. He had forced the earth to yield this much, at any rate—a few cattle would be saved here. And the water-auger he had managed to buy was to be set to work soon; Fred was to have the first use of it, and then it would be sent to Nulalbin.

But he did not stand long to watch the pulse of water; making sure that the windmill was secure and the ditch well mudded, he turned his horse away again, leaving the men there to care for the mill and the cattle. He had other work to do: the creek-beds must be dug out to follow the water as it sank underground, the bigger

K

waterholes must be fenced and made safe so that weakened cattle could not bog there, he must plan how to move the cattle from place to place to make the best possible use of water and feed. Their journey to water was growing longer and longer, as the grass on creek-flats and slopes was eaten out, but they were doing better than he had dared hope. Only the old were dying as yet, but these bitter July winds would weaken the cows, and calving was due to begin soon.

As for the grass, it was going fast. Black earth and rock, the bones of the landscape, showed through everywhere, and the cattle moved as they fed, mouths to the ground, picking up wisps of dry grass and weed loosened by the wind. For weeks that desolate high wind had beaten leaves and twigs from the trees, and there was no sign of a change.

May's fever-pains and neuralgia had returned, and she moved wearily; there were blue marks under her eyes from secret crying. The children, in this bitter wind, caught cold after cold, and it was hard to tempt them to eat, with no fruit or vegetables and very little milk from the cows. The sound of the wind continued night and day, and seemed to fill the house with a reminder of sorrow.

September came and went, and mobs of poor and dying cattle began to trickle down the stock-route from the nearly waterless western country, travelled by men on horses almost too weak to work. They were looking for agistment paddocks; failing this, they camped on the reserve where the stock-route crossed the Dawson, since there, at least, there was water, though the grass had long disappeared. On Nulalbin the stubborn daily battle went on, the digging for water, the felling of the bottle-trees and edible scrub. It seemed there were to be no storms this spring.

Early in October, the westerlies sprang up again, this time with a burning heat and violence, and now the fires Albert had long feared began to break out. It was hard to see the smokes begin; against the white glare of the horizon they were almost indistinguishable. His eyes ached with watching for them as he rode on his ceaseless rounds of the cattle and the creeks; it was easier to see them at night, when the faint red glow showed up against a blessed darkness. He woke many times each night to look for them, raising his head from the saddle, if he were camping out; or if he happened to be at Nulalbin he would slip quietly out of bed to the verandah, careful not to wake May who now slept so little.

On the tenth of the month, he saw a great smoke rising over the range, as evening came on. It looked to be near the Tearaway country, or on the Island. He had moved many of the cattle from there, hoping to save a little grass; when rain fell and there was water again, the cattle from the river could be moved there to live on the standing feed until the herbage began to grow. Somehow he must save that feed.

He rode at a gallop over to the Mimosa where four of the black-boys were working on the creek, gathered them and ran in their horses, cursing the delays. The horses were thin and weak, but this was no time to consider them; somehow they scrambled over the range and reached the fire fifteen miles away, vaulting off their saddles and leaving the exhausted beasts heaving great painful breaths, too much knocked up to move away from the smoke and heat of the fire that blew across them in the gusts of wind.

It was almost dark when the men had reached the fire; they fought it all night, desperately beating it back from the clearings where grass remained, burning breaks, beating down sparks and little flares from twigs that sailed everywhere on the wind. At last, towards morning, the wind dropped for a time; it seemed the breaks would hold the fire awhile, and it was safe to sleep. They dropped to the ground near the horses; they had neither food nor blankets, but they slept.

Soon after sunrise the wind sprang up again, and the fire began to veer in a new direction. It burned more fiercely than ever, and for a time, as he fought down one cape of flame and desperately ran to circumvent another, Albert was afraid it could not be stopped. But it would take all his reserve grass if it got away to the north—and the thought made him forget his charred and smarting hands and his dreadful weariness. Running, beating, burning back against the wind, they had somehow got it under control before nightfall. One of the men from the station had driven out with the ration-cart and blankets, and that night they had a meal, their first for thirty hours.

But there was little time to relax, for by now many of the tallest trees were burning, and the wind blew until midnight; the breaks had to be patrolled and blazing twigs and leaves beaten out. The breath of the fire on the wind scorched their skins and clothes; working too close to it, they sometimes felt the cloth of their shirts unbearably hot, and found a smouldering hole where some spark had dropped unnoticed and burned their clothes, scorching into the flesh before they felt it. In the area of the fire, now circumscribed by their breaks, the flames ran up tree after tree, and logs glowed hotly and poured out sparks, till the night was red with burning glades and towers.

Next day the breaks had to be strengthened; it was not until late at night that Albert finally turned home, weary beyond bearing, blackened and ragged. The other men had been relieved and had had their sleep many hours before, but he had stayed to oversee the last of the precautions and to help with clearing away the cattle and horses that still remained in the neighbourhood. The fire was not safe yet—if another gale should come up, it would spring to life again—but he must somehow get some sleep and a bath and meal. Reaching Nulalbin at midnight, he saw lights in the children's room; Weeta and Arthur were ill again with fever, and May, up looking after them, was white with pain from her neuralgia and the ague-pains that, in this hot dry weather, scarcely left her.

Next day the wind had died down, only to roar up from a new direction that night. He heard it rising near dawn, and sprang up to look across at the eastern sky. It was ominously smoky and red again, and the break that held the fire back against the attack of this new wind was not a wide one. When he and the men reached it, he could see that some of the country must be left to burn; there would be no saving it.

For two more days he stayed there, burning breaks and watching through swollen and half-shut eyes the fire that raged unchecked over his grass in the Tearaway country. Six or seven miles of feed, thin and dry enough but still valuable, had gone to ash, and probably some straggler cattle and horses with it.

This year, for the first time, he had been obliged to renew promissory notes and bills due. He had always taken a pride in prompt payment of his debts, and it was galling to him to ask for grace; some of his notes had already been twice renewed. It was the worst possible time to leave Nulalbin, but this time his mind was set beyond alteration. He would not stay a day beyond the breaking of the drought; if it did not break before Christmas, he would still manage to send May and the children away by then, and they would never return. The place was poisoned for him now, the more bitterly in that he felt the reproach of Bertie's death to be so much his own. Nothing that May could say would cure him of that secret conviction of blame, as persistent as it was useless.

And it seemed now that the country was deliberately playing with him, as a cat defeats a bird's efforts to escape. Storms began again to circle the horizon, but only a few tentative drops fell for all the thunder and lightning. When at last one of these empty storms did break, it was just enough to start the grass, but it yielded no standing water, and the back-breaking digging could not be relaxed.

The stockhorses had now begun to weaken beyond the possibility of work; he and the men walked many miles a day, trying to save them, for they could only be ridden in an emergency. Cattle had long since begun to die, and he counted fresh carcases every day as he walked along the creek-beds; if it had not been for the well, no cattle would have been alive now in the waterless back country of the run. The pitiless wind blew day after day, drying back the first shoots of the spring herbage, and October was almost over.

But early in November the storms gathered again, and at first reluctantly, but with gathering strength, the rain began to fall. He stood beside the creek in the storm, idle at last, and watched the first brown crest of floodwater finding its way uncertainly down from hole to hole; it carried on its shoulders the rubbish of the drought, dead leaves, twigs, branches, small skeletons of bush creatures, bits of rotted hide and hair, carcases dried to insect lightness. The landscape shook off its death and veiled itself again in the quick green of spring.

A few days later, the buckboard and the waggonette were packed and waiting outside the homestead, the children ran in and out, dressed and ready to start, and Albert went to and fro with the last of the bags and boxes. May came out last of all, carrying little Elsie; she and Albert went out through the garden gate for the last time.

The garden, as they looked at it, had a wild and ragged air; the trees that they had bought in Rockhampton from Monsieur Thozet's gardens, on their last honeymoon days, had died one by one over these drought years in spite of the cans of water that the black-boys had brought from the creek under May's supervision. The cherimoya was dry and drooping, the vines had scarcely put out a shoot. But already the weeds and grass had begun growing; a live and riotous green was blotting out the lines of the paths and garden-beds. The landscape through which they drove away was already bright with regeneration.

IF IT WERE not for his debts—that burden now so heavy and threatening, which he could not shake free—Albert could be happy, here and now. May, in spite of her never quite forgotten grief for her eldest son, was gay again; the planning of her new house, the laying out of the acres of garden and orchard as she wanted them, had wonderfully refreshed and cheered her, and the cool sharp air of this tableland country had altered her thinness and pallor already. She was tireless and delighted with her work. Details of the new house occupied her now—where to put their Nulalbin furniture, which looked much smaller and shabbier in these big new rooms, how to contrive enough curtains for the windows and enough coverings for the floors. The children, too, were wildly happy, still exploring this strange new country and finding new flowers week by week, new waterfalls in the deep gorges into which the country fell away.

But it was not easy, as he had hoped it might be, for him to leave the past behind and to begin again, forgetting sorrows. He reproached himself sometimes that the big new house which gave May such pleasure was to him rather an addition to his debts, even though it added value to the property, that the rocky gullies where the creeks began their long descent from the tableland to the sea were not beautiful in his eyes, but meant country difficult to muster, where horses and cattle might be lost or break bones.

The run had a bad reputation—that was why he had been able to get it so cheaply. It lay on the eastern fall of the New England plateau, country that had been later settled than the easier and less forbidding land in the centre and west of the tableland, and was still thickly covered with the forest of small close-growing trees that clung to every hill and slope dark and savage as a thundercloud. He had bought the place soon after leaving Nulalbin, from a friend, who was frank enough to doubt whether it would ever make good grazing land; Withycombe had had bad luck with it, losing many cattle.

Not that there were droughts—this eastern face of the tableland, turned towards the sea not a hundred miles away, caught every cloud that drifted inland from the coast and turned it into mist and rain. But it seemed something was lacking in the land itself; cattle were reputed to lose condition here, take to eating earth and die. Sheep, too, had been tried without success: the thick trees that covered the whole country made it almost impossible to shepherd them without losses, the dingoes were numerous and hungry, and the run was unfenced. These facts, and its roughness and remoteness, had made it cheap enough for him to be able to buy it; not many people were inclined, now that prosperity was becoming general again, to risk their money in so doubtful a bargain.

Yet he thought he could make a good thing of the place, given luck, and if the bank would trust his judgement and continue to provide enough capital. It was a gamble, but a chance worth taking. He would begin by fencing the run; he would clear the trees from its more level parts, drain the low-lying basins that were now swampy and rankly grassed, and then he would try sheep again. He could not believe that sheep would not do well here, on this light fine grass and in this hilly country. And wool prices were high; a few good clips would do much to help him clear his debts.

As for the rougher stony gorges that fell away into steep ridges and spurs towards the coast, he would run cattle there. He had already a plan to counter the losses from soil deficiency; he would begin putting out salt-licks, which he had heard had been tried elsewhere successfully. If he could solve the problem, he was certain that cattle would do well enough here; he would begin to build up a fine herd.

After all, he had not put up Nulalbin for sale. He had felt curiously reluctant to admit defeat; it would have seemed to him somehow ignominious to give way altogether. The season there, after he had left, had grown better; May's young brother Arundel, who had come to manage the station and whom Albert had left in charge, reported well of the cattle and of the prospects for the year. Albert and May had taken counsel and had decided to hold the place for the time being at least; it was worthwhile trying to recoup some of the debts Nulalbin had cost him. If the droughts began again, he would have to sell to meet his commitments, or rather to stave them off, for he was too deeply in debt to hope to free himself for many years yet. But with one or two good seasons, he stood a chance of gaining a little.

It would mean a great deal more work, for now he must travel twice a year to Nulalbin, a journey of many hundred miles, to muster and brand and to take the fats off for sale. It would be hard travelling and hard work; the worry of planning for two runs so distant and so different from each other already weighed on him, and he felt a deep distaste for the idea of returning again to that ghost-haunted country.

And although he dismissed his own weariness, he knew it was no longer true that his body carried its burdens without a tremor. Continual work in all weathers had hardened and strengthened his muscles into a fine machine; he could do a day's work which would have troubled most younger men, and he never spared himself. But he had been driven at a pace which grew fiercer and fiercer with the years, as those years increased their demands, and though he would not hear it, his body had begun to protest. He could no longer spend a hard day after cattle, rising at dawn as he always did and unsaddling at dark or after, and feel his muscles fresh and unfatigued next day. Long spells of work, branding, spaying or among his new sheep, in the cold misty days of autumn here, had tired him more than he remembered ever to have been tired. But he brushed aside his weariness. He had no time for it; he must work now as he had never done before.

If he could only forget his worries, if he could only lift his mind out of its treadmill circling! Round and round it went—over the problem of the children's education, so neglected at present, over the question of the new cattle-buyer's financial probity, or the payments on the water-auger, now working erratically on Nulalbin, over the bank manager's confidence in his ability, and, above all, over those haunting columns of figures in his big account-books. They were all written in red ink, now, and their totals frightened him.

Perhaps, after all, he had been unwise in staking so much in this new run, in deciding, as on May's suggestion he had done, to restock it completely. The cattle Withycombe had sold him with the land were poor nondescript creatures. His experience told him that only good beasts bred to type were worth their purchase money, but perhaps he had been too hasty in selling them at once, and in buying so many new cattle to replace them. His new herd had cost a great deal, there was no denying; the bank manager had looked grave over it. If a disease should break out among them, or if his salt-licks failed to remedy the soil's deficiencies, he was now too deeply committed to recover from the loss; he felt that he walked a knife-edge over bankruptcy.

Yet outwardly, the life he lived now was pleasant enough. May was happy and confident again; she loved to organize, to arrange and create, and this was the greatest opportunity she had yet found for those talents. It was she who had planned and laid out much of the garden, the avenue of pines which was to lead in from the road, the orchard into which the garden merged; the house too, though he and she had planned it together, was in reality more hers than his own. This new home was to be her compensation for the hard Nulalbin years—it was the expression of her wishes, the new Dalwood she had always wanted, and its size and the acres of garden were in proportion to her wishes.

Certainly the house could not be as large or as finely built as she had dreamed it, but at any rate, it was a mark reached, an earnest of the future. Here, she seemed to say, they would find their permanence and importance. The name she had chosen for the run, out of the Dawson Valley dialect, showed the strength of the bonds she was forging for them: translated, Wongwibinda meant 'stay here always'.

He knew all this, and acquiesced in it; if he could have given her more yet, he would have delighted in the gift. But it set his responsibilities even closer on his shoulders. They had put so much money, so much trust, in this doubtful piece of land that it was now his burden to justify them both. Every step he took, every decision he made, was now desperately important; it might mean the difference between triumph and ultimate defeat in the struggle that engaged him. This new tension shut him off from taking pleasure, as May could, in the growth of the house or of the garden, or in the cool bright weather and the green landscape that so much delighted her:

his eyes could scarcely spare time for them from his preoccupation with the goal.

The importance of that goal, now, he would hardly have known how to question. The struggle for possessions and security, wealth and position, had become more and more central in his life as luck and the seasons had seemed to conspire against him. Now, he felt, was the final test of his abilities; the next few years would determine whether he could indeed justify the risk they had taken, whether they would in fact stay here always, or again be driven out.

Now he was working harder than he had ever worked. Time after time he had gone over his plans for the development of the run, searching for ways to make them sounder, for alterations that might make the final difference, for possible flaws and miscalculations. The cattle he had cleared from the run had sold on a lucky market, and he had bought new sheep, rams and breeding ewes. The mob was now on the way from the western districts; they would take six weeks or more on the road, and meanwhile he must leave for Nulalbin and try to get the autumn cattle-work done in time to meet the sheep on his return to Wongwibinda.

He had evolved a plan to put together a good mob of stores at Nulalbin this year, and to have them droved south into New South Wales, where cattle prices were at present high. If he should strike another good market, it would help him a great deal, and just now the season looked promising. With fair water and grass on the stock-route, they could travel slowly enough to arrive in good condition at the Muswellbrook sales; he was proud of the Nulalbin cattle, big-framed and cleanly bred, and thought they should fetch a good price.

His journey to Brisbane to catch the Rockhampton steamer occupied four days. The railway from Newcastle, which was ultimately to connect the New South Wales and Queensland railway systems, was open only as far as Glen Innes. This was the same line that had caused so much excitement in the Hunter Valley in his youth. Since then it had been gradually extending farther and farther north, opening up more and more of the rich pastoral country of northern New South Wales, while each extension was locally marked by speech-making, rejoicings, sprees and grand balls. From Glen Innes he must take the coach for Stanthorpe, and then change into the train again. He was weary when he reached Brisbane and took the steamer there.

At Nulalbin the house, stripped of its familiar sights and sounds, dropped bitter reminders at once into his heart. The sixteen years he had spent there closed in around him; all his old happinesses and disappointments, his failures and griefs, pulled at him wherever he looked. Without May, he was at his own mercy, and he was at once desperate to finish the work and be back with her.

He set to work at a furious pace, riding many miles a day to gather and draft the fats and the store mob. The cattle had done well enough, but nevertheless he found he had been too sanguine in his expectations of a big mob of stores. He had arranged with the Muswellbrook agent for a mob of eight hundred to a thousand; he would be several hundred short of the mark. The drought had cut deeper into the herd than he had expected.

He was dismayed, for he had already promised the trip to a drover; men had been engaged and would soon be here, and the mob was not large enough to make so expensive a trip worth while. It seemed there was only one way out. He must ride round his neighbours and scrape together enough cattle from them to make up the mob to the promised number. Here was another commitment he had not reckoned on—more promissory notes to be met, and on what suddenly seemed to him to be a mad gamble. Would the bank stand by him again—or would it disown the venture? If the trip should turn out badly he would be done for; on the other hand, if it came off, it might be the turning-point for him. In any case, he needed the money too much to change his plans now; he must take the plunge, for he had no choice.

He rode from station to station, looking for cattle, and at last heard of a mob of five hundred store cattle available not far away. He had doubts of their quality, but there was no time to inspect them; he must close at once to get them, and the work was waiting. It troubled him that the quality of his own mob might be lowered by them, and he was inclined to think the price too high, but he wrote his acceptance nevertheless. He rode back hastily to the Benleith yards, where the stores were waiting to be drafted.

The drover was there already, and after a couple of days' drafting a mob of seven hundred, more or less, was ready for the road. Next morning the drover was to leave with them to pick up the other mob on the way south; Albert and the Nulalbin stockmen camped with the drovers near the yard that night, and slept profoundly, in relief that the work was over.

But the omens were bad. With the cattle safely yarded, no watch had been posted, and Albert woke at dawn to find the yards broken and the cattle gone. The men, after their weeks of hard work, had all slept through the night as he had done; the cattle, in this unfenced country, were probably scattered for many miles. In fact, it was three days' work to find and re-draft them; some would not be seen again until next season, and the mob was now far short of the number he had hoped for. 'I have no heart or energy left,' he wrote in his diary, surrendering for a moment to the weariness that filled him. 'I worry myself now with doubts about trifles.'

As he had feared, too, the cattle he had bought unseen were small and uneven in quality, bringing down the appearance of the Nulalbin cattle and making the mob look second-rate. He began to fear that now they might not sell, that he would have the cattle left on his hands after their long trip, with all expenses to pay and nothing but loss from the venture. To make matters worse, the season had turned dry suddenly, and hot winds had begun to blow; if the wester-lies sprang up early this winter, the cattle would lose most of their condition and the grass and water along the route would be un-certain.

His anxiety had made him abrupt and impatient with the men and with the drovers; he had been too willing to pick quarrels, too sombre in his manner, these last weeks, and the knowledge sank him further in his gloom. On his last night at Nulalbin, when the cattle had at last been sent off, and his mare waited in the yard for saddling at daybreak, he sat at the last of the accounts, dejected and angry with himself. These black moods, out of which there was no climbing —he had thought, in the first years of his marriage, that he had over-come them for ever.

Even now, he knew that a return to May's simple and solid world, where no bogies waited round the corners of the future, would drive them off. But here he was vulnerable, a creature pursued by shadows. The jews' harps in the men's quarters droned plangently; on the verandah, Arundel's autophone unwound some tune that reminded him of—he had forgotten what. He could stand this house no longer, this abandonment to solitude, this tearing of his spirit by its own claws.

The journey home seemed longer than ever, and once back he had no time for rest. The new sheep had arrived, and must be counted and distributed into their paddocks; a thousand things waited to be done. The season disturbed him; the westerlies had begun, as he had feared, and he thought uneasily of the cattle on the road. Worse than all, the new thirteen-wire fence, which at great cost he had set up round the boundaries of the country where the sheep were to run, for protection against dingoes, seemed to have enclosed more dingoes than the trappers were able to kill. Reports began to come in of sheep found dead, and now he must go to fresh expense in providing shepherds and folds until the dingoes should be cleared out.

Even with shepherding and fences, sheep were still lost. In the thick-growing timber they strayed easily and were difficult to fold at nights. Occasional losses continued; between these and the threat of a dry winter, he got little peace of mind.

But at the end of May, with the cattle almost at their destination, the weather changed and softened. Clouds drew across the sky, and a week of rain began which he could not doubt was general. For once the luck was his; the cattle reached the sale-yard just in time to meet the sudden demand which the rain had fostered. They sold handsomely. The venture had justified itself, and he would be able to meet the interest on his loans this year, even with the extra expenses of the new sheep and of the fences and shepherding.

He had begun to hope, now, that his sheep paddocks were cleared of dingoes. Riding round the upper paddocks, protected by those expensive miles of fencing, he had found no sheep killed over the last few weeks. It had been a hard fight; the biggest dog, whose tracks beside his mauled sheep he had come to recognize on his daily rounds, had kept four men busy for weeks, laying baits laboriously made from fat and strychnine, riding with loaded rifles on a constant look-out, holding back the mobs that melted so easily away from the cleared grassy spaces into the dangerous timber, counting them into the yard at night. He reckoned that the one dog had cost him almost four hundred pounds.

But now that the killing seemed to have slackened, he felt a little more sanguine. The green mist of young grass that spread to meet the early spring that year promised a good season. He had room for more sheep yet, wool prices were still good, and he had a mob of seven thousand in view for purchase before shearing. He would buy them; it seemed the time was favourable. He hurried on the building of the shearing-shed; it must be ready by November.

He and May rode out together much that spring. The children took up less of her time, now that he felt able to pay a governess for them—he could not afford to send the elder children to school yet. The house and garden were gradually coming into order. The spring was pleasant in early warmth that atoned for winter; a bit of pink and white blossom showed in the newly planted orchard, on the little dry sticks of trees that had looked so forlorn in winter. The cultivations which he had planted for hay, corn and potatoes were pleasant to the eye; the axes of the ringbarkers sounded busily; raw new ditches showed here and there, dug to sweeten the swampy country.

The contrast of seasons, here in this high cold climate, refreshed and a little surprised them both with its vigour. At Nulalbin, the seasons slid imperceptibly one into another; here the spring's announcement of renewal came suddenly and unmistakably. It delighted May; colour sprang in her cheeks as it did on the sticks of apricot-trees in the orchard, and she rode as lightly and daringly as a girl.

They went together up to the hill paddocks to look at the sheep, which grazed quietly there as they should, contented with the season and with their new country. There would be a good lambing, it seemed; it was due to begin early in September, and he counted on it for help with next year's expenses. Apart from that, May and he had decided as they rode that it would be worth while to try again the experiment of a draft from Nulalbin, to catch the summer sales in the Hunter Valley. He must leave again for the north, then, just as lambing was due; he would have to trust the men to take care of that, with May's supervision. But the ewes looked healthy enough, and the grass was good; the little cold creeks of these hills were flowing strongly. Nothing should go wrong.

Riding across the uplands of the Doughboy Range, which stood up like the roof-ridge of the country, they heard on the wind intermittently the dull chock of axes where the ringbarkers worked. Already here and there the little dark-leaved trees, black sally, box and stringybark, had begun to die; brown withered patches had begun to spread in the thick bush over the lower country, and looking down at them he felt a kind of satisfaction like that given by the wounding of an enemy. Grass for his sheep would begin growing as the trees died; the land would carry more and more.

Lambing had just begun when he set off again for Nulalbin. It was difficult to wrench his mind away from the work of Wongwibinda and think of the problems of the northern run, and reaching it, he was vexed to find so much waiting to be done. It was a flush spring and the grass was already well advanced; branding was much behindhand, and the cattle, early in condition with the good season, were difficult to handle. He found he would need a month on the work of mustering and branding, before he could prepare his sale mob for the journey south.

As usual, Nulalbin depressed him. Hot weather and hard work combined day after day, and he could no longer conceal from himself the weariness he felt. At nights, too, the station accounts had to be made up as always; he would sit under the lamp, swaying with fatigue, while the obstinate figures shifted position, vanished and reappeared, refusing to strike a balance. Yet, when the lamp was out at last and he lay down, sleep hung just outside his reach.

Toothache began to torment him; his bones ached after his day's work; he lost his temper and quarrelled bitterly with a neighbour who rode over to complain of strayed cattle on his property. For such things he lay awake, reproaching himself uselessly. As usual, he was lonely. He could not do without May.

Making up his mob with bought cattle again, he started them almost a thousand strong. But it was late in the season; there had been so many delays that it was clear they would miss the best of the market. Early spring and good rain, passing into a rich summer, had stimulated buying, but by the time his cattle reached the sale-yards the demand would probably have slackened or disappeared. The knowledge of probable loss did not help his already downcast spirits, but it was too late to make other plans for the cattle. He saw them off the place, wearily and without enthusiasm.

Another fortnight's work remained to be done at Nulalbin before he could set out for home again. He had found the place neglected, for Arundel was young and as yet inexperienced in the work of management. Albert was tempted to scamp the job a little—shearing was soon to begin at Wongwibinda, and his mind was full of thoughts of what was to be done there—but he knew that he would sleep on thorns until his next trip north, if he did not leave the place in order now. He struggled through the work in fatigue and ill-temper. October was hot and trying, and it was not until late in the month that he set off southwards to catch the coach at Taroom on his way home.

It was a bitter shock to find, when he reached Wongwibinda, that all his expensive fencing had not kept the dingoes out of his lambing paddocks. Not merely one or two, but a whole pack, had broken in somehow; of his year's lambing more than a thousand had been killed in one week. May had set all the men available to driving the paddocks; they were camping with the sheep at nights and lighting fires to keep the dingoes at a distance, and the other work of the station was in arrears, yet lambs were still being killed.

Weary as he was, he forgot his need of rest. In a week or two, shearing was due to begin, and if the dingoes were still at large and killing at this rate when his stockmen returned to their work, his losses would be ruinous. He threw himself desperately into the work, spending his nights in making new strychnine baits, and his days in tracking; he watched every movement of leaf and grass-blade as he rode, until his eyes ached with concentration.

A few of the pack were shot or found dead, but in that rocky and closely timbered country there was shelter for a hundred dingoes, and his persecutors were cunning. They learned not to touch the baits, though hundreds had been laid; they would not drink the poisoned milk Albert set for them, and though the paddocks were

L

driven time after time, scarcely one of them was seen. While the men rode, they stayed quiet, killing few sheep, but when shearing began and they knew themselves no longer in danger, they started their nightly hunting again. Lying awake, Albert could hear their cry faint and far-off, like the voice of the darkness itself.

Gradually their depredations lessened; perhaps they picked up baits at last, perhaps they had merely grown tired of the taste of lambs.

But Albert was little reassured. If his fence would not keep them out, it seemed he must give up breeding sheep; each lambing would be a slaughter. He even began to fear that he might be forced to give up sheep altogether, losing all the money he had put into his new shearing-shed and equipment. He would shear little more than twelve thousand sheep this year, instead of the fifteen thousand he had reckoned on; the price of wool stayed high, but it would scarcely recoup his losses for all that. In his dreams at night, he strained to drag great stones from a debit column across to a credit column, only to find as he turned back again that other and heavier stones had taken their place.

With every year of this constant worry, his dreamed-of prosperity and serenity seemed less and less attainable. The life of the household went on as usual round him, but he was growing too weary and preoccupied to take his old pleasure in it. He felt himself withdrawn a little from the interests and happenings that surrounded him; he knew less and less of the children, it seemed, as they grew older, as though the orbit of the household were May's world and he had become somehow a stranger in it.

The fact was that his work and weariness possessed him more and more. Sheep-work in particular tired and exasperated him. He was not used to it; in his memory it had always been work for old men, despised by the active and young, the swaggering riders. It reminded him of those old shepherds, the crazy fringe of the bush workers among whom he had spent his life—hatters, butts for the shearers' fun, the ragged and lonely. The sheep themselves, with their shallow lunatic eyes, their dirty grey wool, looked like those old men who had oppressed his childhood with pity and an obscure alarm.

And the sheep-work seemed to grow heavier and heavier with each year. Diseases showed up in his mobs; every few weeks, it seemed, it was time to muster and dose them, to put them through the bluestone foot-bath that was supposed to cure foot-rot, to cut away the dense eye-wool that blinded them or to examine them for signs of fly-strike. He grew almost to hate their stupid panics, their stick-like legs that broke so easily, the hopelessness that made sick sheep lie down and never get up again, their continual terrified bleating in the yards, most of all that smell which for him was always associated with the old men and their cranky miseries. If he could keep to cattle, which he understood and liked, his work would be halved; he would not have to go through these weary days of backache and annoyance. But it was wool that made money nowadays; it was the sheep, not the cattle, that were important in the run's economy.

It was a relief to him when the days of cattle-work came round. His herd, at least, were doing well; the salt-licks he had put out were successful, and this year's drop of calves were sturdy and promising. He was building up a good herd, and he took pride in them. With cattle, at any rate, he could trust his own judgement.

It was true, as May often tried to convince him, that he was in fact yearly gaining ground. His debts indeed were as great as ever, but the property itself was growing more and more valuable in counter-balance. The time and work he had lavished on it, the planning and the money, were beginning to bear fruit. Once he would have taken a joy in seeing the land's gradual response, the grass beginning to grow high and sweet on the cleared flats, the swamps draining into firm and fertile country, reed-clumps giving way to fodder grasses, the work of the run beginning to fall into an easy rhythm. But it was seldom now that he could pause in his obstinate round of work and worry to take pleasure in such things. There was too much to be done still—always too much to be done.

12 GROWTH OF A STATION

THE FIFTH YEAR at Wongwibinda came in rainy and warm. It was a summer of rank growth, unusual in this cool country; the grass grew thick and soft in the paddocks where trees had been newly ringbarked and the creeks ran high. Foot-rot was bad this year among the sheep, and Albert passed his days in the yards using the knife and bluestone, in the continual stench of the disease; persistent drifting showers kept the sheep-yards slippery with deep mud and added to the unpleasantness of the work.

This soft weather, too, brought back May's old fever-pains, which she had never quite outgrown. She was still a little weak from the baby's birth six months ago; it had made her ill and low-spirited, as he had never known her. Albert had taken her to Melbourne at last, to have her neuralgia treated by a specialist—an expensive trip which seemed to have done her little good. She was only now beginning to recover her old spirits.

Her sickness had for a time taken him out of himself—it was not like May to be ill and despondent. For a while their roles had been reversed, and he had been the reassuring comforter. The baby's coming had deepened and increased their mutual tenderness and dependence.

Yet even in his deepest concern for her, he could not forget the gnawing of his troubles. It seemed to him that his five years of Herculean work had done no more than to keep him facing a current with which he was unevenly matched. Drought last winter and spring had caught him over-stocked and he had lost numbers of cattle and sheep; all his dosing and care had not freed his flocks from disease, and round the fringes of the run dingoes prowled ceaselessly, sometimes killing only one or two sheep in a month, sometimes pulling down thirty or forty in a night. He had given up breeding sheep, and now only bought mobs to run for wool-growing, but wool prices had sunk again, and at the last shearing his drought-stricken sheep had cut poor and light fleeces. Nulalbin, too, was scarcely paying for its keep. The depression out of which he had lifted himself to meet May's need was now, in this sad rainy weather, closing on him again.

Rain drove him indoors at last. It was time to make up his accounts for the year, a job which he had been putting off from day to day; the mere taking down of those large gloomy leather volumes darkened the days further. Afraid of what he might find, he worked doggedly on through the maze of bewildering figures.

On his own account, he found, he now had debts amounting to thirteen thousand pounds. In addition, Haydon had sent down the accounts for the Vena Park partnership; on these, it appeared, there was an additional debt for more than five thousand pounds. This was worse than ever; he stared at the figures despairingly. He must, at least, try to sell his share in Vena Park; he could not go on bearing this extra burden.

Haydon, perhaps, would be willing to buy him out at a price which might go some way towards covering his debt on the partnership. He would write and make the suggestion, at any rate; the sale could do no more than lighten his load, but it would be worth while to get rid of the worry. He no longer believed in the Gulf country's possibilities, though Haydon kept writing as though prosperity could not be far off.

Haydon's reply was long in coming; the summer meanwhile turned to autumn, with rain still persistently blowing up from east-wards. As he saddled his horse in the early mornings, in yards deep with mud, he could hear the waterfalls pouring strongly in the deep gully behind the house; water oozed and trickled everywhere, rising to fill the hoof-prints of his horse, and he had to watch the ground, as he rode, for the treacherous green of swampy places. Mist alternated with downpours; when the sun struggled out, the drenched landscape dazzled in watery light, and the drops on the horse's mane trembled like stars. The high overgrown grass was weak and sappy; trodden down, it lay where it had fallen, and branches broke away from trees overloaded with leaves and heavy with continual moisture.

The rain brought with it an increase in his work. The foot-rot which affected the sheep was worse than ever; whole mobs were crippled by it, so that it was a cruelly slow job to muster them and bring them limping to the yards for surgery and bluestoning. The weight of water in their fleeces day after day weakened them further, so that the dingoes found them easy prey.

And in this weather his continual war with the dingoes, which had run through these last years like an exhausting undertow that drags at a swimmer, was harder to maintain. Any downpour brought the already swollen creeks into flood, and week after week the flood-gates where his fences crossed them were washed away, leaving great gaps through which not only the dingoes, but the sheep and cattle themselves, might move from one paddock to another, if they were not repaired at once. The flood-gates, then, were a recurrent job too urgent to be postponed; he rode round them after every heavy shower, working often waist-deep in the cold dragging water, chilled and half-naked. Several times his horse bogged in the bright treacherous patches of swamp that were appearing everywhere, and he had to jump for solid ground and drag it out across a raft of branches hastily cut and thrown down; after such struggles he would have to lead the trembling beast until its shock had passed.

The rain and the urgency of his work kept him at home all the autumn. He had meant to leave for his usual trip to Nulalbin; it worried him that he must put it off, leaving Arundel to draft the fats and finish the seasonal cattle-work alone. He must go up early in spring, to see that culling and branding had been properly done, and to examine the new bores and equipment for pumping and for watering the cattle.

Haydon's answer came at last; he was willing to buy Albert out, but the price he offered did not seem satisfactory. Albert had never seen the Gulf station, but he determined now that his best course would be to inspect it before selling, and to arrange the transaction with Haydon personally. He must go up at the end of the winter, then; he would do the Nulalbin work on his way back.

He began to worry out a time-table. To reach Normanton, he must either take the steamer to Townsville and travel inland by coach, arranging for Haydon to meet him with horses and complete the two hundred miles north from the Cloncurry coach road, or he must change boats at Townsville and catch the little cattle-steamer that plied round Cape York to the Gulf ports. The sea-trip would be more expensive, and he would lose eight days by it. He had put it out of his mind, when May intervened. A holiday, however short, he must have; she had become worried by his thinness and his obvious fatigue.

Reluctantly he agreed. Eight days lost—the thought of it troubled him; he determined secretly to finish his business with Haydon as quickly as possible and to waste no time on the journey back to Nulalbin. But gradually, as the damp cold of the winter days began to close on him, he began looking forward to the heat of the north and the sea-trip, as the freezing long for a fire.

He was to leave at the end of June. By that time, he hoped, this winter rain would have cleared to frosty weather. The first five months of the year had been wetter than anyone could remember; in April, riding his water-logged paddocks, he had seen scores of sheep green-backed with sprouted grass growing from their wool, germinated by the constant damps. The roar of the flooded creeks continued week after week, as though a surf were beating unseen; many sheep had been drowned.

But May rejoiced in the garden, which this summer had grown high and rich. The big heart-shaped lawn which Albert had made in front of the house to be a valentine for her was now bordered with flowers; the orchard and the belt of pines, chestnuts and other English trees stood up sturdily in their four years' growth, and the roses May had planted everywhere swung heavy heads of bloom that drooped rain-weighted from the trellises These years that for him had passed so quickly, scarcely noticed in his preoccupation, seemed suddenly to have attained their full importance, starting into life and fruit as the young trees in the orchard had done.

For the first time, Wongwibinda became real to him. No longer future, but present, it stood around him personal and immediate, a fact of which he had only just become aware. He looked at it in surprise, as a stranger might, seeing for the first time the reality of its existence. It was as though the place had grown without his knowledge.

There were the children, too; in his concentration and the increasingly rapid flow of his years he had forgotten how quickly children grow, how long a single season is in youth. His eldest daughter was taller now than May, almost seventeen. Why, she was as old as May had been, that year when across the roomful of people her glance had first transfixed him. And Arthur, now fourteen, seemed almost mature; looking at him, Albert felt saddened, a little cheated. Where had the children gone, whose growth he had once looked forward to, where had the years vanished of which he had once had such hopes? He had seen no more of his own life than if he had been a prisoner locked away from it.

And now he must leave the place that he had so suddenly discovered. This time he would be away perhaps three months or more; it would be far into the spring when he returned, and the orchard would have blossomed again, the children be three months older.

This would be the longest absence from Wongwibinda that he had ever had to prepare for. His mind began to travel ahead along a dozen well-worn paths, anticipating this, providing against that. He made sure that the fences were in order, that the sheep were properly distributed to make the most of the winter feed and that the work with them was up-to-date. He went over the work to be done, with the men, and made sure that each knew all that was necessary; he checked the stores and the orders, tested the station routine to be certain that it was running perfectly.

Arthur was becoming a good hand with stock; he could relieve May of some of the responsibility of seeing that the outside work went smoothly. Naylor, the half-caste head stockman, was a good man and had a head on his shoulders; Maguire was trustworthy enough with the work about the homestead. He hoped that the black stockmen would not take it into their heads to go walkabout before he came back, leaving the place short-handed for the spring work; but nothing could be done to guard against that.

Before he left, the days turned bright and a knife-like wind began to blow from the south-west, rattling the leaves on the trees and chilling him as he rode on his last errands, until his hands on the reins felt like wood. Yes, it would be pleasant in the warm north; he was not reluctant for the journey. A kind of weary slowness of mind and body seemed to obstruct his work this winter; he felt that he needed quiet, time for some kind of recapitulation, he scarcely knew what. This year he would be fifty years old; it was time to pause a little, time for reflection.

Yet there was no more time than there had ever been. He must go on, that holiday-like interlude over; he must work harder than before, an ant carrying grains of sand to build a mountain. The load of debt harnessed on his shoulders pressed more heavily year by year. He regretted nothing, he thought; he asked only for a little time—to be re-wound, perhaps; to find out what he was, what he was doing. Well, perhaps on this trip he would find that time.

At last he packed his valises and strapped them to the saddles. Paddy, the black-boy, would ride with him to the railway station at Guyra, to lead his horse back over the forty-mile journey. It was too long an absence, this time, for him to leave the horse there as he usually did, to wait for him on the return journey.

It was another of those bright days steeled by sharp wind; the sun shook light over the bare winter thorns and stems of the garden, sprinkled brightness on the tossing dark needles of the pines, as he rode away. The air was clear as water, all in rushing motion round him, its chill catching at the throat, and when he looked back from the top of the western hill at the house behind him, it seemed to shrink close into its growing garden away from the wind.

He was glad that it was Paddy who was riding with him today. He had a queer sympathy with the old blackfellow; Paddy could answer his moods with an understanding Albert seldom found among white men, who, intent on their own interests and problems, took little notice of the needs of other people. Maguire or Billy now— if he had been riding alone with either of them, he would have had to exert himself, to try to make some kind of conversation, no matter what. But Paddy seemed to know his need of silence; he would not resent, as they did, his withdrawal and his short replies. Paddy rode now quite happily on his ambling taffy-coloured pony, sometimes at Albert's side, sometimes dropping behind to look more closely at anything that interested him. If Albert spoke, he would answer cheerfully, but there was no need for speech. Secure in his own life, as a wild thing or a tree was, he was simple in acceptance and response, and Albert's mind, so long driven and hurried, seemed to fall quiet in his undemanding presence.

The horses soon took up a steady easy pace, the rising sun grew warmer, and Albert's tense muscles began to relax. Sitting quietly in the saddle, he let his thoughts wander. It was strange, these last weeks, how his problems had begun to fall away from him; it was as though some new requirement was gradually making itself felt in him, changing the rhythm of his life, drawing his energies away into new channels, into himself from the outer world. He had resisted it, dragging his thoughts back to the old paths half in fear, but now that Wongwibinda fell farther and farther behind him, he found himself forgetting the tension and urgencies of the present, finding in his thoughts scraps of long-lost memories, following tracks strange to him.

He must be getting old, he thought; but the idea which a year or two ago would have raised in him such alarm and repudiation now came quite simply to his mind. It was as though the light his mind cast had begun to change its angle, illuminating now a different side of things, casting new shadows. It had been morning; now it was afternoon. That could be understood and accepted. Yes, soon he would be fifty years old.

It surprised him a little, this sudden rearrangement of his perspective, so natural yet so long resisted. Somehow his mind was eased by it, the tension broken that had held him to his wheel. He was free now to feel the sun's warmth, to look about him, to answer Paddy's grin and exchange a few words, to slip back into companionable silence and pursue his new trains of thought. Somehow he had escaped from the imprisoning circle which had for years made up his inner life—his debts, his responsibilities, the thousand details of his work. He could put them aside and follow wherever his thoughts might lead.

The track along which he rode ran through country still sparsely settled; the big land-owners held most of it for winter pastures, and it was still unfenced and as closely timbered as it had ever been. Only here and there a line of fencing showed; one or two new houses had been built lately, the earthen-floored slab shanties of the small settlers, with their big chimneys of clay and rough wood. Before long, he supposed, free-selectors would begin to flood this part of the country; fences would net it everywhere, roads would be built. Another fifty years—could he come this way then—he might not know his road. Even Paddy, then, would not know his own country, its trees cut down, its birds and animals fast vanishing.

That would be partly Albert's own work—his and that of his sons, perhaps, and of his neighbours and their sons. They spent their lives, as his was spent, in destroying one way of life to make another. Yet, he thought—and the thought was new to him—none of them paused to wonder why; or what, in the end, they would make.

What was so important to them—what drove them, single-minded, panting in greed and eagerness, while their lives vanished in the labour? Would his sons, too, be driven in this whirlwind of destruction, and wake perhaps, as he was doing, to ask in the end what had consumed their lives? Money, security, prosperity—those three words had led him on as they led the others, clawing at his very sleep. They had built the cities that had grown so much larger and noisier during his lifetime: on his visits to such places, he felt nowadays discomforted and uneasy. Doubtless they would build cities larger still. Words of power, but not words of life, they had killed Paddy's people, driving them in hundreds over the cliffs of the tableland to die on the rocks below—for spearing cattle, for rebellion against the dominion of money and prosperity.

How else, under that dominion, could they have been treated? he wondered now. What other solution could there have been of the problem they had presented by their very existence? With the land his people needed they had lived in the closest of ties, the most stationary of balances; losing it, as sooner or later it was inevitable they must do, they had had only the alternatives of death or transformation in their very selves—to die, or to serve an idea utterly foreign to them, losing in that service all their own wisdom and traditions; and they had refused to serve.

Even Paddy, one of the survivors, one of the few who had achieved some kind of compromise, kept under his cheerful compliance a kind of obstinate pride of refusal. Deep in him, Albert sensed now a fatal wound that bled continually, a despair at the core, a negative in the end more mortal than the death so many of his tribe had met on the cliffs to the eastward.

Albert was reminded of the queer swarthy native cherry-trees that grew in these hills, always near a certain kind of big gum-tree. When the gum-tree was felled, it seemed as though some mysterious relationship had been abruptly broken; the native cherry began to droop and wither, and in a few months would be dead, though its roots were whole and it seemed to bear no wound. It was in that way that the blacks were dying; quietly, as though they had chosen death. He thought of the Nulalbin tribe, yearly diminishing, and of the incurable invisible sorrow that drove them to the townships and into the hands of the sly-grog sellers and the Chinese opium-dealers with whom they spent whatever money they could earn—seeking forgetfulness, seeking death.

Obscurely he found himself resenting this, as though it were an undeserved wrong done to his own people. Why should the blacks, with that soft obstinacy that was almost gaiety, thus invite their own murder? They refused the conditions his people had imposed; they preferred their own stubbornness. It was unfair, unfair, that such a choice should be given, such an invitation made. 'Kill us, for we can never accept you,' the blacks said; 'kill us, or forget your own ambitions.'

They had scarcely made even the show of resistance. Looking back, he could see how it had been necessary to the whites to magnify that resistance, to keep alive in their minds the memory of the few killings, the few hostilities, to imagine dangers that had never existed. Only in that way could they justify themselves for killing, keep their own self-respect. He thought of one man who had spent his life in laying strychnine baits of flour-cakes wherever he went, wiping out whole tribes, whole camps of blacks; insane, obsessed by a terror far beyond anything that the reality could have inspired, he had died warning the world against 'those treacherous devils'.

Albert began to understand that this was where the danger lay, the mortal wound that the blacks had known how to deal in return for their own dispossession. 'You must understand us or you must kill us,' they had said; and understanding would have meant—something beyond the powers of the white men, some renunciation impossible to be made. Not for many years, it seemed to him, could that wound be healed. It lay at the bottom of the hatred and contempt that so many men held for the blacks, and which, as he thought of it now, he had himself used as a refuge when it was necessary to condone some wrong or other, some injustice convenient to himself.

To forgive oneself—that was the hardest task. Until the white men could recognize and forgive that deep and festering consciousness of guilt in themselves, they would not forgive the blacks for setting it there. The murder would go on—open or concealed—until the blacks were all gone, the whites forever crippled.

He imagined a whole civilization haunted, like a house haunted by the ghost of a murdered man buried under it. The thought recalled to him suddenly the day when he had seen—or imagined—that tall warrior standing on a plain where no warrior could have been, beckoning him across to nothing but a low tussock and the teasing heat-waves of shimmering air. He was overtaken by a deep shudder at that enigmatic memory. Yes, they were all haunted—his generation. Perhaps his sons would be able to forgive, to lay that ghost in themselves; perhaps it would remain forever at the root of this country, making every achievement empty and every struggle vain.

Thoughts like these, a strange revaluation of his life, began to occupy him more and more. Everything he saw today seemed to touch off a new train in him; all was strange and unfamiliar, as his home had become before he left it. It was very many years since he had seen as much as he saw today; the raw ugly little houses of the township, the pretentious stucco of the few stores and public buildings, the sight of teams ploughing in the cultivation near the railway as the train began to gather speed northward, all touched new springs in him and afflicted him with strange feelings. Pity was among them, perhaps, admiration and distaste as well. He was overcome by this queer flood of feeling, this queer alteration in his world.

He leaned his head against the stiff leather cushion of the carriage and allowed the landscape to take charge of him; its subtle variations of colour and detail streamed past his eyes; and through his emptied mind, he knew, the most surprising things were passing. He had not felt like this since that fever-year at Avon Downs so long ago, when he had sat convalescent in the winter sun, weak as water and full of the clarity of the air itself.

This year the railway had at last linked up with the line that ran from Brisbane to the Queensland border; for the first time, he would not need to take the coach at all. It seemed somehow fitting, though he did not try to explain this, that the link should have been completed just now; that the railway which had begun its journey northwards when he was a child should end it in his fiftieth year. Somehow the circle seemed joined, the picture unified by this one detail.

Once, he remembered, he had ridden this way with cattle from his father's northern run, sold to a squatter who had just taken up country on the Darling Downs. Perhaps he had been fifteen then; it was his first big job of droving, his first outside responsibility. He had brought the cattle safely to Patrick's place, after three weeks in country he had never seen; he had had only a couple of young black stockmen and a dog or two to help, and he had scarcely lost a beast for all that. Then there had been few settlers; he had travelled day after day without meeting white men, and the blacks' camps had been numerous on these slopes, for there was some big intertribal corroboree that year. Now, fences had gone up everywhere; the rich soil showed red and black in squares of cultivation and in orchards, and the line of rails glinted ahead.

He listened to the wheels as they rolled over the sleepers; their steady beat was like that of a shod horse galloping continually under him—like the sound of the years, he fancied, as they had bolted with him lately, inexorably forward, faster and faster, leaving no time to breathe, to think, to be. Like the landscape, he had been fenced with iron, bound down with iron; he had been the willing prisoner of his own ambition, of Nulalbin, of Wongwibinda, of those deadly columns of figures that had so oppressed him. It seemed ridiculous, now, that he should not have been happy and calm, that he should have so driven and beaten himself on, been so possessed by fears and distracted by small things. He had May—at the thought of her a loving loneliness moved him; he had the children, of whom he had known, really, so little. For their sake, as well as his own, he must now make himself free.

For ten days or more, he would not have to force his attention and his mind to work; he would not have to wake at nights to listen for dingoes in the near paddocks, or to wonder if the rain would break the flood-gates on Connaughtman's Creek again. He sat here in the train, alone with himself as he had not been for many years; he would begin to find out who he was. He leaned his head back on the head-cushion's slippery leather; the afternoon sun struck dustily through his window and the train hummed and beat steadily northwards. Suddenly he was asleep.

13   *FINAL JOURNEY*

THE MOOD PURSUED him as the steamer carried him northwards. Sunshine and the warm steady breath of the trade wind pressed against him all day, relieving the ache that work and winter had left in his bones. The weather was calm, the sea peacock-blue with a slight coastwise swell, so that the ship rose and fell softly, like the rocking of a chair or a cradle. Serenity immeasurable stretched eastwards and upwards with the sea and sky; he sat on deck and let his eyes rest on the rhythm of that long movement of blue, the perfect horizon.

It was as though the sea itself filled him. Scarcely thinking, scarcely feeling, he began to comprehend how deeply concentrated his anxious mind had been. Depth on depth of tension had loosened in him; now he was abandoned, a weed heaving on the swell, a child grown sleepy after a long day.

It was strange how completely his mind had deserted the problems that had made up his life. Where a few weeks ago his whole vision had been occupied by them, now they scarcely seemed to exist for him; it was as though they had been only a curtain dropped in front of him, obscuring reality, and now simply drawn aside. He did not want to talk to the other passengers, to join the card-players in the cramped saloon; he wanted only to sit quietly, exploring this new space that his mind suddenly offered him. Scenes from the past, long forgotten, kept recurring to him; sentences, conversations, personal relationships which until now he had never thought of at all, suddenly gained a new weight and clarity from this alteration in his mind's balance. He saw his life, his wife and children, as though all were strange to him, with a new and tenderer understanding.

Yet he could scarcely have said that he had learned anything new, or even that in himself he was changed. Perhaps it was only the spell of this little vacant space of days, the presence of the quiet sea; perhaps, faced again with the old problems, he would slip into his old responses, like the bullocks that had worked the mills that ground wheat in the Hunter Valley in his childhood. He would have liked to wait here, in this warm corner of the deck, hearing the quiet straining of ropes and planks, feeling the inexorable motion of slow wave and trough, for a long time; he needed time to explore, to consolidate, to make certain of what it was that he had glimpsed, of what weights had shifted and settled in his mind, of the nature of himself.

Sometimes in his drowsy wanderings he became conscious again of the old life waiting not far ahead. It would close round him soon, he knew, with the inescapable friendliness of custom; it would take charge of him and hurry him on as before. The knowledge pressed on him uneasily. At such times he felt that this strange interval in his life was nothing at all—an interregnum in reality, a loosening of his mind's tightly knit armour, and no more. Perhaps it was as ephemeral a thing as, for instance, his momentary dream of living on that blue island that moved into view on a stretch of blade-coloured water—something which he must reject and forget. Yet he could not help feeling that somewhere in this queer experience he might find a permanence that had escaped him in the rapid flow of his life, a detachment from the thorns and whips that drove him, which he had never been able to achieve.

The Reef flowed past the ship like a blue mirage; islands passed like clouds set on water. At Cooktown he must land for a day, to change from the steamer into the little *Quiriang*, the Gulf boat in which he must complete the journey. The necessity of packing and

M

making his arrangements woke him reluctantly from his quiescence.

Cooktown was young and raw, a town of miners and of cattlemen come in from the hinterland, of Chinese shops and half-castes; blacks and goats wandered through the unmade streets. Coming ashore with his valises, he was reminded of the day when he had landed at Rockhampton for the first time, twenty-three years ago; he smelled again in memory the smell of those new clothes of his—the first he had bought for years, he remembered. It set him again on the track of his own youth, and as the *Quiriang* fussed slowly northwards to Thursday Island, he remembered many things.

He thought of the school at Parramatta—so long ago that it did not seem like a part of his own life at all—and of the day when, a boy of fourteen, he had said goodbye formally to the headmaster on the gravel drive, with the school carriage waiting near; the smell of straw and leather in the carriage was perfectly clear to him. He had sat there absently, as it took him to join the coach for Sydney, trying to mend the broken leather strap of his valise, and struggling with the knowledge that he would not come back to school, for Papa was very poor now.

How it all came back—the gloom of the windowless slab hut, the earthen floor where fungus grew in the darkest corners. He had spent some bad times there; a lonely little beggar he had been. The old grey blanket on the bunk—two sheets of bark and four forked saplings—the cry of the brain-fever bird that had called all night when the moon was up—he had never been able to shoot it. More insistently the memories flooded in.

When the *Quiriang* pulled into the harbour at Thursday Island, the slight breeze of the ship's motion fell; the heat was like that of a still midsummer. He went ashore, to wander among the strange people and flowers and palms, fascinated, drawn by the soft wild faces and the strange mixture of tongues. Black, brown, golden-yellow people thronged here; Malay fishermen, Japanese and Chinese, mingled with the natives; there were half-castes of every colour, faces of every mould. Young girls moved softly along the white sandy roads, dressed in parrot-bright cottons; dark unpupilled eyes from which all light seemed absent glanced at him out of faces yellow as melons. It was a life with which he had nothing in common, a world to which he held no clues.

At little booths in front of palm-hidden houses he bought pearl-shell; there was a little carving for May, necklaces for his daughters, a pearl-handled knife. Then as he turned away he looked more closely at the carving, holding it away to bring it into focus, for his eyes had grown long-sighted lately. It was a tiny, delicately fashioned obscene picture. Behind the bead curtain of the booth, he fancied he could hear a snigger of laughter; he stuffed the carving in his pocket and hastened on, feeling himself flush deeply. At the next booth he stopped and bought another carving, taking care to look at it carefully before he paid for it. On the wharf he would throw that other thing into the sea.

The ship would sail soon after dark; he had left it rather late to return, walking a long distance. Now as he made his way back among the haphazard shanties and houses of the Chinese quarter, night came down; behind the hung screens of bamboo mats little coloured lanterns began to shine, swinging with the evening breeze and making nebulous shadows move across the pale sandy roads. He heard the banjoes and guitars begin. There were all manner of queer instruments here, it seemed; behind the split bamboo screens he could distinguish the sound of a tinkling like water, of a soft drumming, of singing that used no scale that he knew.

On the sand under the palms, where the growing moon cast a vague light, aboriginals and half-castes squatted in groups and began to sing. Sometimes the tunes were familiar, hymn-tunes taught by missionaries, though he could not distinguish the words; sometimes they had the queer wind-like notes of Malay songs, learned from the pearlers; sometimes they were native chants, like the chants he remembered on corroboree nights in the Dawson Valley or at Avon Downs. Men, women and children sang in harmony above a background of strumming banjoes, laughter, idle talk, quarrels; somewhere in the distance beyond, he could hear the cries and stormy wailing that meant a group mourning for someone dead.

Now he was passing a Chinese burial-ground. The tall domed joss-houses stood like anthills among a forest of little dark trees of heavily perfumed creamy flowers; this was the tree of death, the frangipani.

Incense sticks burned somewhere. The scent of the flowers and the scent of the smoke mingled in overpowering sweetness, loading the air like a gas. The cry of the mourners grew louder in its repetition; near the corner of the cemetery he saw them gathered. Their gestures struck him as wildly abandoned, too free, too expressive of their grief. They beat their thighs and breasts, crying to the moon like dogs; they fell to the ground and rolled there.

The heavy alien scent hung in his nostrils like a drug. A few flowers detached themselves from the trees as he hurried on, and fell to lie at his feet. He was overcome by revulsion and a feeling of danger; hurrying on to the wharf more quickly than he need have done, he took out the little carving from his pocket, paused on the gangplank, and dropped it into the black water between ship and wharf. He went below at once, and did not come up again until he felt the ship begin to move and heard the shouts of the crew above.

That night the ship turned southwards again into the Gulf. When he woke in the morning the little grey waves of a different sea beat against the ship's sides, where yesterday the water had been blue and quiet. The weather was still hot and calm, but a slight reviving breeze blew up from the land. He felt relieved that those dangerous languid days were over. It was almost a refreshment, now, to leave behind the beauty of the eastern coasts, the blue and green hills and islands, the reef-filled treacherous seas. About these grey waters and uninviting skies there was an air of business, a return to the hard simplicities that had made up his own life.

He welcomed it, for he felt his weariness had passed. He was anxious to try his new strength, and, invigorated by this altered atmosphere, he looked forward to landing, and to seeing the cattle country of the Gulf stations. Life there was hard and bare, certainly, but it was the life he understood. The melting air, the evening moon, the outlandish music of last night, beautiful as they had been, seemed alien and soft as quicksand; they had been a warning pointing him back to the rigours of life again. Leaning on the railing of the *Quiriang*'s tiny after-deck, he felt with joy the closing-in of the old life on him, not as the trap he had for a while imagined it, but as a loved and familiar routine. He no longer feared it; now he would begin to face it with a new strength and understanding.

The tender met the boat four miles out from Karumba. The bareness, even the ugliness, of the tiny settlement pleased him. The trip up the river to Normanton, hot and uncomfortable as it was, he enjoyed. Yet he reached Normanton weary; perhaps he had over-estimated the good that the trip had done him physically. He would have been glad of a day's rest there; it was already late in the morning, and he had risen very early to get aboard the tender.

But at the hotel he found Haydon waiting with a horse for him. He remembered that in his last letter he had asked that there should be as little delay as possible; he must catch the Cloncurry coach for Townsville this week, for his business was pressing. He did not like to ask Haydon to wait for him now, though the ride to Vena Park—over sixty miles—was formidable to him. And during these last years Haydon and he had quarrelled at times, over the expenses, over the question of management; he felt the coolness of Haydon's greeting, and would ask for no concessions. Accordingly, after a hurried lunch, they set off.

It was long after dark when at last they reached the homestead. The ride had been a hard one, and Albert found that even after so short a break from work his muscles had lost their accustomed ease in the saddle; he was stiff and sore when they dismounted at the yards. The big dinner that the Chinese cook had waiting for them dispersed his fatigue a little, but he cut the evening short and went early to bed. The bunk in which he was to sleep was hard and uncomfortable, and after his days at sea he found the room moving with him disturbingly as he lay awake.

It seemed a long time until he slept, and his sleep was light. Before dawn Haydon woke him. He must ride over the whole run today, and tonight he must settle the question of the sale; the Cloncurry coach made its return trip to Townsville in four days' time, and to reach it he would need three days of riding.

He spared himself nothing, going over the run as meticulously as possible; at night, he and Haydon sat up late over the books and records of the station, and at last an agreement was reached over the price of Albert's share in the partnership. But although they avoided quarrelling, the bargain was not a cordial one; Albert had not spared his criticism of Haydon's management during the years of the partnership, and Haydon had not forgiven him for this. The interview had not been entirely pleasant, and Albert was too weary by now to attempt reconciliation.

It was late when the business was finished; he wanted nothing but to sleep. Next morning he was to set out for the coach road a hundred and sixty miles south. He was taking one of the black stockmen, Polo, who would guide him down to Coobiaby and lead his horse home when the journey was over.

But as he pulled on his clothes and boots by lamplight before dawn, Albert felt half-inclined to put the journey off for a few days, to catch the coach on its journey next week. Instead of hardening his muscles and relieving his fatigue, this second long day in the saddle seemed to have doubled his weariness. If he and Haydon had been on better terms, or if he had not felt unwilling to admit even to himself that he could be so wearied by only two days of work, he might have asked to stay, but the thought of spending another week here now was distasteful to him.

However, he humbled himself so far as to ask for a blanket to be put over the saddle for him, though he knew there would be a laugh over that when he had gone. The horse he was riding was a young one of Haydon's own, big-framed and a good weight-carrier for the distance ahead, but awkward-paced and still raw; he needed constant attention, sidling and pulling painfully. 'He may give you a bit of a go for it,' Haydon warned, 'but there's no vice about him.'

Albert was glad that before he and Polo were out of sight of the station, the horse began to prop and give trouble; he was able to display at any rate a little of his horsemanship, which had always been a point of pride with him. The group of men who watched from the yards would not be able to snigger at his softness, after all.

But the day ahead was long, and though the horse settled down willingly enough after a time, he had no comfortable pace for the long journey. His jerking walk and sawing trot began to grow painful. At first Albert had been interested in the country, in Polo's talk and in the birds and insects of these plains which he had never seen before. But it was not long before he grew more and more silent, enduring rather than enjoying; his muscles had begun to ache steadily, there was rheumatism in his shoulder; at midday the sun burned and at night the great plain was sharply cold. He shivered wakefully under his too-thin blanket, and was thankful when sunrise came and the fire was roused; he drank his tea almost boiling, and longed for more to thaw his cold bones.

At nightfall on the third day's riding he was numb with misery. But now a comforting light shone out ahead; it was in the windows of the pub at Coobiaby, where the coach waited overnight. Here the Cloncurry-Townsville road crossed their track; tonight he would eat a cooked dinner and sleep in a bed again, no matter how rough. His sore bones yearned for rest and softness, after the hard earth and the creeping chill of three nights.

His sleep that night did not seem long enough; he was wakened long before dawn, for the coach started early. Breakfast over, he said goodbye to Polo, who was about to set off on the homeward track with the horses, and climbed to his seat. There were four women travelling; he must sit outside today, if not tomorrow as well.

The day was clouded and grey; over the bleached sparse grass a mid-July westerly came bitterly from the desert. Sitting exposed on the coach's bare top, he felt its full bite and began to shiver. The coach swayed and jerked over the unmade track, and clinging to cold iron bars he regretted his greatcoat left at Wongwibinda; he had nothing warm with him, except the coat of his working clothes. When the coach halted for lunch at a wayside shanty, he dragged it out of his valise and put it on. But it scarcely warmed him; all afternoon he sat dumbly enduring, with chattering teeth, while the wind rose higher and higher, blowing weeds and tangles of dead grass and dust across his face, howling malevolently in his ears. The bare country they were crossing gave no shelter; he began to feel this wind as a personal enemy, intent on snatching away the very clothes he huddled in.

By the time the coach pulled into Hughenden for the night, he was thoroughly chilled. His eyes smarted and his lips burned with the desiccating dust and the perpetual stream of cold air. There was another day's journey tomorrow, before the mountains were crossed and the back of the wind broken. The pub at Hughenden was rough and cheerless, with no fire for the travellers; his bed that night was dirty, and the worn blankets would not keep out the night's frost. It was as though he were travelling in a nightmare of discomfort, and, to crown it all, he had begun to feel that he was in for a bout of fever. He could not stop shivering; his teeth chattered although his forehead burned with heat.

Well, if it was fever, it would be a great nuisance certainly. But he was confident of his ability to shake it off quickly. He had not had fever since that year at Avon Downs, and he felt that he had been initiated then into all its terrors; he was sure of his comparative immunity. He would go on to Townsville, catch the steamer there tomorrow evening, and get his attack over and done with during the two days on board. He could not afford to miss this steamer, for the next chance of a boat to Rockhampton would not come, perhaps, for weeks, and he had wired Arundel to have the cattle ready for him in four days' time.

He dressed in the morning as warmly as he could, in all the clothes he could manage to put on, for he heard the wind raging outside as wickedly as ever. He had hoped for a seat inside the coach today, but again they were all occupied by women and children. He had no appetite for breakfast, but drank enormously—the strong sweet tea was the only thing that seemed to warm him, and put a stop to these fits of shivering, of which he had begun to be almost ashamed.

He begged a few old bags to put over his feet during the journey, and climbing up made himself as comfortable as possible. But in an hour or two the wind had chilled him deeply again, and his shivering was growing uncontrollable.

The coach laboured slowly on, through the hills to Charters Towers and over the Hervey Range, following the river's course. He looked round now and then, when the wind abated a little and left the air clear of dust, but his eyes smarted and watered too much for him to take much interest in this country, which he had so looked forward to seeing.

Once he saw a camel train passing, loaded for the inland beyond Cloncurry; he had never seen camels before, and for a moment stared at them lightheadedly as though they had been creatures in a dream. Another time, at the edge of the scrub that bordered the road, a group of brolgas were dancing, gravely occupied, ignoring the coach that passed near them. Their long legs and necks, their delicate plumage grey as clouds, their queer posturings, struck him suddenly in his fever as unbearably beautiful. He strained round in the teeth' of the wind to watch them as long as they were in view.

In Townsville that evening, it seemed a scarcely tolerable effort to book his passage, to find his way to the wharves and aboard to his cabin. He was certainly in for a bad day or two. His head ached abominably, and once or twice when he had to stand still for a time, beside the counter in the booking-office, or as he waited for the steward to show him his cabin, his legs seemed to totter and the earth to tilt and waver under him.

He climbed into his berth at once, not caring to undress; he would do that later when he had had a rest. But although he was so tired, sleep would not come. He forced his eyes shut and lay as quietly as he could, abandoning himself to a chaos of whirling darkness and broken terrifying dreams.

The steward in the morning thought him merely seasick, though the weather was calm enough. It was not until the ship had nearly reached Rockhampton, and Albert had not responded to several summonses, that it became evident he was really ill. After a consultation with the doctor whom the captain hurriedly called on board he was carried ashore and to the hospital.

Ill as he felt, he would not have May hear of it. He was still convinced that this was only a fever, picked up that treacherous night at Thursday Island and aggravated by his long journey—it would be over in a day or two and he would be none the worse. The doctor, a busy man, looked doubtful, but the symptoms were not definite yet. It might be malaria; perhaps there would be no harm in waiting to see.

But when the week was over, it was clear that this was a case of pneumonia, and that it was growing dangerous. Arundel, who had come to Rockhampton on hearing the news, sent a telegram to Wongwibinda. It would be best that May should come as soon as possible.

But it would be some time before she could catch a steamer from

Brisbane, and the overland trip, with its delays and roundabout roads, was unthinkable. Ten days at least must pass before she could reach Rockhampton.

For Albert, however, time had now altered its whole character, becoming an uncertain quantity which telescoped and expanded: weeks seemed to elapse in the space of an hour, whole series of days disappeared altogether. It was better not to try to remember what day it really was, or to goad one's fading consciousness too much; awake, the pain was worse.

In the doctor's cant phrase, he was putting up a great fight for it; his splendid physique, his body which was still almost that of a young man, seemed at first unconquerable. But now he was growing weaker; the long days of pain and difficulty through which he was struggling began to seem too much. He sank deeper and deeper into marshes of burning dreams and nightmare; the lucid moments when he knew himself and recognized the present moment grew fewer and fewer.

Some responsibility weighed on him. For a long time he struggled to discover what it was, but at last in one of his hours of consciousness he made a nurse bring his diary and a pen. What was the date? he asked, and finding it in his diary turned over twelve pages left blank since his last entry at Hughenden. He had always been meticulous in keeping that diary, the record of his work, of his transactions, of the weather, of his hopes and his despairs.

He began to write, taking infinite pains to keep the pen steady. He must set down as well as he could the record of his commitments, of his debts and obligations, of the money to come in and to be paid out; he marshalled his mind with painful effort, and the pen seemed as heavy and needed as much skill to guide it as if it had been the long stockwhip to which his hand had been more used. At the foot of the page it was no longer possible to keep the wandering nib between the lines; he knew that the words were staggering and scarcely legible. It was beyond his power to lift the pen to the top of the next page; he let it drop and fell back again, closing his eyes. Back to the darkness again; it was easier to sink down, to fall away from effort.

In the maze of his dreams, among beckoning darknesses and sudden scarlet warnings of pain, like fires breaking out in the night across the range to burn his grass, he kept meeting a small boy whom he could not identify. The boy was dressed for a journey; he looked at Albert with a strange smile and was suddenly taken away, sometimes on a boat, sometimes in an old brown-painted carriage. Though Albert called to him to wait, the boy never spoke, but stood and looked at him always with that strange smile.

At the end of the boy's journey, Albert knew, something waited shrouded in darkness, but though Albert tried to warn him, the child would not stay; inexorably the ship began to draw away, the carriage disappeared. Time after time the same scene met him, whatever the subject of his dream; perhaps he would be taking cattle through the Gogango Scrub, riding the fences in the Mimosa, watching the rain on the lagoon at Collymongool, dancing with May in the old drawing-room at Bickham on the night of Mary's wedding, when as he turned his head for a moment the boy would be there, watching him intently with that strange and quiet look.

Where was the boy's mother, he wondered? His heart was filled with reproachful grief at her desertion. She should be here; she would comfort the child, she would save him from the waiting darkness. Now the dreams began to change, and he was searching for her desperately, though he often forgot the object of the search. He went from room to room of the old house at Bickham; sometimes no one was there at all, sometimes it was filled with people—old Bennett the shepherd, Sallie Dickinson, his headmaster at the Parramatta school, the old Madman singing his songs, red-haired Lily from the shanty at Clermont, old Captain from Nulalbin—hundreds of them crowded round him. But the person whom he sought for was not there—she had gone away. He must find her, for the boy needed her; and the search would begin again. He would wander through the big summer-scented garden at Dalwood where the rose-hedge bloomed, and among the green vines where grapes hung, or in the orchard where heavy fruit fell suddenly, sounding like footsteps, and startled him into looking round—but the orchard was empty. Through all these dreams, like an urgent background, fell the red light which he knew to be pain and in which day and night were equal. He must go on searching continually, for though she was not in this place, she would surely be somewhere near.

It was out of one of these long-repeated wanderings that he woke one afternoon, lifting his eyelids very slowly in an effort to shake off the dream and remember who and where he was. For a moment she mingled with the last of his dreams; it was a sudden shock of strange familiar joy to see her there, sitting so quietly as if resigned or weary, her eyelids drooped, her head half turned away. It was the woman he had been looking for, the mother; the search was over, and now he was free to sink back into the darkness, no longer troubled.

He lay a moment looking at her, at the pretty and decided curve of cheek, at the curled brown hair and strong wide shoulders, while the mists of his sleep cleared away. Then she turned and looked up, and became May.

14   THE END OF 1890

THE DIARY LAY in front of May on the big roll-top desk. The rest of the papers she had brought back to Wongwibinda—Albert's agreement with Haydon, the letters she had written him during the journey, the little leather folder that held her picture—were stacked on one side. She opened the diary and set herself to read the entries he had made on the journey; all those days were precious to her now, the last days she would ever, even so vicariously, share with him.

She read carefully, slowly, taking note of every word. There was not much to read; he had set down little more than a record of the weather, the ports the steamer had touched at, his interview with Haydon. Then came the brief record of his painful journey eastwards, ending with the entry made at Hughenden. After that the blank pages stretched ahead, broken only by his final unsteady entry made that day in hospital, the writing of which she could not recognize and could scarcely read.

She had to steel herself to look at it without tears. This was important. She took notes as she deciphered the straggling record of debts, payments and commitments, examining each word carefully to make certain of the meaning. Only when she was sure of the last word he had written did she at last allow her head to fall on the desk and the repressed tears to come.

But she did not let herself weep for long. It was months now since the funeral, months since her return to Wongwibinda; it was time now to pick up the dropped threads, to discipline herself back to work again. There was a great deal to be done. She opened the pages of the diary at a date some days further ahead, and wrote in a steady hand, 'This day my beloved died.' . . . Further on yet she turned, and began her own entries.

Shearing would soon be starting. She had found a temporary manager, a young man still learning, who would work for a smaller wage than an experienced man would ask. She herself knew enough already to guide him in the work. When the shearing was over and the year drawing to a close, she must make arrangements for the future; already her relatives and her creditors were pressing her to sell Wongwibinda, to buy a cottage in town and devote herself to educating the children. It was time she made her decision. It seemed that everything and everyone was against her plan of continuing to work the run and to live at Wongwibinda, yet she found herself more and more reluctant to leave.

'My dear May, I have no doubt that you are a very capable little manager,' Albert's mother had written. 'But after all, you are a woman, and cannot accomplish a man's work as well as your own. Your youngest boy is not yet two years old; your first thoughts must surely be for the children. . . .' It was a chorus that rose from all of them—her sisters, her friends, Albert's sisters and brothers. 'Of course you will not remain at Wongwibinda beyond this year . . . a nice little cottage, cheap and pleasant . . . you must think of the children. . . .'

It made May impatient to hear them. Certainly, she thought, the children were all-important. Why, but for them, would she wish to stay here, Albert being dead? It would be better for the children, surely, to stay at whatever sacrifice, rather than to move to some poky cottage in a town, to live on the slender income which the sale of the runs would afford after all debts had been paid (if, indeed, anything should be left at all). It would be better for the boys to learn to work hard and early on their own land, even if they were always to be poor and to scrape for a living, than to take some narrow and humiliating job in a city office. And if the bank were willing to trust her judgement even a little, she felt, she would manage somehow to make it possible for them to stay here, to carry on what Albert had begun. Somehow she would bear this terrifying load of debt, meet the payments, find the rent, see to it that the children did not suffer.

Indeed, the thought of losing Wongwibinda had been the final cruel screw put on her grief. She had put into the place and into her plans for its future so much of her own life that to give it up now would have broken roots which she felt she would never be able to put out again. She knew every joint and rafter of the house that had been built under her supervision; the habits of the chimneys in every kind of wind, the sound that each door made as it opened and shut, were dear to her.

Outside her bedroom window she had planted a climbing rose; it had grown high, and now the scent of its summer roses came to her softly as she lay awake and lonely in the big double bed, and seemed like a kind of comfort. The place, for her, was alive; it breathed with her own breath; she would not give it up except in the last extremity.

She began searching through a heap of old letters and papers that she had preserved in a drawer of the desk which she and Albert had shared. At last she found what she wanted—a crumpled piece of paper, kept from some party that she and Albert had gone to, on a visit to the valley when she was still a young married woman, thirteen years ago perhaps. They had played a game fashionable at the time: each of the guests was to write down as frankly as possible the character of one of the others—a malicious little game, she recalled, that had led to some trouble. She hardly knew why she had kept the scribble she had been given; it had amused her, though Albert had been a little annoyed by it. Now she smoothed it out and read it over.

'Character of May Wright, 1877.

'Irritable temper and disposition; inclined to be vain and fond of flattery, but pleasing in manners and kind-hearted. Inclined to gossip and be sarcastic. Good hand at business and shrewd at making any bargain.

'Likes her own way and generally gets it. Not at all *goody*, but conscientious. Disposition on the whole good.'

It was no longer the criticism of her faults that interested her.

She knew herself well enough now to give this its fair due and no more, and she knew too that her determination and the strength that lay behind her charm had often caused petty jealousies and enmities. That was unimportant now; what she sought in this crumpled piece of paper was some kind of reassurance, a backing for her own confidence, an acknowledgement of her ability. 'Good hand at business and shrewd at making any bargain'—she re-read that. 'Likes her own way and generally gets it.'

As for her shrewdness and pleasing manners, they would make useful weapons in the pursuit of what she now wanted. The faded little piece of paper seemed at this moment an ally, perhaps her only ally; she sat awhile absently folding and unfolding it. Finally she placed it carefully in the diary, as though it had been some precious document, and turned back to the notebooks, the business records, and the big account-books, those dusty volumes over which Albert had toiled so long.

She knew already that the debt incurred on Wongwibinda and Nulalt in was altogether almost equal to the value of the two properties as they now stood. The knowledge, though it dismayed her, had not daunted her. Land values, she felt, were too low; they would surely rise if she could only hold the properties a few years longer. The railway through New England, the new roads, the gradual inflow of settlers, all were in her favour. She was confident enough of meeting her debts if her creditors would only give her time. But if they were to refuse to risk their money further, or to put their trust in the management of an inexperienced woman, there would be no alternative to giving way.

Well, she would need all her charm and wit, all her capacity and knowledge, to persuade them that she was worthy of trust. Certainly she was still good-looking, still young enough to interest men's eyes; her poise and knowledge of men, she knew, made her a good judge of their capacities and prejudices, clever at handling people, tactful in her approach to them when she wished to be so. As she herself would have said, given time and opportunity she could twist most people round her little finger.

But she could not rely on that alone; she must show, when the test came, that she knew thoroughly what must be done and how it should be done. She must draw up from her memory, if she wished to keep Wongwibinda, everything she had ever heard or learned about the work of the run, about its routine, its whole economy, every detail of the enterprise; she must have clear in her mind not only the past and present, but the future; she must be able to summon at will any detail of what had been done, what was being done, what needed to be done yet.

It was an immeasurable advantage that, no matter how much of her time the children and the housekeeping had taken up, she had always made room in her attention for the affairs of the run and had always looked for Albert's confidence. She had so much valued his praise that she had made sure that he should find her a partner worth consulting, even in these busy last years since they had left Nulalbin. Whenever it had been possible, she had ridden out with him, making it her business to know how the cattle were doing in this or that paddock, how the sheep were responding to this or that treatment, whether the new bull's first crop of calves was satisfactory or where their faults lay.

She was more than ever thankful now that Albert had been so willing to call on her for help and advice, and that she had not allowed herself to sink wholly in the circumscribed routine of family and domesticity. She understood Albert's plans for the herd, knew their faults and virtues, and knew enough, too, of the technicalities of points and breeding to rely on her own judgement of beasts. In the business of buying and selling, whether of sheep or cattle, she had perfect confidence in herself. She went methodically over her knowledge of the year's routine, of what must be done at each season— the dosing, the bluestoning, the eyewooling and crutching, the shearing—and how it should be gone about.

As to the run itself, she knew almost as well as Albert himself its geography, its soils and grasses, the aim of the improvements that Albert had made. She knew that the men now finishing the ringbarking in this paddock were next to move to that other, and she knew what trees were to be destroyed and what left. She knew that she must make certain that the posts for the fencing which was to be done this year were of a particular timber, length and quality, that they must be put in to such and such a depth, and she knew where

N

the soil was shallow and rocky and the fencers were likely to scamp the digging if not watched. She knew when and where the salt-licks were to be put out for the cattle, and which cows were to be put with which bulls next season. Yet she went rigorously now over every detail, checking her own knowledge and foresight as closely as she could against Albert's records and documents.

The morning was almost gone when she closed the books and filed away the papers. Soon it would be little Phillip's mealtime; she always liked to feed him herself and to put him to sleep afterwards with the old nursery songs and rhymes the children had always loved. She would go out to the garden for a little while to clear her mind, and to probe it for certainty in her decision. The work she had done this morning had made her understand more clearly the magnitude of the responsibility she was taking on herself; for a moment or two, at the thought of so heavy a burden on her shoulders alone, she had hesitated.

She walked out through the house and down the wide handsome flight of steps that led to the garden. There had been showers these last few days, and the air was washed and softened; the roses were shaking off their load of raindrops and the sky was sober but breaking here and there into blue. In front of the house the carriage-drive curved elegantly round the heart-shaped lawn which Albert had laid out and made for her. It was edged now with a gay border of verbena and delphinium; the green grass glittered with fallen rain and the colours of the surrounding flowers made the whole as bright as a valentine, as he had intended it to be.

A rose brushed its cold rain-filled petals against her bare arm; there was a scent of lavender that reminded her of the scents of the Dalwood garden, and in the young springing trees beyond the flower-beds thrushes sang and wrens scuttled like mice. In the house behind her, Weeta was at her piano-practice; outside, she could hear dogs barking where Arthur and the men were bringing in a mob of sheep to the yard at the shearing-shed.

Possessive love burned up in her. All this was hers by right; this was the life she had helped to build, and it was in danger. She would not let it go; she identified herself with it. To give it up would be to betray Albert, to betray the children.

She walked half-absently down the slope of the garden, pausing now and then to pull a weed from the riotous borders, or to notice how a rose-bush or a young shrub grew. Her mind was busy with the future. The challenge that presented itself was one that roused in answer all her latent powers; without self-flattery, she felt herself capable of meeting it. She thought of sacrifices to be made, both material and spiritual.

The children must forgo their schooling for a time; Arthur she would need here, for he was old enough to help with much of the work; for the younger children, perhaps, she might scrape a schooling later on. There would be no margin to spare at present, even with the strictest economy. She must forge the whole run, her family, the men whose work she could not do without, into the closest of units; she would tolerate no shirking and no extravagance. For herself, she did not care how hard she must work or how heavy the strain would be.

It was typical of her that she had scarcely paused to wonder whether her powers and strength would be sufficient to do all that she now planned. She had seldom met any person whom she could not win over if she gave her mind to it, and had seldom attempted any task in which she had failed. She was already, in her small circle, a commander, and she was not used to opposition. Albert had been proud of everything about her, accepting her judgement without question and delighting in the equality of their relationship; it was a matter of course to her that others would follow where she led. Now, pausing at the foot of the carriage-drive, where the rambler-roses hàd already begun to cover the arch Albert had built, she searched her mind and found herself decided. She would stay here, no matter what difficulties she might encounter.

She turned back to the house again, walking now more quickly. In the young pine-trees the thrush and magpie vied with each other in a last burst of singing, before the afternoon silence should close down. Her mind, as she went up the curving flight of steps again, was detached and clear; she always found that out-of-doors her problems fell into place, her vision was refreshed and her emotions settled into firmness.

She had still a few moments before she must turn her mind to the household routine. Turning back into the little brown-panelled office, she put back in its place the diary for the year—the diary which Albert had left unfinished—and took down a parcel just arrived from the stationer's. It held, she knew, the diary for the coming year.

The parcel opened, she riffled once or twice through the volume's stiff pages; never yet opened, they yielded unevenly to her fingers. It gave her a strange feeling of power, as though the year itself were given into her hands, white and untouched, to be filled with the record of actions still to be performed, decisions not yet made. She turned to the first page and dipped her pen; some memory of a verse, read she had forgotten where, had caught at her mind, and she wrote it down firmly and clearly.

'When all the blandishments of life are gone,
The coward seeks for death; the brave live on.'

'The brave live on!' It was a gesture, a throwing-down of the glove—too dramatic, unlike her usual matter-of-fact attack on life, it embarrassed her a little as she read it over. Nevertheless, the moment seemed to require it; it was a seal set on her decision, an earnest of the future. To make an oath, even privately in one's diary, so definite as that, was an action that might keep one's resolve from sinking, one's heart from giving way; irrevocable, black on white, it stood there in her best handwriting.

She stared down at it, musing. 'All the blandishments of life are gone'—for months now she had felt that to be true, and felt that it would be true always. Yet in the sudden access of confidence that had come with her decision of this morning, she was sceptical enough to question it a little. She had the children still; she had just determined that she would have Wongwibinda.

She believed in time and hard work as certain remedies for sorrow, and had often enough recommended both to the unfortunate among her friends, feeling robustly as she did that fate was meant to be out-witted rather than submitted to. And she thought of Bertie, her lost and mourned-for darling; though her love and grief, when she remembered him, seemed no less than at first, she could not help admitting that the busy years since his death had thrust his memory deeper and deeper into her being, until now she scarcely ever met, as she had once continually done, his small image in her path.

Was it possible, then, that life might lead her across the breadth even of this second grief? Its size and darkness daunted her; she had been a passionate woman and had found in Albert something which continually renewed her feeling; it was, now, as though she had been stripped of all her defences against the bitterness of loss. Until now, she felt, she had passed her time in a warm and sunny shelter, like a plant growing by a wall. With the wall so cruelly and abruptly taken away, she stood exposed to the full force of winter, bewildered and weakened by her loss. If the plant of her life were to survive, it must be strengthened; she must prune herself mercilessly of all that flower and foliage, she must send out deeper and more obstinate roots, hold fast to the soil she grew in.

But the day, the precious day was passing too quickly. She had a thousand things to do; she closed the desk and locked away documents and books, moving with her usual quick precision. Now the baby must have his meal and be put to sleep; after lunch Arthur must saddle her horse, for she would ride round the fences to see that all was in order, have a word with the contractor about the line for the new stretch of fencing, inspect the sheep the men had just brought in for tomorrow's work.

The sheep from Connaughtman's paddock had always been more liable to liver-fluke, and she was anxious to see if the last dosing had improved their condition, for Albert had tried a new formula lately. Then tonight she must discuss all the arrangements for the shearing with young Mr Murray, the new manager, to make quite certain that he had understood everything that was required. And most important of all, she would write to the bank manager.

She thought with a wry smile of his last letter, so dryly and delicately hinting that it was time she decided—taking it for granted that she would not wish to stay at Wongwibinda beyond the new year. . . . 'I'll settle that,' she thought, turning through the door; and as she walked quickly up the causeway that led to the kitchen quarters, she was already planning her attack. She would go to visit him as soon as the shearing would let her—perhaps it would be best to arrange to be in town at the weekend, and to manoeuvre a visit to his wife, whom May knew slightly. A private interview, outside the dry business atmosphere of the bank—a personal appeal, joined to the other arguments she had marshalled—a talk as between friends.

She thought of him intently, sizing him up—a dry little man, a capable little man, with a sense of his own importance; tears would only repel him. But she could see already how he should be handled—a touch here and there of carefully concealed flattery, only the very slightest reference to her widowhood, the rest pure business. Her knowledge would impress him; she must take care to ask his advice wherever possible, to imply a suitable awe of his financial mysteries. Thinking and planning in this way, she moved round the kitchen, setting the baby's tray.

Now that she had at last come to a decision, she felt in some way lightened and clarified. For months she had been given over to mourning; she had clung to others, had been dependent, had withdrawn from life, unable to think of anything but the wound that drained her best blood and left her dried and weakened. Now she stood alone, in command of herself again. Merely to plan, to look forward, had worked the miracle in her; she tested the muscles left so long unused, began to bring others into play, to feel power welling up again from some source now unsealed. She had always secretly enjoyed the pleasure of opposition, the sharp tang of a fight to be won; droughts, floods, other set-backs had roused her where they made Albert miserable and depressed. The thought of the struggle ahead began to excite her, as though she stood in a great gale of wind.

As for her grief, she had already begun to lock it away, a sad treasure only to be brought out when she was alone or sleepless. Like the lock of Bertie's hair and the straggling childish letters he had written her from Sydney during that last separation, it must be kept apart from her daily life, allowed its full dominion only in secret.

She put on the baby's egg to boil; slicing and buttering bread, she began to explain to Mrs Maguire the best way of making the apricot jam and how the jars should be covered.

15   *VISIT TO DALWOOD*

THIS, THE FIRST winter since Albert's death, seemed a formidable enemy, reinforcing with its cold abridgement of life the grief that still lay every night beside her, a chilly vacancy in the big double bed. But the cold, so saddening and limiting by night, spurred her on during the days; it was a whip that drove her to work early and late.

Not only winter, but a widespread depression, had descended on the country. The very bounty of the season that had just ended seemed to aggravate the evil; prices had sunk lower and lower with the progress of summer and autumn, with the growing perfection of the culminating season, and were still sinking now. Yet Wongwibinda for the first time had begun to produce to its full capacity.

The haysheds were full to overflowing, and ricks stood round the cultivations, for there had been more hay than could be housed; the paddocks of corn that May had had sown in spring stood now ripe to be picked, each tall bleached plant bearing three or four cobs of perfect yellow grain; the potato crop had been the heaviest ever known, the calving had been exceptional, and the grass in the cleared country and on the flats stood rich and sweet. The country was ready to carry more sheep than ever before, and they were healthy and full-wooled; the cattle stood knee-deep in grass, and their red and white coats bloomed with well-being.

Riding over the run in autumn, on horses fresh and fat with good grass, hearing the song of the replenished creeks and seeing how the land had responded to these years of work and improvement, May had felt a triumphant delight only darkened by the knowledge that Albert was not there to share it with her.

But the trouble was that the season had been equally good every-where. The whole country was a great cornucopia filled to over-flowing; all the work done since the first settlers had taken it from the blacks seemed to have culminated in this extraordinary year.

Everywhere the grass was rich and the water plentiful; every run was fully stocked and even over-stocked, studded with dams and wells and windmills, cleared and tidied, burgeoning with the promise of wealth and rewards as yet unheard of. And in this very year the markets had begun to fall—catastrophically, uncheckably.

It seemed incredible to May that the Wongwibinda cattle, so carefully bred and improved, should now bring less than the roughest scrubber would have fetched a few years ago—less, in this incomparably promising season, than in the hardest year of drought prices. The autumn draft of fats from Nulalbin—beautiful beasts, so Arundel had written, and a bigger lot than had been got for many years— had scarcely found a market at all; after long delays, they had at last been sold for a most miserable price. Beef values were falling weekly; the market reports showed that even the wool market was staggering and uncertain.

But May still held her determined optimism. This final stroke of bad luck could not last long. She studied the newspapers and market news with concentration, laying her plans to circumvent fortune; it seemed that wool was still a little more steady than beef prices, and she bought more wethers, selling cattle to make room for them, even though the price the cattle fetched was scarcely worth the trouble of droving them. Everything depended on what price the wool shorn last summer would fetch. It was soon to be offered; she would hear the result, probably, in late July.

If it met a bad market, she scarcely knew how she would manage for the rest of the year—there was the rent on the leasehold land to be met, interest on her debts, on which she was already behind, and all the year's running expenses to be paid. She worked out the minimum price that would allow her to carry on; surely the wool would bring her that. She determined to hope for no more; the bare sum would satisfy her. Meanwhile she continued her work with even more spirit and energy. There was no use in worrying.

But she was tired, and this winter her old neuralgia and sleeplessness had troubled her more than usual. There was so much to think of, so many details that wore away her day. She must have a hand in everything, be perpetually vigilant, delegating responsibility only where she could not avoid it. Later, when the boys were old enough, she told herself, she would relax a little of her generalship, but now she never felt secure unless she knew all that was being done on the station, and was sure that it was being gone about in the right way. The turnip-paddock was being sown, the orchard pruned, baits laid for the dingo suspected of lurking in Middle Paddock, yards being repaired out at the Bora, the Doughboy sheep being inspected for signs of fluke, and on all these she must keep a watchful eye. Meanwhile the work of the house could not be neglected either, and she and Weeta must cut out and sew the children's summer clothes, must make and mend and darn and polish and clean.

Weeta was teaching the younger children, but sometimes May would hear them their lessons. Little Phillip was growing fast, and must be watched and kept out of mischief. The sudden widening of the field in which she worked, the strain of unaccustomed problems and continual forethought, weighed on May heavily. It was difficult not to do too much and end the day exhausted, lying awake sleepless to con her problems over and over; deprived of Albert, she felt starved and comfortless.

She had had letters from her sister in the Hunter Valley, and from Dalwood and Bickham, urging her to rest for a few weeks and to visit the valley. With her usual clearheadedness, she knew that without a change and holiday she was in danger of illness from overwork, and she could not afford to be ill. The valley rose up in her mind like a friendly oasis in this sorrowful winter; she thought of the soft airs that had blown in her childhood through the Dalwood garden.

Perhaps, when the mid-winter pause descended on the work of the station, she would take the children and go for a few weeks, leaving the run to the superintendence of young Mr Murray. Nothing much could go wrong at this time of the year.

More and more, as the unlucky winter went on, she thirsted for the valley and for the companionship of old friends, of her family, of her clan. It was as though, welcomed back again, she would find there some kind of strength to carry on in the warm matter-of-fact atmosphere of those houses where she was remembered as little May Mackenzie.

For Dalwood she longed particularly. It was all changed now, she knew. Much of the big house was shut up and beginning to fall into decay, the vineyard and the great stables had fallen on bad days, and it seemed as though this depression, if it went on long enough, would put an end to the Dalwood story. She must see it again, impressing on her memory perhaps for the last time the sight and feel of the place she remembered as so stately and beautiful. The springs of her own life, she knew, lay there.

If the sight of its decay saddened her, that would be in keeping with this new phase of her own life, this end of her youth and of her youthful happiness. It would be fitting, she felt obscurely, to renew her links with the past before she took up again with determination the hard journey into the future.

She had only one thing to wait for before she set out. She had sent a sale mob of sheep travelling towards the western districts in the hope that they would strike a better market there; they had been on the road almost a month, and there had been no offers. Soon, however, they would reach the Moree sale-yards, and she hoped to hear of some buyer who would take them at a price, however low. If they found no sale this week, she would have to arrange to rent grass for them; it would be a loss. But she could not believe they would not sell; they were a good and even mob, and she had had high hopes when she sent them away.

Day after day, no word came from the agent, and at last the drover telegraphed to say that the grass on the stock reserve was giving out. She would have to arrange for agistment, then, while the mob waited for a sale. Against her will, events had begun to convince her that this depression would not be, as she had hoped, a temporary one that would pass away with the beginning of the new season. It even occurred to her that the sheep might not sell at all, or that she might have to offer them at a price that would scarcely pay for droving expenses.

As she waited from mail-day to mail-day, more bad news came. A selected mob of young bulls had been sold from Nulalbin earlier in the season, and the agents had not yet paid over the money due. It was little enough, but she had been counting on it to pay certain urgent bills. Now, a letter informed her, the agents had been declared bankrupt. She might, if she were lucky, get ten shillings in the pound on her money, but it would not be for a long time.

This was a blow, certainly, and for the first time May began to feel really alarmed. Rumours of banks about to close down, of big firms tottering, of further falls in prices, now filled the newspapers. She reckoned up her own chances. Wongwibinda was painfully vulnerable, and a few more such losses would put her in a position from which she could never hope to recover.

Accordingly, when a week or two later the agents wrote with an offer for the sheep, she telegraphed acceptance immediately, although the price would have seemed to her ridiculous a few weeks earlier. There would be no profit at all from the trip, after the drover and the agistment fees had been paid, but she felt herself lucky to have escaped so lightly. She would not send stock travelling for sale again, she vowed; she had been really frightened.

For a little while she wavered over taking this holiday; it seemed an extravagance at such a time, even though she need spend nothing except the train fares. But there was little she could do at Wongwibinda until the spring began; all work was up to date, and the worry of this last month had made her more than ever anxious for some respite in which she could gather her forces again. The children, too, were eager for the holiday.

At last the waggonette was brought out and cleaned, the packing was done, and she set off with the two girls, and Cecil and little Phillip. Arthur could not be spared from the work at Wongwibinda. Fifteen years old now, he was growing tall and serious; he looked thin and hard-worked, she thought with a pang, watching him as he rode alongside the waggonette. He was to come as far as Armidale and would drive the waggonette home again.

The spare bleached slopes of the winter landscape, crowded with small dark trees and ringbarked skeletons, rose and fell as the horses trotted briskly along the track to Armidale. It was a journey she had only taken once since her return from Rockhampton, and the change after her long seclusion pleased her, in spite of the memories that sprang up painfully at the sight of each familiar landmark.

With the horses doing a steady six miles an hour, they would reach Armidale in the early afternoon. She had business in the Lands Office and with the stock agency, and she occupied herself with planning out the afternoon as she drove, while the children chattered. They left Wongwibinda so seldom now that this trip and the thought of the train journey ahead was an excitement scarcely to be borne; even the long hours of the road did not quell them.

They had started early, and frost was still whitening the hills and steaming up in vapours along the eastern slopes when they had passed through the gate at Wongwibinda's boundary fence. The track was still unmade, passing through lonely country, most of it still leased by the few settlers for low-rent cattle pasture, houseless and unfenced. Few free-selectors had yet come here to trouble the leaseholders, for this part of the tableland was isolated and difficult of access, cut off from the coastal settlements by the steep gulfs and ridges of the plateau's edge, and from the closer towns along the tableland railway by bad roads and rough hilly country. The soil, too, was light, and water not plentiful; it was uninviting land, compared with the richer and more closely settled western side of the tableland.

Still, a few huts had gone up lately; the first of the invaders had moved in. She looked at the poor little dwellings with misgiving; brought up as she had been in the almost feudal atmosphere of Dalwood, she did not like the idea of this influx of landless men, who, so it was said, would pick the eyes out of the big runs. She thought of the expensively-cleared country along the track that ran through Wongwibinda, and bristled to defend what she held.

She had never shared Albert's attitude towards the bush workers and small settlers; she had been inclined to regard his stand in the shearers' strike, the year before his death, as altogether too soft. But she was thankful now that he had gone against her advice, employing union labour for the shearing and refusing the non-union men who had been employed by so many of the other run-holders they knew. It had seemed to her at the time that the strike, and the great maritime strike which had accompanied it, were blows aimed at the very foundation of her world; such things had never before been heard of; she had been more than a little indignant at his decision.

But last year it had certainly made her own task easier. The strike had been broken, but there had been stories since of much trouble in the sheds which had employed non-union labour—of ill-shorn fleeces, of delays and small defiances. She had had to contend with none of that.

Yet she felt deeply and instinctively that this influx of the small selectors was part and parcel of all that trouble. It was something she must stand against—a breaking down, a change in what (it seemed to her) should be immutable.

As the sun began to slope downwards from the zenith, and they drew nearer to the town, the signs of settlement increased. The road now ran here and there between fences, and from a faintly-marked track had become a wide and worn road. Patches of cultivation were to be seen here and there, where the confluence of slopes made room and shelter; the clearings grew more frequent. The small crowded black sallies and white gums of the higher eastern country had given place to box and stringybark trees, whose leaves with their lighter blue-green tints made this landscape seem less dark, more frank and open, than the hills and gullies of Wongwibinda.

It pleased May secretly, when they had reached Armidale and she set out to do her errands in the town, that the glances that greeted her were as respectful as ever and that the deference paid her was not merely that which, as a widow whose fortunes were known to be perilously in the balance, she might now have expected. This was not the easy and ordinary lip-service paid to property, whether secure or not, nor even the sympathetic admiration, half-sentimental and half-patronizing, that she had expected to find. She knew that her decision to keep Wongwibinda had aroused a good deal of comment, for it was not usual for women to take such work on themselves, and that few had expected her to succeed.

She could not help knowing that this new friendliness and respect sprang from genuine feeling. Indeed, she was already building up something of a reputation; her acuteness and the knowledge she had displayed of the work she was doing were now common gossip. She was said to be 'as good as a man' with stock, and not to be imposed upon in a bargain.

This acceptance, which secretly flattered her as much as a compliment on her looks or on her children could ever have done, went far towards increasing her confidence and assurance. If men with a life-long knowledge of stock asked her advice on a line of wethers or discussed with her the trends of the market, it was plain that she had already conquered some of the prejudice of which she was always a little afraid. Only on this basis of mutual equality could she establish her right to carry on the work which was now so important to her future and that of the children, and the knowledge that she was succeeding raised the colour in her cheeks and animated her talk.

Indeed, her very air and figure now carried a kind of mature authority, increased by her new responsibilities. When with Albert she had first come to this little town, on the way to Wongwibinda six years ago, she had still carried the marks of those bitter last years at Nulalbin; thin, tanned by the years of drought and heat, quieted by her lingering grief for her eldest son, it would have been possible to pass her over as merely another of the anonymous crowd of country women, hard-worked and undistinguished. who saw the town only at gala seasons. Now, with the six years of this keen pleasant climate, her figure had grown full and handsome and her air decisive; even this last year of loss and trouble had not taken the colour from her face nor all the gaiety from her brown eyes. She had grown conscious of the extent and limits of her power. Voices were lowered as she passed, strangers gave her a second glance, and she accepted this with a secret pleasure.

It was a delight to her, too, to be among other people again, after her long seclusion. She had already made many friends in the town, and families of her own relatives, too, now lived in the district, for the clan of the Wyndhams and Mackenzies was large and growing. She always drew strength from her contact with her human world, as she did from her love of the natural world.

It filled her with pleasure to know herself liked and admired, and though her tongue was often sharp and her perception of the weaknesses of other people even sharper, she contrived to keep and increase her popularity. She did not need to force herself to be amiable and gay, since the company of others always roused her and whetted her wit; she could, when she chose, be an excellent companion.

Still, in spite of her pleasure in the greetings and conversations that halted her on her way up and down the shopping street, it was not so pleasant to find that everyone seemed to regard the depression as worsening rather than improving. She heard many stories of runs already hard-hit, of acquaintances deep in trouble, of businesses bankrupted and abandoned; people shook their heads and were inclined towards gloom, and more labour trouble was predicted. Nevertheless, the town still seemed prosperous and calm enough, and though there was less spending than usual, there did not seem to be any lack of goods in the few shops. She decided to discount a good deal of the talk.

When she had packed herself and her children into the train next morning, she felt gayer and more alert than she had done since Albert's death. She had certainly been right to take this holiday; it was already beginning to soothe her again into normality, to restore her to ordinary life after the grief and strain of this last year. Things had begun to slip back into familiar perspectives; the world, she found, looked much as it always had, in spite of the blow which had so long deprived her of its companionable and reassuring warmth. Though the old happiness had gone, she had glimpsed again the possibility of a life not too intolerable, and her return into her world and the nature of her reception had restored the sense, which she found so necessary, of her own place in it.

Even the railway porter had given her especial attention; she and the children had a compartment to themselves, and the day promised to be pleasant. She settled down gaily with the children, joining in their games, telling them stories, pointing out through the train window the boundaries of properties whose names they knew, and the houses of the owners.

On the tableland, even since she had first come this way six years before, settlement had grown quickly. The railway line had helped to foster its growth; crossing the country, it now threaded on its length a series of little towns, whose bare English trees looked cold in the light westerly wind, whose ungainly little weatherboard and iron houses huddled together along rough streets that had once been bullock-tracks.

Along the creeks, willows had been planted here and there; they stood among the dead ringbarked timber whose wild and sombre gestures made the landscape seem desolate and bewildered. All seemed uncertain, in transition; the pale and shallow winter sky behind these timbered hills and untidy clearings seemed to echo their uncompromising bareness.

Yet May felt a sympathy for the very ugliness and newness of the unpainted houses, and for the evident narrowness of the lives they sheltered. This was a landscape at least of safety and of settlement; though clearly tamed by force, it had at any rate been tamed. To her the little towns seemed to triumph over the sullen opposition of the country; their ugliness was incidental and temporary, it was the conquest that counted.

She was pleased with every fresh mark of victory that she saw— the cultivated river-flats at the foot of the Moonbi Ranges, green with winter lucerne, the big haystacks, the windmills, the wheatfields. This was progress—the stream in which she herself moved, the struggle that she herself played a part in. She felt the pride of membership, of vicarious possession.

Fifty years ago, the Dalwood bullock-waggons, her mother with them, had travelled through this country, roadless then and largely unknown. The first few huts of settlement had scarcely appeared on the inland side of the Liverpool Range, and only a few cattle had then grazed on these plains. She remembered how, in her own childhood, the plains over the range had seemed to her wild and uncivilized, almost a legendary place; bushrangers had ridden there, hiding in the unexplored hills and valleys of the range, so that her uncles, riding north to Bukkulla, had always gone armed, and tales of Thunderbolt had haunted the valley with excitement and alarm.

It pleased her, now, to remember and tell the stories her grandmother had told at Dalwood long ago of the great waggon expedition and of the three years of wandering. The tales sounded strange against this altered landscape; so much had been done since then and so much had vanished that she could scarcely believe in some of her own memories, and it was hard to recognize places she had once known. Yet she was not yet forty; it was curious to have slipped so suddenly from one age into another, to find one's old world already gone and its features scarcely remembered.

The valley, too, she found when she had reached it, had changed. It was quieter than she remembered it; the old atmosphere of busy prosperity had gone from the little country centres. The depression had affected the new farms and the remaining old pastoral properties alike.

It was with these last that she felt herself allied; they were the remnants of the old life she had known; and it was against them that the bad times had struck hardest. Like Dalwood, they had shrunk into anachronisms; year by year they gave way to the smaller farms or disappeared entirely. The whole constitution of the valley seemed changed; the emphasis now lay with the big southern towns and the port at Newcastle; the coalmines had brought with them a different atmosphere and different interests.

Even the landscape she scarcely recognized, looking in vain for the landmarks of her childhood. With the passing of the big houses and the station families, and the springing up of small farms and cottages, the trees too had disappeared. Clusters of houses now stood where she remembered timber and pasture-land; the slopes and hills, once tree-covered, were now bare, and here and there marked with the slight scars of water-eroded gullies. The rich flats of the riverside, which had once been an unbroken plain of wheat, were criss-crossed with fences and patched with the alternating dark and pale of corn and plough. Set against her memory of it, this landscape seemed constricted, grown narrow and small.

The change was not only external, she found; the life of the valley had altered subtly with the landscape itself. Of the people she remembered, the dancers at those half-forgotten balls and parties, the singers at those evening gatherings and Sunday picnics, many had left or lost their homes altogether, edged out by the encroachment of the farms and the rising value of land, by drought or flood.

Southward the city flourished, and there were plenty of young people who left the land in impatience or ambition and went to find a different life there; northwards and westwards land was cheaper and more plentiful, and the old pastoralists had tended to leave the valley and begin their work again where the little farms and towns did not crowd them so closely.

Still, there remained enough of May's old friends and of the clan of her relatives to make a secure and welcoming circle into which she could pass, as if into protection. Her mother had died long ago, but of the cousins and sisters with whom she had grown up a number remained; at Bickham, too, the old life went on little altered.

Among her friends and contemporaries, the sorrow and tension which had darkened her last year fell away further; she ceased to be the head of a household, the director of an exacting enterprise, and became instead little May Mackenzie now grown into a woman. It was an exquisite relief at first to sink back into such mere womanhood—to join in the long quiet gossiping afternoons of sewing, to relax in confidences and reminiscences, to cease doing and thinking. This was what she needed; soon it would make her impatient and even a little scornful, but now she gratefully let herself be gathered into the strong web of kinship and common feeling, into the thread of women's talk, which, during her long years away from the valley, had continued binding all the happenings of clan and district into a strong and homely fabric that held the past securely to the present, the present to the future.

Safe in that web, she felt warmed and strengthened. It made up the background of all lives, and in it her own life was woven; the bitterness of this year and the joy of that other year when she had first met her husband were balanced in it impartially, merging equally into the threads woven by all the other lives there. No sorrow, no catastrophe, no success but took its place there, and the weaving continued for ever.

Moreover, she had to an unusual degree a respect for kinship and family ties; perhaps the old days at Dalwood among the crowd of Wyndhams and their relations had confirmed it in her. That large yet intimate group, with their ramifications in time and space; the English background of which they had always been so proud, keeping up correspondence through the years; the very fact that her own family was poor and a mere satellite of the big house—all had strengthened in her the respect for such ties.

She saw herself, in consequence, always as a member of a group united by common bonds; the size and importance of the group was a comforting assurance of her own security, and any defection from it or denial of its ultimate rightness had always pained her like a betrayal. To renew, as she now did, her membership in it was an additional fortification.

She began to find her life moving more and more into a clear perspective, her own preoccupations receding into the background. Day by day, the sharpest edges of her grief were blunted, as the thread of family talk, confidences and recollections wound it round. Death itself, to this continuing unit, the clan, was merely a well-known visitor; solitude became bearable, hardship a passing incident, unimportant in the long journey of a lifetime. She had been plunged again into the whole continuing story of humanity, and it had refreshed her being.

Yet, as she grew healthier and more normal, she began to be more and more eager for her return. Her renewed enthusiasm and energy did not easily tolerate the merely domestic and feminine routine of other women, and began to show itself in occasional caustic criticisms and small ironies uttered rather from impatience than from malice. The hard work and routine of her life at Wongwibinda were offset for her by one compensation; there she had the authority which she needed.

And after her comradeship with Albert, it irritated her to live in this atmosphere which implied a feminine submission and a male domination. In spite of the welcome she found everywhere, she felt a kind of censure mixed with the outward admiration of her friends, which was all the more annoying because it was seldom open. The word "unwomanly" was not exactly spoken, but there was a hint of it in the tone in which her cousins spoke of her bravery in taking on 'a man's work'. She felt the unspoken assumption, and fretted against it; she would be glad to be at Wongwibinda again, free to dictate her own terms to life and model it according to her mind.

The mail, at last, brought her the news she had long looked for with anxiety; the wool clip from last year's shearing had at last been put up for sale. She was almost afraid to open the envelope when it came, so much depended on this news. After her run of losses, she hardly dared expect any success. She was half-incredulous when she found that the whole clip had been sold, at a price much higher than she had dared to hope.

The Wongwibinda sheep, well cared-for and carefully chosen, had in that cool climate begun to do well; they had grown bright fleeces, with wool of a long fine staple. Until now, there had not been much demand for fine wools, but now, it seemed, they were coming into request. The heavier and coarser clips put up for sale that year had not done well, but about the Wongwibinda clip her agent was quite enthusiastic.

This unexpected success enormously raised her spirits. It seemed like an omen for the future, and her hopes and plans surged up again. She would have no need to worry now over the payment of this year's rents and interest; there would be a surplus out of which she might even hope to send Cecil to school next year, with careful management.

She grew more than ever anxious to return to Wongwibinda and take up the new season's work; the first hint of spring was in the wind, and on the hillsides wattle began to show in gleams of yellow. The cattle would be near calving soon, and the spring sowing must begin.

She had only one more visit to make; she must spend a day or two at Dalwood itself. She scarcely knew why she had put off her visit there until the last. Now she would go.

Old Dalwood had passed to one of George's younger sons and his family. With the depression, they could not afford to pay men to keep the place in its old order; half the rooms were closed, and as she drove up to the house with the children, their locked shutters and the silence struck unpleasantly upon her heart. She remembered how alert and gay the big house had always seemed when Grand-mama was alive, every window open and polished like a jewel, the paths bordered with meticulous flower-beds and the lawns scythed until they looked like moss. Now the house had an indefinable air of loss, and the shape of the garden had changed with the growth of trees and shrubs; something about the place seemed woebegone and old.

She was saddened too, to find how little of the land was left to the old estate. The pleasant slopes and flats where she had ridden as a child among the trees were fenced off and sold; shoddy little farms, rough cultivations ignorantly handled, stood there instead.

Little was left of the place, except the vineyard, and that too was falling on bad days. Depression had already halved the wine sales, and the brothers with obstinate pride refused to lower their prices to meet the times, or to make cheaper wines. Going through the big cellars, May saw hundreds of barrels stacked there unsold; half the hands had been turned off, and few men worked in the vineyards and cellars, where she could remember a perpetual bustle of coming and going. She thought of the prosperous days, when at harvest the vineyard had swarmed with cheerful workers, cutting the grapes, loading them and bringing them in; all now seemed mean and cheerless in comparison with those shining harvest-times of her remembrance.

The seventy acres of vines, some now more than fifty years old, looked untidy and neglected in their winter bareness. She walked down the long rows, leafless and brown, remembering how Albert and she had walked here in that autumn of their first meeting, among green leaves and great ripening clusters. She knew where the different vines were planted, and the wines they were fittest for—Hermitage, Burgundy, Lambruscat; remembered the sweet fermenting smell of the pulp and grapeskins that lay to rot near the presses, the cloud of tiny dancing ferment-flies that hovered there, the heat and translucence of those days, the stained hands of the men as they pressed out the grapes. All was silent now in the bareness of the last winter cold.

The house, bereaved as she herself was, had lost its grace and welcoming air; it gathered brooding in stone round the courtyard, where grass grew among the flagstones, and the pump at the well was broken. There were few flowers in the garden; it was too big to be kept in order in these pinched days; the lemon hedge that Margaret had planted in the garden's first years was old and diseased.

But the lavender-bush May remembered near the great heavy side-door had multiplied itself and grown riotously. She bent to it before she went indoors that evening, and rubbed a leaf in her hand. She would take a root to plant at Wongwibinda; it would serve to remind her of the old house, where she might never stay again.

For it was clear to her that Dalwood was sinking beyond hope of recovery. It filled her with helpless indignation to think of its loss, as though the place had somehow been betrayed. Too many people had leaned on its former security; family conflicts had weakened it, a combination of bad luck and mismanagement had completed what those dissensions had begun, and now the depression was bringing final ruin.

The thought of Dalwood ruined disturbed her far more than she cared to acknowledge. All her life the place had stood as a symbol of the rewards which her own race had won, and was still winning, from this new and savage country, and indeed from life itself. Progress, achievement, security, were to her the outward signs of the fulfilment of an inward trust; she had grown up with the struggle; those around her had built and conquered from mere wilderness a prosperous civilization. This was the creed on which she had based her life, and it was intolerable to find that what had been won with such difficulty could slip so easily out of the hands that should hold it—that victory could turn into failure, not because of mere external disasters, but through some hidden inexplicable weakness in the victors themselves.

This piece of land, brought in the space of one generation from untouched forest to obedient fruitfulness, should have remained, she felt inarticulately, as a glorious possession and memorial. Now George's struggle to found a house that would endure, as the English houses he knew had endured, was nullified as soon as his own life had ended. She rebelled against the thought of this; it was unbearable to imagine that perhaps Albert's work and her own would go for no more—that everything they had done might turn to chaff on the winds.

No, she would never believe that. Dalwood would be remembered; she herself would build up some memorial to it, though she scarcely knew what. She, at any rate, would profit by the lesson; she would build Wongwibinda more strongly than Dalwood had been built; there would be no betrayal there.

Leaving the old house, she took with her the root of lavender; it would be planted, not in nostalgia for the past, but as a promise for the future. Dalwood was lost; Wongwibinda would be held, a fortress against the years.

16 *THE SHOW, 1896*

SUMMER, PAST ITS height, was turning towards autumn. The grass in the paddocks, high and rich this year, had begun to bow with the weight of seed; every plant in the garden seemed absorbed in a fury of flowering; yellow light held the whole landscape still. Pears were ripening, and the apple-branches almost swept the ground, weighted down with fruit not yet sweet. Silver-eyes and rosella parrots descended on the orchard in flocks like blown leaves, and rose screeching at the noise of Paddy's shot-gun; as for Paddy himself, he stalked them through the trees in stealthy delight, hunting birds and ripe fruit at once.

The earliest of the apples must be brought in for jelly-making as soon as the Show was over, May decided. It made her indignant to find how much of the fruit already was pecked and knocked off the trees. But this had been a wonderful season for fruit; no late frosts had come to cut the blossoms and neither hail nor gales had spoiled the summer's growth. Her store-room was crowded with the jams and preserves that she and Weeta had made and bottled; the cherries that ripened in November, the apricots, the peaches and nectarines of full summer, the black and red currants, stood there in neat and richly-coloured rows. The shelves round the walls were quite full already, and more must be put up.

But there was no time to think of the apples now. She could only give the trees a passing glance of appraisement as she went on her way down to the yards. Arthur had brought in the cattle for the Show, for their final looking-over; tomorrow morning he would set out for Armidale with them, for the Show began in six days' time, and they must travel slowly or they would lose condition on the way.

She could see Arthur moving round the yards; his big chestnut tied nearby whinnied and stamped, full of the well-being of the good season. Arthur was a grown man now, she realized suddenly; slender and young as the shape of his body was, he walked with the horseman's give at the knees, and the muscular shoulders of the man accustomed to hard work. At this distance his attitude reminded her of Albert for a moment, touching a nerve in her that still too easily responded. Elsie and Phillip perched on the top rail of the yards, watching; as they caught sight of her coming down the slope from the house, they scrambled down to run to her, and she heard Arthur's reproving shout as the cattle moved in alarm.

It always pleased her that the children so readily left their own occupations for her company; she felt a possessive pride in them and in their straight and healthy limbs and comely looks. Elsie was thirteen now; May planned to send her to school in Sydney soon, for that could be afforded. Phillip, seven years old, was outgrowing his childish shape and beginning to shoot up, although she liked to think him only a baby still. But all her children, she thought with pleasure, were good to look at; all of them were tall, strong and straight-boned. She took unconscious credit to herself for their physical development.

In the yard the three Show beasts, grass-fed and brought in only lately from their quiet paddocks, moved uneasily as she approached and then stood still again. She leaned cautiously through the rails and ran her eye keenly over them while she and Arthur talked. They pointed out to each other all over again the merits of each beast, recalled their breeding points, discussed their chances and the possible opposition they would meet.

The sun beat down warmly, and the cattle stirred the dust in the yard as they moved round, till, growing accustomed to the unfamiliar sound of voices, they gathered sleepily in the shade of the young pine beside the yard fence, twitching their tails against the dancing summer flies.

May savoured the moment with zestful satisfaction. This was a time of reward, and she was entitled to enjoy it. Her eyes, moving over the pretty red and white heifer and the shapely and solid young bulls, found nothing lacking; the fine full uniformity of flesh and colour in each beast, the bloom on their even coats, delighted her. In the existence of each beast, bred on her own land and by her own forethought, she had a controlling hand; it was the pleasure of creation that filled her as she looked at them. The smell of the yards, of the cattle, the jingle of the horse's bit as he stamped and tossed his head against the flies, and the children's voices, made a familiar background to her pleasure.

They were fine cattle, no doubt of it; they were, also, the tangible representation of her work, the fruit of her years of difficulty and self-denial. 'For lo, the winter is past, the rain is over and gone'— the words occurred dimly in her mind as she moved round the yard to inspect Beauty's shoulder; she had torn it a little on a stake, as a calf, but the mark now scarcely showed. May went on discussing with Arthur the question of how they should be fed when they reached the showground.

This Armidale Show was to be a great occasion; the first to be held for years, it celebrated both the passing of the long depression and the beginning of what seemed likely to be a time of such prosperity as had never before been known. It was, too, to be May's private celebration of her own victory. Wongwibinda was now hers, secure and beyond doubt.

Land values had soared so high, now, that the debt under which she and Albert before her had laboured so long was wiped out almost overnight. And she had not compromised at all; nothing of Albert's original plans for the run's development had been neglected, no matter how she had pinched and scraped to carry them out. All had gone towards the building up of the station, and now she stood triumphantly justified. Arthur was twenty years old; much of the burden had fallen on him, and he had never had the schooling she had hoped for him, but Cecil she had managed to send to Armidale to school, and he would soon be old enough to leave and return home to help her. The heaviest of her tasks were over.

This was the first time she had decided to enter cattle from the Wongwibinda stud, in the Show. It was as though she had been reserving that moment, waiting until she was certain that the gesture was justified and would not be annulled by fate. Accordingly she felt it now almost as a rite of thanksgiving, a kind of solemnity, a harvest-home.

When Arthur had left with the cattle, her own bustle of preparation began. There were clothes in the making, to be fitted and finished; the waggonette must be new-varnished, the harness cleaned and dees and buckles polished till they shone. Bags and valises must be packed with the family's gala wear: Weeta's ball-dress, which had been a centre of excitement for weeks, May's own new dresses, in which she had allowed herself unaccustomed expense and frivolity, the children's clothes, immaculate and stiff with newness; all must be folded just so, the pleats pinned, the ruffles laid straight in paper backings. All these she and Weeta had made and were properly proud of.

The wooden frames containing Weeta's paintings were packed and screwed down with special care; they too were to be entered in the Show, with the preserves and jellies that had turned out especially well. The children felt the whole gravity of the occasion; their excitement was hushed by it until anticipation seemed almost too great to bear.

The waggonette, when everything and everyone was disposed in it, was so full that every corner was taken up. Mrs Maguire and her children were fitted in somehow. Bill Naylor and his family were to drive in in the station buckboard. Paddy and Minnie and the rest of the station blacks were taking the old buckboard and the cart. The morning was benevolently warm, and the few clouds drifted high and calm, promising a run of fine weather.

All the morning, while the horses trotted at a steady and energetic pace, the waggonette's passengers went through their repertoire of songs. Everyone sang, down to the youngest of the Maguires—Christy Minstrels' favourites, old choruses and rounds, sentimental drawing-room ballads and the hymns May loved to lead. At lunchtime they pulled up at a creek-crossing, unpacked the big basket of food and boiled the billies. When they passed Paddy and Minnie and the rest, who had started early with slower horses, they shouted and waved as though they had met old friends whom they had not seen for months.

It was late afternoon when they reached the town. The streets were crowded with every imaginable kind of vehicle; the hotel yard, when they reached it, was full of smart sulkies and buggies, and the yard hands were busy unharnessing and feeding the horses. Inside the hotel there was a buzz of excitement and greetings. The Show did not begin until tomorrow, but most of the country people were in town already. Everyone knew everyone else; and for those whose holidays were rare there was a sense of release and jollity in the air, of prosperity and open purses.

There was a circus in town, and its handbills fluttered everywhere in startling reds and blues. Parties were in full swing. The bars of the main-street hotels were filled with a riotous crowd, where young and old men, land-owners, stockmen and bush workers besieged the counters with cheques in which a year's hard and monotonous work briefly fruited. May as she walked through the street listened distastefully to the inhuman babble of noise from the bar doors, and drew the children to the other side of the road rather than pass them, for every now and then they swung apart and a noisy irruption of shouting men tumbled, pugnacious or maudlin, into the street.

She had found in the hotel a crowd of friends and members of her own clan, with their children; a dinner-party was arranged, and tonight everyone was to go to the circus. But first of all she must go out to the showground, for Arthur would be established there with the cattle by now; send, attling the children on the balcony of the hotel in Weeta's charge, to watch the crowds in the street and to fraternize with cousins who were almost strangers to them, she slipped off alone.

The cattle were paddocked and safe, down at the showground, and when she reached them Arthur was forking hay from the waggon-load left at the ground for the Show. She took a handful and smelt it, but she was satisfied; they were not palming off mouldy stuff, as she had feared. Again she and Arthur looked the cattle over; they had stood the trip well, and though they had snorted at first when the hay was thrown down for them, preferring the green grass and clover of their rearing-paddocks, they had taken to it at last and were eating as they should.

Now Arthur must escort her on a tour of inspection of the cattle they were to face tomorrow in the judging. There were other owners here on the same errand, but she was the only woman among them; they greeted and talked with her in embarrassed equality, but she knew that there were not many among them whose knowledge and judgement were greater than her own when it came to cattle, and she took no notice of their uneasiness at a woman's presuming in this way to walk through the territory of men. She and Arthur looked over the cattle and discussed them, deciding at last that the three from Wongwibinda were not likely to disgrace the Wrights.

'Beauty is sure to win her class,' May said at last, 'if the judge has a pair of eyes; and Dandy has a good chance. I haven't seen anything to beat Hercules yet, though they say that big animal is a certainty; Hercules is far deeper at the shoulder. Now you'd better fix up here and come back to the hotel with me; it's time to dress for dinner. Your room looks rather dark; if you can't see to tie your tie properly, you'd better knock on my door and I'll do it for you.'

At the circus that night, she found her heart miraculously light—light as it had not been for years. She sat straight in the chestnut-coloured silk which she knew matched her eyes and brightened her hair, where yet was scarcely a touch of grey. Phillip beside her sat holding her hand and gazing raptly at the clowns. Along the bench beyond sat the rest of her children—well-dressed, good-looking, a family to be proud of; and on the other side sat a family of cousins, with whom at the moment she felt on the best of terms, for Bertha had admired Weeta's eyes and complexion, and everyone had been very amiable at dinner.

In the sawdust ring the clowns and performing dogs tumbled, and she laughed out like a young girl; how many years was it since she had been to a circus or a theatre? She could scarcely remember.

Next day the sun rose hot and the air was still; at the showground, everyone was certain, it would be scorching. Cecil helped the grooms to harness the horses early. The ground was not a mile away, but it was the thing to take one's own vehicle there. With the horses unharnessed and tied in the shade, the waggonette would serve as a meeting-place, a shelter in case of rain, and a shade from the promised heat of the day.

Along the rough sapling rail that marked the show-ring, buckboards, waggonettes, gigs, even a few carriages, had begun to range themselves. Children ran everywhere, the girls in starched sunbonnets, the boys in straw hats; family groups arranged themselves, people wandered from group to group, greeting friends, introducing newcomers. The later arrivals hesitated, clotted, gravitated finally to their places, invisibly sifted by the meshes of social acceptance, some into the sections where the land-owners congregated, some to the other side of the ring near the sideshows, where the townsfolk and the bush workers mingled.

Here had risen a motley row of stalls and tents, where spruikers dressed in red flannel shirts, in white cord kneebreeches and spangled caps and cummerbunds, shouted and gestured in hoarse invitation. Pies steamed on trays beside smoky wood-stoves, braziers sent up wavering trails of heat, an ice-cream stall and a booth where jam-tarts and gaily-coloured sweets were ranged did roaring business.

The mixture of competing voices, the music of the barrel-organ where the hurdy-gurdy merry-go-round stood beyond the pavilion, and of the gipsy band that played outside the fortune-teller's tent, the cries of children and the occasional whinnies of horses or bellowing from the cattle-yards, all joined in a joyous background of noise, indistinguishable and overwhelming as the din of a waterfall. The children darted everywhere, intoxicated with the unfamiliar noise and colour, open-mouthed and with burning faces; restricted to the line where the vehicles stood and sternly forbidden, as yet, to go farther, they scrambled and tumbled between the wheels and round the shafts, unable to keep still.

Soon the cattle were to be judged, and May chose a judicious resting-place for the waggonette, where a tree would give shade towards noon-day and where the cattle-yards were easily in view. In the ring, the horse events had begun, and horses were trotting like polished toys that glittered in the sun; but May, having settled everything to her liking, went across to the yard where the cattle were one by one being brought in to meet the judges' eyes.

The first class, for bulls under three years, was being judged; Hercules was entered in this, and May looked over the beasts as keenly as the judges themselves, discussing points and breeding with the owners who watched with her. The bulls, brought in from their paddocks without stabling or handling, milled uneasily in the yards, while the men in charge of them manoeuvred them carefully here and there to give the judges a clear view. It seemed to May that they were taking an unnecessarily long time.

There was Arthur now, with Hercules; the bull was moving well. The local stock agent paused beside her as he bustled through the crowd. 'A fine beast, Mrs Wright,' he said approvingly. 'I've a buyer for him; I think we should get a good price. He looks the winner to me.'

And sure enough, after a brief conference, the judges turned to Arthur with the blue ribbon. There was a brief burst of claps from the crowd around; May's heart swelled as Arthur came to the yard rails and gave her the ribbon. First, in the first event of the day; and as she answered the congratulations of the little crowd that formed round her, she felt the colour burning in her cheeks.

If only Albert, and old Grandfather Wyndham, could have been here today! Momentarily, she felt near tears, remembering the days when she had ridden among old George's cattle on Dalwood, learning from him the points of a good beast; Hercules was descended from those cattle, as were all the Wongwibinda stud. That was something for pride, she felt; and she and Arthur looked at each other with a mutual understanding.

Dandy's class came soon, and she had another ribbon to add to the first; for he took second place. Well, that was what she had expected; and now she had to wait what seemed a dreary time until the females were judged. Beauty was her especial pride; and when her class came in, the judges hardly hesitated before adding another blue ribbon. May had already had two offers to buy her, but she was not for sale at any price; she would be taken home to the stud, for her calves would be valuable.

May went back to the waggonette, receiving congratulations all the way. She fairly glowed with pleasure. As she had hoped, this was her day, her compensation and reward. Arthur had had an offer for Hercules which secretly staggered him after the years of depression and low prices, but when he came to consult her she held out decisively for more. She knew that she would get her price, and now the agent reported that the buyer was coming round and would probably pay what she asked.

Dandy, too, was sold. Apart from this, she knew that her triumphant morning had been a good advertisement for the Wongwibinda cattle and that she would now be able to demand higher prices for her stud beasts. But, above all and more secret to herself, there was her own more personal reward—the new respect and admiration of the eyes that turned on her, the taste of importance and influence that warmed her like wine.

For she had not forgotten the head-shaking of her world when she had decided to keep Wongwibinda and manage it herself. It could not be done, they had said; impossible to manage a station, bring up a growing family, and remain womanly; impossible in any case to cope with such a load of debt; she was headed for certain failure. Now, no doubt, the jealous ones would find other matter for criticism; but she had won her victory and could afford her pride. Momentarily, at least, she was the centre of admiration and praise, and holding her head high she drank it in. It was what she needed.

Now she could spare time to look at the rest of the Show; she would go round the ring to the iron shed that served as pavilion, where the handicrafts and cookery exhibits, flowers and vegetables were displayed. Weeta's pictures were there, and the Wongwibinda preserves, and the judging must be over by now; and Phillip was growing restive to see the sideshows and visit the ice-cream booth.

The elder children had gone off with their own friends, and were roaming goodness knew where, among the gipsies' fortune-telling tents perhaps, or where the Indian dancer and the giant from Africa stared from luridly-painted canvas, three times as large as life. She gave Phillip a shilling to spend, and sent him off with his young cousins, and she and Bertha walked off round the ring, glowing with warmth under their raised parasols, and greeting acquaintances as they went.

The pavilion was crowded; its iron roof reflected the heat downwards, and the rough undressed plank floor was already littered with paper, half-sucked sweets lost by crying children, printed handbills and advertisements screwed up and thrown away. She saw Weeta and her friends just disappearing from the other door, too far away to be called back; the judging must be over. She and Bertha edged along the rows of trestle-tables.

There stood the bottles of jams and jellies, labelled in flourishing copperplate handwriting, and the Wongwibinda collection was well to the fore here too. She stopped awhile, commenting and comparing, then dragged Bertha on past sponge-cakes and iced plum-cakes, embroidered cloths, sprays of artificial flowers made of fish-scales and nutshells, prodigious pumpkins and melons, heavy staring dahlias as big as cabbages, rank-smelling bunches of prize marigolds.

The sun sent a wide beam slantwise through the door, picking out in dusty limelight a bunch of paper flowers, a bottle of home-made cherry wine from which a trembling red light fell. All seemed to swim in the dusty haze under the dark cobwebbed cave of the roof. And there among the painstaking crayon vases of flowers and the copies of Landseer reproductions she ·saw with delight that Weeta's pictures were prominently displayed. 'First Prize,' she read, leaning over someone's shoulder, and shone with renewed delight. Really, the Wrights were doing wonders today; not that she had expected less, as she explained to Bertha. Her cup was overflowing.

Round the tables and along the tiers of shelves the crowd shuffled, oh-ing and ah-ing, disparaging and admiring. There were Paddy and Minnie, leaning on a trestle; Minnie held a fat red velvet pin-cushion (Now how had she got hold of that? It was to be hoped that she had not let her fingers wander again, as she had done with May's rhinestone stick-pin); Paddy wore a vivid blue and purple handkerchief round his neck. Eating toffee-apples, they beamed shyly across at her and May waved back.

But across the way May saw the roped-in space where agricultural machinery was being displayed. She had looked at embroideries long enough; the shed was stuffy and hot. 'Come along, Bertha. I see that new disc-plough is over there; I must really go and look. Arthur thinks it would suit our depth of soil.' 'Oh, May, don't be

so practical. Just wait a moment, I want to see how that stitch is done
—oh, very well, I'm coming.'

But though May edged out thankfully with the crowd into the
open air, she was already promising herself that she would come
back again this afternoon and look at those pictures once more. It was
the blue ticket underneath that had pleased her most. 'First Prize,'
she murmured to herself, and briskly began asking the machinery
salesman searching questions.

Among the tents and their violently-coloured signs, the children
wandered, fingering sixpences. The barkers with their hoarse voices
and wooden grins, the women with red-and-white cheeks and bright
sateen skirts, with swinging necklaces and gold buttons, the nobly-
stripped boxers, the balancing acrobats, the trapeze artists, the stalls
of clay dolls and brandysnaps, the shies and the barrel-organs assailed
every sense and tempted every weakness.

Soon their money would be gone, and the day was scarcely begun.
Soon they must go back to the rows of buckboards and sulkies, for
it was almost lunchtime. Flushed and exalted, throats rasped with
dust, they put off the moment as long as they could, and struggled
back at last with their trophies, only anxious for another dole of
sixpences and freedom to wander off again.

Back at the waggonette, May spread out the brown rug in a patch
of shade, Weeta unpacked the basket, Cecil went for boiling water,
carrying the tea-billies. All the related and friendly families had
joined forces for lunch, sitting on rugs and travelling-cushions around
the spread cloths; they made a great ring, a magic circle of conservatism, excluding the outer world.

There was unspoken rivalry among the women as the baskets
were unpacked; chicken patties, cakes and biscuits were handed round
with jealous watchfulness. 'You must try a piece of mine; it's a
new recipe.' The gentlemen opened their waistcoats, stretched out
and began to make jokes; the children broke into squabbles and
were rebuked.

Lunch over and the baskets and cloths packed up again, May
felt the day becoming desultory, a mere aftermath to her morning.
She settled herself in the waggonette to chat with cousins and to
watch the horses. Tonight was to be the Show Ball; she wavered for

a while over whether she would go, or whether she could leave Bertha to chaperon Weeta.

But no, everyone cried, she must go, of course she must. It would be good for her, just for once, to have a little gaiety; how many years was it since she had been to a ball? Why, not since she had been a child of seventeen with her hair still not put up; for before she had had the coming-out ball her grandfather had promised, she was already engaged to be married. All the more reason, everyone said, that she should go tonight.

But dressing in the evening for dinner and the ball, she looked without pleasure at the mirror between the twin candlesticks. Settling her hair carefully into the conventional curls and folds, she went over the events of the day; her victories won, she felt somewhere in her heart the twitch of sadness, and for a moment tears were not far away.

After all, she was forty-one—forty-one, and Albert dead six years. If he had been here—then her triumph would have had worth and meaning. And yet if he had indeed been here, the triumph would not have been, as now it was, her own.

She dismissed the treacherous thought at once, as she dismissed the threat of weariness, and neither of them was there any longer. Finishing her toilet, she turned decisively from the mirror. The acetylene gas-flame roared and flickered on the other side of the room, where Weeta sat mending a stitch gone in her day dress. Her mother thought she looked charming in her new ruffled cream-coloured silk with the little yellow roses; and as for May herself, she knew that the brown velvet suited her, strictly though it was cut; and Weeta pinned a bunch of pansies on the shoulder to set off her eyes.

After all, the evening promised to be enjoyable. The pleasant buzz in the hotel dining-room, the tables crowded together, the air of festivity and the prosperous look of new and rustling evening-gowns and dress-clothes, raised her spirits again, and she had her table in fits of suppressed laughter as she commented on the day's events and the get-up of acquaintances as they came into the room.

Then came the ball, in the draughty barn-like town hall where bunches of ferns and gum-tips were nailed on rough unlined walls.

But as soon as she went in, with Arthur and Weeta beside her, she was launched immediately and in her element, the centre of a small crowd, congratulating, complimenting, almost competing.

That in itself was delightful; and when she caught an unexpected glimpse of herself in a mirror set among the leaves on the wall, she was surprised at her own youthful look. Tall and neat-waisted, the dominating figure in the smart brown velvet smiled with a gaiety of gesture, spoke with an animation, that made her think her own image a stranger for the moment.

No, she was not dancing, she answered the eager gentlemen; she had only come to chaperon her daughter and watch the ball. But when she turned round, Weeta had already vanished with her partner and Arthur was nowhere to be seen. Well, just one or two, perhaps. . . . But by the time the supper waltz began she was glowing; she had danced every dance. Where were Arthur and Weeta? For a little while she had quite forgotten them.

Dawn was not far off when at last she settled into bed with a sigh of comfort. She was tired enough by now, but she lay awake for a time while the excitement of the night died down in her blood, musing over all that had happened. The flattering air that had blown round her she accepted at its true worth; her shrewd eye had seen through much of it easily enough. Nevertheless, it had its significance. This was her moment; she had climbed the wave and now she rode it.

After today, what was there left for her to do? With one son now a man, another soon to become one, must she step back bit by bit from the leadership, resign it to her children, move farther and farther into the chimney corner?

No, there was something in her now that demanded more yet—much more. She had scarcely begun to taste the joy of power; she had only just found out what strength she had to call upon. Today had been only the first milestone; there would be many yet. No one need think she would be content, after this, to sit and sew like her sisters, like her friends; she had other things to do.

She thought of the sly rumours which, although she had pretended to ignore them, she knew very well were going the rounds. Such and such a gentleman was very attentive; perhaps after all the handsome widow's devotion to her husband's memory might be overcome. . . . No, that she could not even consider. The thought of remarrying made her withdraw in disgusted rejection.

None of the men who had danced attendance on her tonight, none of the men she knew or could imagine knowing, were fit, to her mind, to hold a candle to Albert. She mocked them mercilessly at the very thought, remembering this one's conceit, that one's weakness, the other's bullying manner. No, she was alone and strong, and would remain so. If she needed men to carry out her plans, had she not three sons?

Grey dawn began to move into the room; her velvet dress hung inert against the pallor of the wall, a mere shape without detail in this disenchanting light. Well, the Show was over, she thought drowsily, and slid gradually down into deep sleep.

17   THE DECISION

AFTER THE CLIMAX of the Show, the rest of her year passed quietly, through winter to spring and on in familiar rhythm to early summer. Outwardly her life was as usual, but within she was restless and preoccupied. She had not forgotten her resolve that her work must continue, and now, in the uneventfulness of the accustomed routine, she had begun to feel Wongwibinda's new prosperity, her own comparative ease, as a threat to the balance of her life. The load which she had carried was falling away bit by bit; soon Arthur would be twenty-one, and she knew that already her leadership of the family had ceased to be so necessary to them. She felt a bitter though obscure sense of loss and disappointment as the burdens slipped from her shoulders.

She remembered how much alone she had been when Albert died—how shelterless. The children still so young, the plans Albert had made, and left uncompleted, even the sapling fruit-trees and the young plants in the garden, had all seemed to demand her saving care and protection. In the effort she had made to meet the call on her, she had not spent herself but had rather enlarged and strengthened her own powers. Now in this first period of calm, she looked up to find the saplings grown into trees, the children taller than herself and as strong. Once again she was surrounded by sheltering arms.

In the very promise of that shelter of which she had once been so bitterly in need, she found the cause of her new uneasiness. She wanted it no longer; it irked her to feel the cramp and restriction of ordinary feminine bonds again descending on her. It was her habit, now, to hold her own; she did not wish to let the direction and leadership pass into other hands, even though they were her sons'.

Over these six years since Albert's death, she had altered more than she acknowledged to herself. Sometimes that gap of time seemed to close, and she would remember with piercing clearness a gesture or a look of his, or something he had once said. At such times her

P

grief would break out again for a little, with a strength that took her by surprise; and then only hard absorbing work, the sense that she was needed and that her capacities were being used to the utmost, drove her sorrow back into the privacy where she felt it to belong.

It was work, hard demanding work, that had kept her from weakness and over-indulgence in her grief; and the sense that idleness now threatened her—or, if not idleness, then a life that left unused half her capacities—frightened her in part because of the gap that would be made in her defences against loneliness. She had known lonely and unwanted women; looking into the abyss of their lives she shrank back at the thought that she should ever be like them.

Accordingly her mind was busy, as the year passed. She allowed herself no relaxation, working on though it was no longer so necessary; riding through the paddocks on her grey horse, with a keen eye everywhere as usual. Albert would have been proud of the station, if he could have seen it now, his plans for it brought to fruition.

The ringbarking he had not lived to finish was all done, the pastures growing, the landscape altered. He would scarcely know the orchard and garden, the trees had grown so tall; dozens of small changes in the place itself would make it unfamiliar. He would scarcely know the children themselves, especially little Phil whom he had known only as a baby. Everything had grown; all outlines had blurred and altered with time until the world itself seemed a different place, its very aims and ambitions subtly changed.

And perhaps, fiercely as she would have combated the idea, the greatest change was that in herself. The plant that had grown in shelter had altered its form and habit, its shelter taken away; of necessity she had learned her new air of authority and decision, even though her old charm and gaiety could still flower as they had done before. She had had to remember so much, to encompass so much, that she felt that in a sense Wongwibinda was her own creation.

Every detail of its organization, every crop taken off the cultivations, every calf born, every mob of sheep bought or sold, the shape and function of each fenced-in paddock, the map of each creek, its watershed and direction, the cost of each piece of clearing and fencing done and the reason for it, rose exactly into her mind as they were needed, and she dealt with her problems with clarity and precision.

She had not failed the tasks that the land had set her, and in wrestling with them she had come to love them.

Now she was maturing other plans. She had mentioned them to no one as yet, but she had quietly prepared her ground, sitting late in the little office room and calculating as nearly as she could what assets she now had, what money could be raised if there were need, and what margin of safety she could reckon on. She felt a decision waiting for her, ripe to be taken.

It was towards the end of Cecil's final school holidays. She woke early, with a feeling of controlled excitement. Today she would ride, with Cecil and Elsie, up to the Doughboy paddock to see how the new sheep were settling down. The Wongwibinda boundary fence crossed the hills there, some nine miles from the homestead—that fence that Albert had had built to keep out the dingoes, at such expense, and had so agonized over.

She would ride the boundary to make sure that no wires were broken or repairs slummocked; men were camped on the clearings, suckering the new growth on the ringbarked trees, and she would look at the work and estimate how much more needed to be done. Then she would ride across to Burke's selection and ask if Mrs Burke's sprained wrist were better, and make final arrangements for the Burke boys to take on the rouseabouts' jobs at the shearing which began next month. She dressed in her well-worn riding-habit, and began to brush her hair—still bright brown, still long and wavy—with vigorous strokes, while she planned the day.

Outside her window, the square of garden it overlooked still lay in the shade of the young pine-trees, pale with dew, but on the eastern side of the trees she could see the first of the early summer sunlight, and magpies sang and squabbled on the lawns. Dressed, she went briskly out into the long hall, noting as she went the familiar morning noises and the meaning of each. The younger children were up and dressing; she must put out another shirt for Phillip, for she had noticed a rip in the blue one yesterday.

In the dining-room she could hear a rattle of crockery and spoons where the little half-caste housemaid was laying the breakfast-table. From the yards came Arthur's voice, discussing the day's work with Naylor. She moved about the house quickly, arranging this, putting that in order. It would be a beautiful day; thrushes and magpies outside in the trees joined in a burst of song to which half her mind listened with pleasure. Birds—she had always loved them. She distrusted Weeta's tribe of cats on their account, keeping a watchful eye on their movements and hunting them from the garden where her pretty diamond-sparrows and double-bars and finches nested.

She went up the wide concrete causeway that led to the kitchen buildings, and to the courtyard around which the store-rooms and dairy were built. Grapevines were trellised along the causeway and over the yard—pink and purple Isabellas and long black muscatels, and as she went towards the kitchen she caught sight of a great spotted caterpillar, horned and green, clinging to the stem of a grape-leaf. She pulled it off as she went by—the vines must be sprayed and examined this week, for the fruit was setting. She must look out the sulphur and make certain Maguire remembered how it should be used.

In the kitchen Mrs Naylor stirred a great panful of scrambled eggs and a big iron pot of porridge. Toast crisped and plates warmed on the whitewashed brick shelves beside the big range; pans of dough for the day's bread-making were set under white cloths to rise. May crossed to the range and threw the caterpillar quickly into the fire that roared red-mouthed between the polished black doors of the range. She stood talking with Mrs Naylor a few minutes, while her quick glance went round the room.

Its tables, shelves and floors were scrubbed to meticulous bareness. On the open porch outside stood piles of clothes in wicker baskets, for yesterday had been washing-day at the laundry shed that stood down by the creek below. Today they would be ironed, and Minnie, early for once, stood already at the ironing-table damping and rolling them, and singing quietly to herself. The washed clothes smelt clean and pleasant even through the more urgent scents of breakfast.

From the eastern window a pattern of moving leaves and sunlight fell from the grape-trellis and a noise of bees came in at the window from the bushes of Spanish broom and cabbage-roses that lined the yard fence. It pleased her that for a moment her own house reminded her of a bee-hive, busy at satisfactory tasks, each member in some proper place. The day ahead was planned and easy stretching out with a quiet assurance of work to be done and leisure afterwards.

The day's orders given, she went outside to talk to Maguire, who had finished the milking and was washing in the yard before breakfast. First the vines must be sulphured; she made sure that he understood what was to be done. Then there was the garden—the vegetables that must be sown for succession, the seedlings to be transplanted, the lawns that needed mowing again.

'That native cat was about again last night, Maguire,' she said. 'Arthur went out with the gun, but it was too dark to get him. He was round the chicken-roosts again.'

'He's a troublesome one, frightening the hens that way. I'll lay up with a gun for him when the moon's fuller. He can't get into the yard, though, Mrs Wright.'

'Well, I was looking at the roof there only yesterday, and there's one place where the pickets are loose. I think you'd better fix that up before this evening, Maguire; we don't want him to get in, with the two hens sitting and everything just beginning to lay so well. Come down and I'll show you what needs to be done.'

The two black hens sat in their coops silent and watchful as she pointed out the weakened pickets. Green acacia trees planted for shade were just bursting into creamy bloom. The other hens and cocks, let out to scratch, strutted along chuckling and murmuring. Yes, these two pickets needed replacing, and another wire had better be run right along the fence. She over-ruled Maguire's arguments; certainly it would take an hour or two to do, but the cabbage seedlings could quite well wait until tomorrow to be transplanted.

In the dairy young Ned Maguire was finishing the washing-down of the shelves and floor; hearing his whistling as she came back along the flagged path where honeysuckle flowered, she turned in through the door. The eggs were kept in the dairy for coolness, and she had suddenly remembered that the pullets had begun to lay; she must make sure that their eggs were not put away to be preserved, but kept for the table. Elsie and Phil loved the little brown eggs.

Cold air hung like a pool of water over the dairy's stone floor. Under the shelves big earthenware crocks stood, slowly filling from day to day with salted butter to be kept for winter use; the buckets of warmed milk from this morning's milking were set under clean butter-muslin for the cream to rise, and from the weighted cheese-press lye slowly dripped into a pan. A dishful of eggs, tenderly-shaped ovals of pink and brown, stood by the cream that was to be today's churning, for today Weeta would make the butter.

The still cold air pleased her, and the scent of honeysuckle from the vine over the door. She stood a moment or two to talk to young Ned, who stood bashfully wringing out his steaming cloths, his hands red and boiled-looking. But far down in the house the break-fast-bell began to ring, and she went quickly back along the stone pathway under the vines, calling out as she went a good-morning to Naylor, who had come to breakfast with his wife and daughters and the Maguires in the big kitchen dining-room.

Down in the long dark room with its great cedar table, the children and the guests stood behind their chairs and waited for her to come in. The clock on the mantelshelf began to chime as she went quickly to her big chair at the head of the table—seven o'clock. Then the chairs were pulled out and everyone began talking.

The dining-room was high-ceilinged and long, with French windows opening to the front verandah, where yellow climbing roses and a few last sprays of wistaria were now in bloom. The big dining-table almost filled the room; its white damask table-cloth shone dully with starch, and the silver dishes and cutlery shone too. The whole room was repeated upside-down in miniature in each bright spoon, and the knives and dishes reflected the red of the tasselled plush curtains. In the middle of the table, Weeta had arranged a bowl of roses and larkspur, which May noticed with approval as she took up the big silver ladle to serve out the porridge.

She always liked meals to have a certain dignity, the solemnity of a family ritual. Even in the hardest years, she had managed to preserve something of that dignity in her household, a reminiscence of the great family dinners at Dalwood, where she had once sat as the least of the hierarchy and observed the ceremonies on which George and Margaret had always insisted.

Now that money again flowed freely, she had begun to spend it on the things that were dear to her—beautiful table-linen, good silver, rich-looking curtains and plain heavy furniture. The dining-room was beginning to look as she would have it; nothing was skimped or scanted, nothing over-extravagant. It had about it the air she wanted—an air of ceremonial intimacy.

She herself enjoyed, as she sat in her big chair at the head of her table, her own acknowledged ascendancy. She knew herself not merely the nominal, but the real head of the family, the beloved and obeyed. It was always her opinion that clinched an argument, her way of thinking to which in the end the household was converted, her advice that was asked in large and small matters; and her relationship to her five children was a treasure of which she was both proud and jealous.

That they should not be loyal to her was unthinkable; but in return she was unshakably loyal to them. The praise of guests and friends, whether for Weeta's painting, Elsie's piano-playing, or the boys' abilities, redounded to her own credit as well as theirs and enhanced the value of their position among them, but her love for them was not merely possessive but self-sacrificing. Such praise warmed her and forged her bonds with her children even closer, and this was one reason why she so enjoyed dispensing hospitality, now that she could again afford it.

Yet it was not only for this reason that Wongwibinda was so open and generous a house, and that cousins and friends so continually came and went nowadays. She had not forgotten her promise to herself, that, in her life at least, Dalwood should find its continuity. Dalwood now was lost to the Wyndhams; she did not like to think of the old house's humiliation, but it solaced and rewarded her to be able to sit at the head of this long and crowded table, to be able to recreate even a little of that old atmosphere of rich security that she remembered.

And Wongwibinda was her own creation—less than Dalwood it might always be, but it belonged to her. As Margaret her grandmother had done, she reigned over the house and the big garden and took pride in each detail of her housekeeping, as well as of the work of the station itself.

When breakfast was finished and the day's work begun—Arthur gone to the yards to handle a young colt destined for work in the waggonette, Naylor and Paddy down the Falls country to bring back a mob of cows and calves for a buyer's inspection, and Cecil and Elsie to saddle up the horses—she pinned on her hat and went out to the kitchen for the parcels of sandwiches and cakes that Mrs Naylor had made up for the riders' lunches.

Minnie, at the week's ironing, slid her flat-iron hissing and steaming over the expanses of starched white damask tablecloths and napkins. Mrs Naylor was giving the bread-dough its second kneading, and the great bowlful sprang white and elastic under her neat dark hands. Mrs Maguire had come up to help with the ironing, and stood near Minnie, pressing the shirts and dresses. Beside the paper parcels of sandwiches she had put a few cherries, picked from the trees near her cottage.

May saw them at once and tasted one—she had had no idea the cherries were so near ripening. Well, Saturday would be a good day for picking; they would make a party of it, and on Monday the jam would be made. She lingered to ask Mrs Maguire about the baby's cough, to suggest remedies, but outside the screen of yellow broom-blossom she saw Cecil and Elsie waiting with the horses, her grey Possum saddled ready. She went out gaily between the cabbage-roses at the gate, and mounted as easily as a young girl.

Even so near the fullness of summer, with a glowing sun drying the heavy dew from the shade, the wind on these hills of the table-land still held an undercurrent of cold, a pleasant sharpness. The trees of orchard and garden were heavy with unripe fruit. Beyond the pines that marked the avenue the wind bowed the tall standing oats in the cultivation-paddock. The horses moved off willingly, playing with the bit and dancing a little with pleasure in the day.

They followed a line through the trees that led southward across the road, once an important wool-track to the coastal ports, which cut Wongwibinda's paddocks into two sections. This road, always rough and difficult and traversing many miles of empty country, had fallen into disuse since the railway had come to the tableland; the wool-drays no longer groaned along it on the steep and painful journey down to the coastal ports of the northern rivers. It was now only a local road for the few settlers who lived on this wild edge of the tableland. Nevertheless, cutting the station in two as it did, it was something of a vexation to May.

When the tide of selectors, now mounting, should at last thrust its extreme ripple into this stronghold of hers, the road would make her vulnerable, for it ran through much of her best sheep country, and along it the selectors would certainly choose to settle. She felt a cloud of distaste and irritation at the thought, and was glad to canter on up the long gentle folds of hollow and slope, towards the blue mound-like hills of the Doughboy Range.

These slopes, once uniformly dark with the low black sally-trees and stringybarks of the original timber, now opened here and there into clearings of dry silver skeleton trees, ringbarked to Albert's plans, where grass crowded to the base of the dead trunks. Luxuriant summer grass had almost overgrown the network of little earthen paths beaten out by the sheep, but along them, heavy with wool, the sheep still moved or stood, looking like the small rocks of grey granite that cropped out here and there from the grass.

Now they gathered in alarm at the sound of the horses' hooves, staring with witless yellow eyes towards the noise that interrupted their quiet. May and Cecil rode cautiously up to each small mob, looking them over sharply for signs of fly-strike or sickness; the mob would hold their ground awhile, stamping at the dogs when they came too near, then would break and run all at once, disappearing into the dark crowds of sally-trees among olive-green trunks and fallen branches.

The horses climbed gradually higher, until they reached cleared uplands where the force of the wind struck them, sharply cold at this height even through the thin burning of the sunlight. Above this shelf-like plateau, whose outlines seemed worn down to gentleness by thousands of years of wind and storms, the line of curious square hills stood up a few hundred feet higher, loaf-shaped and steep-sided. They might have been the remains of old earthworks built by some vanished people; in fact they were the last stumps of a decayed volcanic range. Not long ago they had been clothed with dense bush, but now they were greyed with dead trees, and sheep had begun to terrace their grassy sides with narrow tracks.

From this side of the range, the country fell softly away westwards in folds like drapery, to the wide plain and the westward hills, floating now like outlines of a blue whose pallor matched the sky. Usually May would pull up her horse here to look with pleasure at the wide view, but today she scarcely glanced at it. Her mind was fixed on the other side of the range.

The horses pressed on round the flank of one hill and down the track that led from its shoulder. Now the view was southward, a long downward prospect through a widening valley. A few miles farther, she could see the line of clearing where the fence of the Wongwibinda boundary ran; beyond this, all was as yet heavily timbered with the original bush.

The contours of the slopes dropped away into the basin of heaving ridges and low hills, closed in by the curve of the range on one side, and to eastwards by the taller barrier of the main range which shut it from the coast. Today, in the cool clarity of morning, the view was distinct for many miles. Wind poured over the range like a stream of cold water, rippling round horses and riders with a keen chill.

Ten miles or more beyond the Wongwibinda boundary ran the main road which joined the inland towns to the coastal ports. She could just see its course from this high point, and she showed Cecil and Elsie where it ran. But her gaze was concentrated on the land which bordered it. She knew it to be one of the largest holdings in this part of the country, and to be up for sale.

She reckoned out with her glance the shape and size of the holding, the direction of the slopes that bordered its main creek. It was well-watered, evidently; a little clearing had been done, though not much. She had lately set herself to find out unobtrusively all that she could about its acreage and carrying capacity, and about its present owner and his reasons for selling, and she had collected a multitude of different opinions on its possibilities. Looking at it spread out below her now, she did not doubt that it was good country; and, best of all, bordering the main road as it did, it was easy of access from the coast or from the inland towns—easier than was Wongwibinda.

Her plan seemed at every moment more and more logical— presented, the more she thought of it, further and further advantages. If she were to buy Wallamumbi, it would be easily worked in conjunction with Wongwibinda; a track led down from this range towards it, steep but practicable even for sulkies.

Sheep should do well there, and it would provide her with room for the increasing stud of cattle and for the herd beasts which were bred for sale. It lay within a few hours' riding distance from Wongwibinda; and from all she could hear, the present owner was not competent to manage it, and could probably be brought to sell at a price she would consider fair.

And once bought, it would be for years a sufficient outlet for the growing energies of her sons. She could see no flaw in her plan.

It would be a big risk. She would be deliberately jeopardizing the security she had so lately won, for in order to buy so large a property she must go into debt again, and there would be little margin for bad luck or bad management. Another fall in prices, another bad drought—but she would not think of that. She had been deep in debt before and had come out victorious; the game once entered on, the plunge once taken, it was best to commit oneself entirely.

The idea began to take possession of her like an excitement in her blood. She did not speak of it to the children—it was Arthur's privilege to hear and discuss it first—but as she sent her horse on down the track to continue the day's work, she was unusually lively and talkative. The sense of a new struggle waiting ahead, new problems to be faced, worked in her exhilaratingly, and the day of wind and flying clouds seemed to urge her on.

As, late in the afternoon, they rode homewards, while Elsie and Cecil amused themselves by jumping their horses over fallen logs, she allowed herself the luxury of arranging a future. If Wallamumbi, once bought, should turn out as good an investment as she believed it would do—if all went well with this plan—why should she stop there? She began to imagine a chain of stations linked to Wongwibinda and Nulalbin, a famous stud, a family firm—May Wright and Sons, perhaps: hundreds of thousands of acres under her own control and that of her sons, and she herself reigning still at Wongwibinda, the centre of all these activities and the focus on which they all converged.

Her imagination took fire afresh at the idea. This would be her way of setting up a memorial to Albert and herself, of completing the life that Albert had left unfinished. She thought of that bark hut that Albert had told her of, where as a boy of fourteen he had lain awake contending with visions of poverty and death; she thought tenderly of his whole after-life, its hard work and solitude, of the things he had never had.

It pleased her to imagine his life's work as leading ultimately to this; and in the background was always her memory of Dalwood and the promise she had made to it. Now she had begun already, in secret, to direct all her force and will along this new channel she had chosen for it.

At dinner that night she fretted in impatience, more talkative and sharper of tongue than usual. She could scarcely wait for the moment when, the meal over, the guests settled, the piano opened in the drawing-room and the songs fairly begun, she could take Arthur's arm and draw him to the door. 'You won't mind our leaving you for a little while—Arthur and I have some business to discuss.'

Then, sitting down in the office—that comfortable brown-panelled room where Albert's picture, serious and remote, hung watching them from the wall—she would begin. 'Arthur, I've been going into it, and I think it would be a good idea if we were to make an offer for Wallamumbi.'

EPILOGUE

IT IS THE autumn of 1929. She is seventy-five years old. There she sits on the garden seat, in her cave cut deep in the branches of the big laurel-tree, looking across to the valentine lawn with its trellised roses. In front of her the red rose-tree wears its last blooms and the towers of white chrysanthemums begin to topple from their heights.

She has left her office this morning in impatience; perhaps after all she will never write more than a sketch of her memoirs. Writing tires her —words, too many words and not enough action. And the office is too dark and crowded, on this fine day, too filled with documents and tied-up bundles of papers, with paperweights and ornaments brought back from the trips overseas, from Italy, from England, from France and America; too thickly hung with photographs of prize bulls with ribbons hanging from their necks, with old pictures of tennis-parties, picnic-parties, family gatherings (the ladies in high necks and narrow waists) fossilized for the incurious stare of a new generation.

Now she wants to sit in the sun, to refresh herself with the sight of the autumn roses, and the twittering and scuffling of the birds for which she loves to scatter crumbs. She breaks a stale piece of cake for them and they fly to her shoulders, to her lap, round her shoes—her little finches, her diamond-sparrows and native canaries, coming back to nest in this garden year after year. She talks to them, smiles at them—that smile that still, even in her old brown face, illuminates and warms.

This year begins the second century since Dalwood was founded, and since, with it, her own story first began. She has just been writing of her childhood and her mind is full of it still; Dalwood stands in her memory as serene, as welcoming as ever, ruined and degraded though the old house itself is now. A century—and only twenty-five years of it are not really her own. A century is not so long after all; for she contains the story of all that time within herself.

Her memory is as good as ever, she is still strong, her eyes are still keen though long-sighted. A solid, active old lady, she crumbles cake for the birds; yet within her the trees of a century fall, the people of a century come and go, a million things die and are born.

Everyone knows, at this moment, where she is—the maids, the chauffeur, the gardener working a little faster in the strawberry beds, Weeta, who is playing the piano but who will soon come out with cushions to sit with her. Beloved, beneficent, dogmatic and more than a little feared, it is not possible even for her grandchildren to forget where she is, to dismiss her as old and negligible. She knows all that, but chirruping to her birds she has left Wongwibinda behind and is wandering in her past.

Everything has happened as she planned it, as she worked for it. No, not everything; disappointment and failure and grief spare no one, and death waits always near. But a great deal has happened as she planned—more, perhaps, than she herself knows. The world that she has built, the century that she encloses, combine to warm her with the sun of this last autumn.

For it is her last. By the end of the year she will have gone to her grave on the hill-slope near Wongwibinda—the grave she chose, as though even in death she must overlook what is being done on her beloved property. As for her world—perhaps by then it will have fallen and smashed with the prices on the world's stock exchanges, perhaps it is already vanishing from round her on the quickening tide of change. But she at least is secure; whatever changes, she and her century are unalterable now.

She is entitled to her triumph, then. No one can rob her of her conquests, of the awe that she is held in, of the love that is rendered to her by right. She may expect, perhaps she does expect, that not only her children but her grandchildren and their children too— for who knows how far ahead the ripples of her influence may travel? —will all carry a certain stamp, a mark that singles out even the most distant or rebellious of them for her own.